sartre on violence
curiously ambivalent

ronald e. santoni

the pennsylvania state university press
university park, pennsylvania

Library of Congress Cataloging-in-Publication Data

Santoni, Ronald E.
    Sartre on violence : curiously ambivalent / Ronald E. Santoni.
      p.   cm.
    Includes bibliographical references and index.
    ISBN 0-271-02300-7 (cloth : alk. paper)
    1. Sartre, Jean Paul, 1905– . 2. Violence.
    I. Title.

B2430 .S34S315 2003
303.6—dc21   2003005786

Dedicated to all

who struggle and all who will struggle

with the issue of violence

Each adversary, however repugnant he may be, is one of those inner voices which we might be tempted to silence, and to which we must listen in order to correct, adapt, or reaffirm the few truths we catch sight of in the same way.

—Albert Camus, "Défense de *L'homme révolté*"

contents

We—and, of course, our children and, for many, our grandchildren—have inherited a world of turmoil and injustice. This world, too often, has been committed to violence, war, terror, and the threat of each as means for settling disputes. We have lived in a century in which, it is estimated, a hundred million people have died needlessly through horrors that human beings have inflicted on human beings—world wars, the Holocaust, genocides, regional conflicts, insurrections, and revolutions—usually carried out in the name of justice. Leaders of nations—including our presidents—appear to have cultivated a ready and easy disposition to call their nations' causes and killings "just," while downplaying or virtually ignoring the causes and sufferings of others. "Self-defense" and "necessity" have been characteristic words offered to "justify" violence. At the time of my writing, the whole world is on edge: no part of the world seems safe from the horrors of violence, savage destruction, the threats of mass bioterrorism or nuclear annihilation. The horrific terrorist elimination of the Twin Towers and thousands of people inside them, in the traumatic "event" now chillingly referred to as 9/11, has shocked North Americans into recognizing that they, too, are vulnerable to unimaginable violence. President Bush's "War on Terrorism" and rapid military incursion into Afghanistan have, in turn, raised a cluster of issues about the *justifiability* of retaliatory and "self-defensive" use of violence or Terror against violence and Terror—especially when hundreds, perhaps thousands, of innocent lives in a destitute country are expunged. And in the Middle East, to use but one other example, a small, historically oppressed yet now technologically sophisticated people, intimidated by killings and "suicide bombings" and other threats to its security, has, in the name of *necessary* "self-defense" or counterviolence, demolished the offices of the Political Authority as well as major towns of a neighboring poor and oppressed people striving to attain legitimacy as a state. Violence and counterviolence,

Terror and counter-Terror, by both the Palestinians and the Israelis, in a seemingly endless and escalating dispute over historical claims, suggest a developing war between civilizations, perhaps even an "Armageddon."

In a word, *violence* is the issue of our time. And the intensifying violence in our current world raises and reraises philosophical issues of gnawing importance. What is the nature of violence? What are its varied forms? Is it to be distinguished from "force," for instance? Does the concept of violence have a moral dimension? Can violence or Terror ever be justified morally? If so, where would its moral limits be? Is oppression unequivocally a form of violence? Is violence that is used to dismantle oppression or other blatant forms of dehumanization in the world morally justifiable? Are self-defense, counterviolence, and necessity (military or other) acceptable *moral* grounds for using violence? Is it ever morally defensible, in an unjust world shamefully divided between the privileged and the "least favored," to employ violence in order to rectify injustice and create what some have called a "new humanity" and more humane world?

Though bold in its claims to provide rigorous clarification of terms and issues, the dominant Anglo-American philosophy of the twentieth century—and now of the early twenty-first—has been markedly slow to confront these vexing issues. Jean-Paul Sartre, who both engaged with and initiated a divergent philosophical perspective, ran counter to this trend. The concerns I have articulated in the preceding questions pervade his philosophical life and work. My book-length study that follows strongly corroborates this point. Moreover, in closely examining Sartre's overall thinking on violence, this book can provide the reader, whether or not the reader agrees with Sartre's views, with valuable insights, criteria, and philosophical arguments—pro and con—with which to refocus on and rethink the many issues concerning violence and Terror that the seemingly deranged contemporary events have imposed on us. Although this service did not constitute my initial or primary motivation for the present work, it can be, I hope, a highly worthwhile by-product. Having expressed this hope, I turn to the specific philosophical and personal considerations in my own existential trajectory that moved me to write this book in the manner and order in which I have.

For over a quarter of a century, I have been actively engaged in writing and scholarship in two main areas—the philosophy of Jean-Paul Sartre and issues related to violence and the terrors of our age, actual or anticipated. While my writing on violence has centered on my attempts philosophically to debunk the "just war" tradition and radically to challenge any attempt to justify nuclear deterrence or any resort to nuclear warfare, my writing on Sartre—my primary project—has focused on untangling the knotty ontological concepts and challenges of *Being and Nothingness*. Although both projects have engaged demanding existential issues, I have had or seized little opportunity to interrelate my scholarship on Sartre with my abiding distaste for violence and the traditional justifications offered in its behalf. That is hardly because Sartre never dealt with violence or endorsed it. From early in his work to its conclusion, he confronted violence regularly: he analyzed it, discussed it, indicted it, often defended it, and, on occasion, appealed to it as emancipatory and part of the way to a new humanity. There is no question that Sartre was deeply troubled by the violence that pervaded human societies, yet receptive at times to the use of violence—even Terror—to break down the humanly created structures of de- and subhumanization.

Thus, in my passion both to understand Sartre's challenging thought and to rebuke the repeated violence and Terror that have defaced humanity in our century, it was inevitable that I should be baffled and disconcerted by some of Sartre's pronouncements on violence. How could violence or Terror be condoned or philosophically justified? became my frequent question. Although in my continued reading of Sartre I sympathized deeply with his passionate concern for the oppressed, I could not fathom his fusing of "Fraternity" and "Terror" (*Fraternité-Terreur*) in the *Critique of Dialectical Reason*, or his emotional defense of violence and Terror, both there and in his Preface to *The Wretched of the Earth*, for instance, as necessary and "justifiable" means for the colonized natives' passage to humanity. Given Sartre's unrelenting embrace of an ontology of human freedom, as well as his repeated denunciation of all that violates or suppresses it, I readily suspected—at least on first reading—a tension within his overall thought. How, I asked myself, could his acceptance of violence and Terror, however noble the ends, be reconciled with his delicate analysis in the *Notebooks for an Ethics* of the meaning and anticommunitarian, non-coexistential, consequences of violence? I saw merit in the affirmation by Raymond Aron and other critics that Sartre's social and political theory was transforming a philosophy of freedom and liberation into a philosophy of violence. Although Sartre's declaration toward the end of his life—in the highly controversial *Hope Now* (*L'espoir maintenant*) "interviews" with Benny Lévy—that "violence . . . is precisely the opposite of fraternity" gave me some renewed personal satisfaction, it also added to my bafflement regarding the coherence of Sartre's position on violence and its justifiability. Not only did some of his earlier views seem to me questionable, but, as even passing readers of Sartre had suggested, his overall position on violence did not appear to pass the test of consistency.

Although in 1993 I had already published an article ("On the Existential Meaning of Violence") attending favorably to Sartre's discussion of violence in the *Notebooks,* my reconsideration in 1996 of Sartre's apparent about-turn in *L'espoir maintenant* (*Hope Now*) (1991), together with the sometimes acerbic debate (with Simone de Beauvoir at the forefront) that followed the publication of these controversial "interviews," stirred a want on my part to get Sartre right on violence. I wanted now to center my own discomfort with violence and its alleged justifications on Sartre's writings. Were my earlier assumptions and inferences about his views correct? Were some critics—and also passing readers—right in alleging that Sartre often "exalted" violence, or that Sartre's overall philosophy was scarred by an attraction to violence? Did a deep-seated inconsistency or double-talk infuse his apparent accommodation of violence and Terror to his socialist ideal of creating an autonomous humanity, or "city of ends"? Was Sartre's final disavowal of violence and Terror in the *Hope Now* interviews to be taken as his decisive position and an important, but largely overlooked, part of his legacy?

These questions, among others, prompted me to write the present book. My deep engagement with both Sartre and the unsettling issues of violence virtually required that I do it. No other available book focused exclusively on Sartre's views on violence throughout his *oeuvre complète.* So, in 1997, although still in scholarly dialogue about issues I had raised in *Bad Faith, Good Faith, and Authenticity in Sartre's Early Philosophy* (1995), I grasped the bull by the horns and began this study. In effect, I decided to start over. My intent was to confront, understand, and articulate in detail Sartre's most important and representative philosophical discussions of violence from very early in his work to the end. I decided to follow and study the trajectory of his thinking on violence, to compare and contrast the key moves in that trajectory, and to determine whether any noticeable tensions in his dialectic could be dissolved, or at least alleviated, by an eventual overarching, if unsteady, coherence.

My almost single-minded inquiry into this topic during the past four years led me to follow paths that, until then, only tempted me. For example, to comprehend the background to Sartre's developing views regarding conflict and violence, I could not ignore Hegel's account of the Master-Slave relationship. And to understand further some of Sartre's most extreme statements concerning the regenerative or humanizing functions of violence in specific circumstances, I regarded it as imperative to reconsider his relationship to Frantz Fanon's *Wretched of the Earth*. Further, it became clear that I must now do what I had often wanted, but neglected, to do: namely, write in greater detail about relevant passages in some of Sartre's masterful plays—especially those that contrasted with related statements in some of Camus's engaging and beautifully written literary works.

The preceding consideration demands that I note a more crucial and—what turned out to be—more pivotal consideration. As I progressed in telling the detailed story of Sartre's uneasy, troubled, and seemingly ambivalent confrontation with violence, I increasingly recognized that no responsible attempt to comprehend Sartre on violence could justifiably ignore the painful, acrimonious, and mutually self-demeaning 1952 quarrel between Sartre and Camus over Camus's basic contentions in *The Rebel* (*L'homme révolté*), published only a year earlier (1951). My engagement with the complete protracted debate—a bitter exchange carried out openly in the pages of *Les temps modernes* but as of mid-2002 still not published in its entirety in English—strongly confirmed what I had earlier surmised; namely, that the tragic "break" between Sartre and Camus was rooted predominantly in their deepening philosophical differences over the existential meaning and justifiability of violence.

With that confirmation, I could not do otherwise than as I did. I decided to devote a whole part of my book, not just a subsection, to this historical confrontation between two of the towering intellectual figures of our era. The confrontation was, for me, an integral part of Sartre's trajectory on violence, preparing the way for what he would go on to say in the *Critique* and his Preface to *The Wretched of the Earth*, for example. And, to my mind, the reader needed to view the skirmish principally in terms of Sartre's impatience with Camus's increasing disapproval of revolutionary killing and any justification of it—a position that Sartre saw as "bourgeois" and insensitive to the violent conditions of oppression that permeated the structures of bourgeois society. Toward that end, I attempted not only to acquaint English readers with all segments of the debate—including the contributions of Francis Jeanson, one of Sartre's closest intellectual collaborators—but also to show both the diverging backgrounds to violence that nurtured the confrontation and the role the debate played in Sartre's strong endorsement of violence and killing in the *Critique* and the Preface. In my judgment, the justifiability and limits of violence, over which Sartre and Camus quarreled so vehemently, constituted one of the lingering unresolved issues that Sartre later tried to address more explicitly and bring to relative closure in his

"Rome [or "Gramsci"] Lecture Notes" of 1964. For that reason, among others—including my wish to test my findings further—I decided not only to include this still (2002) unpublished lecture as a fitting topic for Part II of this work but also to treat it here as a rich and climactic set of "notes" that every student of Sartre on violence and Terror ought to consider and study carefully. Nowhere in Sartre's philosophy does he deal more directly with defining the limiting conditions for the use of Terror. In this regard, the "Rome Lecture" challenges, tantalizes, perhaps even incenses, anyone who is existentially and philosophically involved with the traumatic "event" of September 11, 2001, for instance.

The title of my book gives away the repeated finding, as well as the theme and the conclusion, of my study: Throughout his probing oeuvre and life, and through the twists and turns in each, Sartre's attitude toward violence is markedly and—after a while—predictably ambivalent. Even in his last days, when he baffled his "family" at *Les temps modernes* by presenting violence and fraternity (and human community) as opposites, he offered—under the rubric of "necessary evil"—his approval of the "violent struggle" of the "tortured" Algerian people against the French. Early in his writing, Sartre had stated that violence is "curiously ambiguous." I believe that if the reader has the determination to follow Sartre's trajectory with me, she or he will recognize that Sartre's approaches to violence evoke both parts of the repeated ambiguity and that they conduce to an overall position on violence that is, without question, "curiously ambivalent." In his struggle with violence, Sartre, in my judgment, shows both his optimistic side and his darker side, both his unwavering commitment to human freedom and his willingness to see it abused. But whatever side he exhibits at any particular time, one thing seems sure: Sartre never abandons his deep concern for and dedication to the oppressed, exploited, colonized, disadvantaged, and "least favored"—indeed, for the "wretched of the earth." For that reason, however one might respond to his periodic attempts to condone or justify violence and/or Terror, one may continue to pay tribute to him and resolve to persevere in his project to bring about an integral, autonomous humanity.

For me, it is not the case that "tout comprendre, c'est tout pardonner." Accordingly, the reader is entitled to know that, as much as I may understand some of Sartre's reasons for his occasional defense of violence and Terror, I do not—for reasons that I have already implied—find them compelling. Unlike Camus, Sartre did not always appear to recognize or take sufficiently into account some of the dehumanizing dimensions of violence.

Thus, written at the *end* of one century and the *beginning* of another, both marked by overwhelming violence and Terror, my book on Sartre's confrontation with violence will, I hope, encourage the reader to rethink carefully and systematically the question of violence and its alleged justifications and to ask whether the use of Terror can ever be justified in behalf of a better and more just society or world. Like them or not, these are the questions that Sartre and our frightening times demand that we confront. And our communal answers to them may determine whether humankind will survive.

Ronald E. Santoni
March 2002

acknowledgments

I want again, as in the past, to acknowledge first my indebtedness to my father, the late Fred Santoni, and my mother, Phyllis Tremaine Santoni, who, at the time of writing, lies virtually bedridden in a Kingston, Ontario, nursing home. Without their vision, sacrifice, inspiration, and determination, both my career and my scholarship would be but a dream. For their five children they provided a home in which love and laughter tempered family discussion, disagreements, and intensity of debate. They opened for me and my four siblings (Terrence, Brian, June, and Carole) opportunities that they never had the privilege to enjoy. May this book be yet another token of my deep and abiding thankfulness.

Second, I express once more my deep gratitude to my wife, Margo, and our six children—Christina, Marcia, Andrea, Juanita, Jonathan, and Sondra. Each one continues to sustain me. My life partner and truest friend, Margo remains an uplifting spirit, a paradigm of "amazing grace" and selflessness, an intelligent and loving nurturer who knows who she is and inspires integrity, compassion, and moral concern. She has been the "without whom" I could not have done. Our children—now all out on their own—are living proof that, given a mother *extraordinaire,* the progeny of a philosopher can survive the erratic challenges and demands, the endless discussions, the "ins" and "outs" of students, the mind-boggling views, and the many other idiosyncrasies of a somewhat disorganized academic home. Together, my wife and children—and now, also, their children and spouses—remain the bedrock of my support. Among other blessings, their counterchallenges, concern, help, and humor keep me in place.

Third, I want again to thank fellow scholars and friends in the field from whom I have learned much and with whom I have been in continuing discussion and lively exchange on professional panels and in published materials. Joseph Catalano, Thomas R. Flynn, the late Phyllis Morris, William McBride, Ronald Aronson, Robert Stone, and Tom Rockmore—among others—come readily to mind. And for the inspiration, friendship, and encouragement of Hazel Barnes, surely the doyenne of North American Sartre scholarship, and the late Maurice Natanson, one of the first American expositors of Sartre's ontology of *Being and Nothingness,* I am deeply grateful. Moreover, I cannot fail to add appreciation to two close friends, David Sprintzen and Karsten Harries, who, though focused mainly on other writers and areas of philosophical specialization, were among the first to show—as they continue to show—close interest in my early writing on Sartre. I am additionally indebted to Sprintzen for sharing with me important materials he and his collaborator Adrian van den Hoven had translated in the preparation of their own forthcoming book. Moreover, in this context, I thank two other "groups": (1) the two highly able and very careful readers of my manuscript—whom I now know to be William McBride and Tom Anderson—whose perceptive suggestions and references have made this book a better one; and (2) all the unmentioned members of the North American Sartre Society, the Sartre Circle, Le groupe d'études Sartriennes, and the Society for Phenomenology and Existential Philosophy, who have contributed to my thinking—sometimes without knowing it—by treating my work seriously and by nurturing the creative and growing dialectic in Sartre scholarship around the world. Finally, I express my gratitude to Concerned Philosophers for Peace and International Philosophers for Peace, two engaged groups of inquirers who have spoken, written, and worked against the widespread violences in our world. I count as a rich and undeserved privilege the opportunity to have served, on separate occasions, as president of these two organizations.

I must pause for a special consideration. As I note early in this book, the comments of Phyllis Morris, in 1997, on an earlier article of mine encouraged me to pursue this study on Sartre and violence. Two years later, Phyllis died prematurely of metastatic breast cancer. Her untimely death marked a significant loss to Sartre scholarship and to me personally. Coming from similar philosophical backgrounds, and sharing many of the same interests in Sartre, Phyllis and I were in philosophical dialogue for twenty years. I—and, I'm sure, many others—have already missed her careful, analytic, philosophical eye, her perceptive commentaries, her intellectual integrity, and her genuine friendship. I give thanks for her life and her solid contributions to the understanding of Sartre. At least in part, this book is dedicated to her memory.

Next, I wish to express appreciation to those persons and institutions who provided environments and means for the preparation of this book: the

Robert C. Good Faculty Fellowship Committee, the Faculty Development Committee of Denison University, and the Denison University Research Foundation, which supported me with awards and grants; the Governing Body of Clare Hall, Cambridge University, and the Faculty of Philosophy at Cambridge, whose appointments and accommodations have permitted me to write and work, at rather regular intervals, in the intellectually stimulating and culturally rich conditions of Cambridge; the administration of Denison University—in particular, past president Michele Myers and past provost Charlie Morris and their successors Dale Knobel and David Anderson, as well as Associate Provost Keith Boone—who, while likely regarding some of my interventions as an annoyance, have given tangible evidence of appreciating my teaching and scholarly work; my present colleagues in philosophy at Denison—Anthony Lisska, David Goldblatt, Steve Vogel, Mark Moller, Barbara Fultner, Jonathan Maskit—who, as a group, integrate rigorous philosophical inquiry and exchange with friendship, goodwill, and mutual support; George Pattison, former dean of King's College, Cambridge, who provided me intellectual and spiritual stimulation, as well as friendship, during a number of my stays at Cambridge; the librarians and staff of Denison University, who have tolerated my mess and have allowed me to make the library my "second home" (in particular I thank Mary Prophet, who located for me some source material on which I had given up); the librarians in the majestic Reading Room of the University Library, Cambridge—especially Colin Clarkson and his expert staff—who have devised helpful ways of accommodating my overload of books; the staff of the Beinecke Library at Yale, who facilitated my access to and use of the marvelous "John Gerassi Collection" of Sartre interviews and manuscripts; John (Tito) Gerassi, himself, for generously donating his documents to the service of Sartre scholarship; those courageous workers who have accepted and met the unenviable challenge of converting my scarcely legible handwritten yellow pages into attractive computer drafts: I include among these stalwart souls Pat Davis, our longtime and faithful maintainer of order in the Philosophy Department at Denison, whose eyes have doubtless worn from exposure to my scribble; Karen McPeak Politinsky of the Denison staff and Lori Klimaszewska of Cambridge University, whose adeptness at the computer evoked my sense of awe and of my own technological incompetence; and Ann Hodgson of Little Shelford, England, who, during two of my summers at Cambridge, saved me from technological despair.

To all of these, I offer my profound thanks, but perhaps to none more than to my students of four decades. Students have been the "spice" of my academic life: they have given me remarkable creative joy and an occasional migraine headache, and have also sustained the youth in me. Continuing interaction with them—with their interests, questions, challenges, vitality, and affection—forever persuades me that the vocation of teacher-scholar is among the noblest and most existentially rewarding available.

Last, but not least, I express my gratitude to Sanford Thatcher and the dedicated staff of Penn State Press. In my judgment, Sandy Thatcher stands tall among press directors, university or commercial. I am grateful for his competence, thoroughness, reliability, honesty, and encouragement and am proud to be publishing with a press guided by his direction and standards. That he continues to pursue the interests of his undergraduate thesis on Sartre is reason for thanksgiving from any Sartre scholar. Moreover, the meticulous care given to my manuscript and its topic by an extraordinary copyeditor, Keith Monley, is also cause for my thanksgiving.

These acknowledgments in no way implicate any of the preceding "bene-factors" in any deficiency in this work. And offering excuses would hardly be appropriate for a Sartre scholar!

part I   sartre's trajectory on violence

introduction

In *Hope Now: The 1980 Interviews*,[1] the controversial "conversations" that took place between Jean-Paul Sartre and Benny Lévy just months before Sartre's death, Lévy quotes back to Sartre some of the extreme statements he made regarding violence in his introduction (normally called Preface) to Frantz Fanon's *Wretched of the Earth*.[2] In particular, given both Sartre's insistence during these "interviews" that we are all brothers born of the same "mother-humanity" and his plea for a "true fraternity" in which "what I have is yours, what you have is mine," Lévy reminds Sartre of his characterization in that Preface of the "colonized man" as a "son of violence [who] draws his humanity from it at every moment." Pressing Sartre to acknowledge the tension between these two positions and to admit that,

---

1. Jean-Paul Sartre and Benny Lévy, *Hope Now: The 1980 Interviews,* trans. Adrian van den Hoven, with an introduction by Ronald Aronson (Chicago: University of Chicago Press, 1996). The original French, from which this translation comes, is *L'espoir maintenant: Les entretiens de 1980* (Lagrasse: Verdier, 1991).
2. Frantz Fanon, *The Wretched of the Earth,* preface by Jean-Paul Sartre, trans. Constance Farrington (New York: Grove Press, 1968); originally published as *Les damnés de la terre* (Paris: Présence Africaine, 1961).

in this latter statement, "violence [for Sartre] is the midwife," Lévy asks Sartre whether people can be "brothers inasmuch as they are the children of violence." He also asks whether violence can ever "have the redemptive [or regenerative?] role" that Sartre attributes to it in his Preface. With Sartre on the defensive and now acknowledging that "violence . . . is the very opposite of fraternity," Lévy notes further "a profound tendency toward an ethic of violence" in Sartre's philosophy and wants Sartre to account for his "exaltation of violence" in selective situations. In addition, as if to push the knife in a little deeper, he asks Sartre why he didn't "work out an ethic of regenerative violence" at the time of the Resistance.[3]

This is not the time or place to give the details of Sartre's answers to these questions or to offer a close assessment of section 10—entitled "Sons of Violence"—of *Hope Now*. I give detailed consideration to these questions and the Sartre-Lévy exchange in the concluding section of Part I of this work. I have offered the statements above mainly as a starting place for introducing my own concerns about the continuity and coherence of Sartre's overall position on violence. Regardless of the style of Benny Lévy's questioning or his oft-debated idiosyncrasies of dialogue, I believe that Lévy is raising some of the right questions and is justified in introducing the issue of consistency with respect to Sartre's views on violence. Indeed, as I shall show, other scholars (not to mention passing readers) have raised such a concern.

My own recent reconsideration of the Lévy-Sartre "conversations,"[4] together with Phyllis Morris's written response to an earlier article in which I invoked Sartre's analysis of violence in the *Notebooks*,[5] has prompted me

3. All quotes in this paragraph are from Sartre and Lévy, *Hope Now,* 89–95 (*L'espoir maintenant,* 58–66). I suggest "regenerative," in the square brackets, as a possible additional connotation of the French word *rédempteur* (p. 62) in this context.

4. Ronald E. Santoni, "In Defense of Levy and 'Hope Now': A Minority View," *Sartre Studies International* 4, no. 2 (1998): 61–68.

5. This response, to Ronald E. Santoni, "On the Existential Meaning of Violence," *Dialogue and Humanism,* no. 4 (1993): 139–50 (also in *Violence and Human Co-existence,* ed. Venant Cauchy [Montreal: Montmorency, 1994]), came in the form of personal correspondence dated February 4, 1997. Though expressing agreement with my position on violence, she confessed to having "real reservations about tensions within Sartre's own position" and encouraged me to pursue my projected work—which we had discussed earlier—on "Sartre and violence" as part of my wider project on violence. Once more, I express gratitude to her for our philosophical dialogue, her probing questions, her careful work, and our friendship, though I am saddened to report that between my original writing of this note of appreciation and my completion of an early, incomplete draft of Part I of this study three months later, my good friend Phyllis Morris died of complications related to metastatic breast cancer. She worked conscientiously on Sartre's philosophy until two days before her death. For my fuller "Appreciation" of Phyllis, see *Sartre Studies International* 4, no. 1 (1998): 101–6 (R.E.S.).

to do an intensive inquiry into Sartre's thought regarding violence. Accordingly, in the study that follows, I formulate, interrelate, and compare Sartre's views on violence in selected works in which he deals most directly with violence—namely, *Cahiers pour une morale* (*Notebooks for an Ethics*), *Matérialisme et révolution* (*Materialism and Revolution*), *Critique de la raison dialectique* (*Critique of Dialectical Reason*), his Preface to Frantz Fanon's *Les damnés de la terre* (*The Wretched of the Earth*), *L'espoir maintenant* (*Hope Now*), and the unpublished "Rome Lecture Notes." Although I do not pretend to cover the entirety of Sartre's thinking on violence, I believe that I present enough of it to reflect the diverging and contrasting positions—what I call the "curious ambivalence"—that Sartre exhibits in regard to violence through representative stages of his career. In addition, I attempt to show that there is consistency within each side of the tension, or dialectic, that seems to mark Sartre's overall discussion of violence. Put another way, I think there is a wobbly continuity and coherence within the shifts and apparent inconsistency. While not entirely eliminating the tension, this continuity tends to relieve it. For one thing, the "altered view" on violence that Lévy directs Sartre to announce just before Sartre's death in *Hope Now* is, I submit, noticeably similar to the main, but not exclusive, position Sartre expresses in his rather unsystematic, sometimes unfairly dismissed, but highly important, *Notebooks for an Ethics*,[6] which he wrote in 1947–48, at the formative stage of his philosophical oeuvre. If my suggestion is even generally correct, it should lend support to Sartre's insistence in *The 1980 Interviews* that "my contradictions were unimportant and . . . in spite of everything, I have always held to a continuous line [*malgré tout, je suis toujours resté sur une ligne continue*]."[7]

---

6. Jean-Paul Sartre, *Notebooks for an Ethics,* trans. David Pellauer (Chicago: University of Chicago Press, 1992); originally published as *Cahiers pour une morale* (Paris: Gallimard, 1983). It is important to note that although Sartre wrote these *Notebooks* in 1947–48, early in his career, they were not published until 1983, three years *after* his death. It is also of interest to note that, in contrast to Haïm Gordon or, to a lesser extent, Joe Catalano, both William McBride and I, writing in separate works, used the word "gold mine" to describe the benefit of these posthumously published *Notebooks*. See William McBride, *Sartre's Political Theory* (Bloomington: Indiana University Press, 1991), 63, and Ronald E. Santoni, *Bad Faith, Good Faith, and Authenticity in Sartre's Early Philosophy* (Philadelphia: Temple University Press, 1995), xix. Please note that all subsequent references to the *Notebooks for an Ethics* are cited as *NFE,* followed by the page number(s). References to the French original use the abbreviation *CPM,* followed by the page number(s). Unless otherwise indicated, I use the Pellauer translation.

7. Sartre and Lévy, *Hope Now,* 57 (*L'espoir maintenant,* 26).

After viewing some preparatory materials from Hegel's *Phenomenology of Spirit* and Sartre's *Being and Nothingness,* I begin my systematic inquiry of Part I with Sartre's analysis of violence in *Notebooks for an Ethics.* I then consider, in chronological order, his sustained discussions of violence in his other representative works. But let me say at the outset that the reader must not assume that my study of Sartre on violence will terminate with the conclusions I reach on Sartre's trajectory at the end of Part I. For, believing that no responsible inquiry into Sartre on violence should ignore the acrimonious 1952 exchange between Sartre and Camus over the latter's views in *The Rebel,* I devote Part II of my study to this "confrontation." To my mind, "violence" and revolutionary killing, in particular, are at the core of that mutually self-demeaning exchange (in *Les temps modernes*). I expect that the analysis of Sartre's evolving views of violence that I provide in Part I will elucidate the philosophical bases for Sartre's assault on Camus, even though some of these views come to fruition only *after* the dispute. In addition, I expect that this 1952 skirmish will bring to a head the dividing issue of the justification and limits of violence—the issue that will mark my culminatory concern in Part II of the book—and allow me to draw on Sartre's rich, though not yet published or fully translated, "Rome Lecture Notes" of 1964.

Before addressing the relevant details of Sartre's *Notebooks for an Ethics* or any of Sartre's other major discussions of violence, I think it is imperative to provide a brief account of the background and framework out of which Sartre's sustained confrontation with violence may be viewed. Because—as commentators on Sartre usually note—Sartre often invokes Hegel and in *Being and Nothingness* calls upon Hegel's analysis of the Master-Slave relationship to generate his own account of our "concrete relations with Others," it is important to begin with a brief summary of Hegel's famous account. Sartre saw this relation as having "profoundly influenced Marx,"[8] with whose philosophy Sartre seemed to have been in dialectical engagement during most of his philosophical development and oeuvre. And he himself refers or responds to Hegel's specific account of this relationship in numerous places other than *Being and Nothingness,* including *Notebooks for an Ethics.*

---

8. Jean-Paul Sartre, *Being and Nothingness,* trans. Hazel Barnes (New York: *Philosophical Library,* 1956), 237; originally published as *L'être et le néant* (Paris: Gallimard, 1943), 293. In the footnotes that follow, I use the abbreviation BN for *Being and Nothingness* and EN for *L'être et le néant.*

theoretical underpinnings 1

Hegel and the Master-Slave Relationship: A Pivotal Analysis

From Alexandre Kojève's brilliant lectures and commentary on G. W. F. Hegel's *Phenomenology of Spirit*—which were gathered as lecture notes by the poet and novelist Raymond Queneau at the École des Hautes Études between 1933 and 1939—we can gain the crux of Hegel's driving Master-Slave relationship.[1] In his "nascent state," the human being is never *simply* human being. "To speak of the 'origin' of Self-Consciousness [or For-itself] is necessarily to speak of a fight to the death for 'recognition.'"[2] I want the Other to "recognize" my value as his value; and conversely, the Other has the same desire. Each is willing to risk his own life and the life of the Other to satisfy this desire for "recognition." Their confrontation can only be a "fight to the death." Thus, human reality "comes to light," is "formed" and realized, for Hegel, only in and by "the fight" that culminates in the Master-Slave

1. Alexandre Kojève, *Introduction to the Reading of Hegel: Lectures on the Phenomenology of Spirit,* assembled by Raymond Queneau, ed. Allan Bloom, trans. James H. Nichols Jr. (New York: Basic Books, 1969).
2. Alexandre Kojève, *Introduction to the Reading of Hegel,* 7.

relation. The "revelation of human reality," the "truth of man," prerequires it; as Kojève puts it, "it is only through the risk of life that freedom comes to light,"[3] that man moves from "animal" being, or "nature," to human being, or Being-for-itself (in Hegel's sense). Human reality is necessarily either Master or Slave, rooted in conflict or mutual opposition. It is presupposed here that this struggle does not end in death: human reality cannot come into being as "recognized" reality unless the antagonists in the fight stay alive after the fight. Self-realization demands recognition by the Other. This means that they must adopt different behaviors in the fight and "constitute" themselves as "unequals." The one must fear the Other, submit to the Other, refuse to risk his life for the sake of satisfying the Other's desire for "recognition." He must be willing to "recognize" the Other without being "recognized," to "recognize" the Other as Master and himself as recognized only as the Master's Slave.[4] In short, the Slave becomes the "defeated adversary" who has refused to adopt the Master's principle: "to conquer or to die." In refusing to risk his life, in choosing to remain alive, he has chosen the life of Slavery over death, of "dependent consciousness" rather than "autonomous consciousness." His fear of death, his dependence on Nature, gives him a sense of Terror (*Furcht*) and of his nothingness and "justifies" his dependence on the Master. While the Slave remains at the natural bestial level, the Master is already recognized by another consciousness—is already "mediated" and freed from Nature by his "fight to the death" for "pure prestige." The Master becomes "Consciousness for-itself" mediated with itself by a "slavish consciousness" that is bound to Nature and is afraid of death.[5]

But this fight has not yielded the authentic recognition that the two adversaries mutually seek. Although "Man was born and History began with the first Fight,"[6] in the ensuing appearance of Master and Slave neither of the adversaries receives the kind of recognition he or she wishes. Although the Master has been recognized in "his human reality and dignity,"[7] he has not accorded the same recognition to the Slave. So he is recognized by someone whose humanity he does not "recognize." But his wish for recognition can be satisfied *only* by one whom he recognizes as worthy—by another "human," not a Slave or someone the fight has turned into a thing. So the Master is condemned to an "existential impasse."[8] Although

3. Ibid., 12.
4. Ibid., 7–9.
5. Ibid., 16, 18, 47.
6. Ibid., 43.
7. Ibid., 19.
8. Ibid., 19, 46.

he can force the Slave to *recognize* him as Master, he cannot get the *human* recognition that he wanted when he engaged in the fight to the death. For, if recognition must come from "another man" and the Slave is not human, then the Master can never be satisfied. "The Master is fixed in his Mastery" and cannot accept any Other as Master. He prefers death to having to "recognize" another as Master. Only the Slave, who does not want to risk his life to be Master and does not "bind himself to his condition as Slave" (he has good reasons for wanting to leave his servility), is ready for change: he is, "in his very being," "change, transcendence, transformation, 'education.'" He wants to transcend himself and attain autonomy.[9] Thus, in an ironic twist, the details of which are beyond the scope of this background summary, only the Slave—the being who has known Slavery, who is predisposed to go beyond it, who struggles to surpass it, and who *does* overcome it "dialectically"—is capable of achieving satisfaction and bringing History to completion. And, as Kojève points out, this is why Hegel says that History belongs to (*the work* of) the Slave and that the "truth," or "revealed reality," of the Master is the Slave.[10] In the Terror of the Master's rule and domination, the Slave discovers his humanity as something negated and oppressed.[11] Mark Poster's way of putting it—in addition to his suggestion that Marx (as well as Sartre, I might add) is indebted to this Hegelian insight—merits repeating: "The slave is the secret of change in history and his desire for freedom from oppression is the ground of man's becoming more human"[12] (an observation relevant to Sartre's defense of Frantz Fanon). In "overcoming" his Master as Master, the Slave "overcomes" himself as Slave and reveals reality; in surpassing Slavery, he achieves satisfaction, authentic freedom, and self-transformation.[13] So if History is, as Hegel claims, a "dialectic between Mastery and Slavery," then this "overcoming" by the Slave starts a new "period" in History in which the postfight domination of the Slave by the Master is replaced by the Slave's "determination" of human existence. In this way, Mastery, though an "impasse," is "justified" as a necessary stage in human History. On this dialectical account of History, the end or completion of History could come about only with the

9. Ibid., 22. In this paragraph I rely not only on pages 19–22 of Kojève's introduction but also on Kojève's excellent summary of the relevant part of *The Phenomenology of Spirit*, on pages 43–47 especially.

10. Ibid., 20, 22, 47.

11. Mark Poster, *Existential Marxism in Postwar France* (Princeton: Princeton University Press, 1975), 14. I express gratitude for what I have gained from this book.

12. Ibid., 13. See also Kojève, *Introduction to the Reading of Hegel*, 19–20.

13. Kojève, *Introduction to the Reading of Hegel*, 27; see also 46–48.

realized synthesis of Mastery and Slavery.[14] If and how and in what form this ultimate transition would take place becomes the issue for Hegel and those who—like Sartre—are both unsettled and motivated by Hegel's analysis. For so long as Master and Slave exist and are in opposition, human existence will not be satisfied, for neither Slave nor Master will be universally recognized.[15]

Although Sartre does not totally endorse this Hegelian account of the Master-Slave relation, its influence and reverberations are evident in Sartre's initial pessimism with regard to the possibility of authentic human relationships and the likelihood of overcoming interhuman struggle and violence. Moreover, the fundamental violence related to material scarcity in the *Critique of Dialectical Reason* does, I believe, echo some of Hegel's analysis. Further, insofar as part of the Sartre-Camus dispute pertains to the relation of violence (and revolution) to the "end," or "completion," of history, it too echoes Hegel's analysis. Yet this is not to assume that Sartre *finally* agrees with Hegel's perception that *conflict* is necessary to the development of human consciousness, or For-itself.[16] In passing, let me note that Sartre is said to have heard Kojève's discerning lectures on Hegel: how faithful he was, however, to attendance at those lectures—or, for that matter, to the content of those lectures—remains a matter of disagreement among his intellectual peers of that period.[17]

But to gain some preliminary insights into Sartre's subsequent views on violence, we must proceed to a brief background sketch of Sartre's account of the genesis of interhuman conflict in *Being and Nothingness*.

Conflict in *Being* and *Nothingness*

Anyone familiar with even a skeletal account of Sartre's phenomenological ontology recognizes that Sartre's study of the "phenomenon" in the intro-

14. Ibid., 44–45, 46–47.
15. Ibid., 48.
16. For a discussion of this point, see, e.g., Linda A. Bell, *Rethinking Ethics in the Midst of Violence: A Feminist Approach to Freedom* (Lanham, Md.: Rowman & Littlefield, 1993), 161–63. I have reacquainted myself with this engaging book after my completion of the *core* version of the present manuscript. I recommend it to the reader's attention. In fact, I look closely at a part of this book—specifically chapter 5—toward the conclusion of my present study.
17. Poster, *Existential Marxism*, 145. Note also that earlier in this informative book Poster suggests that although Sartre was enrolled in Kojève's lecture class on Hegel's *Phenomenology*, his

duction to *Being and Nothingness* leads him to affirm two radically different "regions of being." Adopting Husserl's axiom of intentionality—namely, that all "consciousness is consciousness *of* something,"[18] that all consciousness intends or posits an object outside of itself—Sartre contends that any phenomenon points to the existence of two *transphenomenal* beings: the transphenomenal being of consciousness and the transphenomenal being (or foundation) of the phenomenon. To these divergent beings Sartre gives, respectively, the names—already suggested by Hegel—"being-for-itself" (*l'être-pour-soi*) and "being-in-itself" (*l'être-en-soi*).[19] This basic distinction pervades, even directs, *Being and Nothingness* and recurs, with contextual modifications—some quite significant—in virtually all of Sartre's writing. *Being-in-itself* is "object" being or "thing" being: it *is* what it is, has "identity," is not conscious, cannot refer to itself, has no possibilities or projects (human reality has projects for it), coincides with itself, is one with itself. In radical contrast to being-in-itself, *being-for-itself* is conscious, self-aware, and self-referential being. As distinctive human reality, being-for-itself is *not* what it is and *is* what it is not.[20] It is not a "what" or object or thing. That is to say, since it is *not* what it is, it lacks identity or "a certain coincidence with itself"; it is always at a distance from itself; it has no fixed essence; it is "no-thing." On the other hand, since it *is* what it is not, it is its possibilities, its continuous potential for transcendence, its future undetermined projects. In short, then, the *being* of human reality is *not* what it is and *is* what it is *not*, because it is *free*. Although human reality is "born supported" by a being that is not itself (and is other than itself), it is always evanescent and self-surpassing. In a word, being-for-itself, or human reality, *is* freedom. "What we call freedom," Sartre says, "is impossible to distinguish from the *being* of 'human reality.' . . . there is no difference between the being of man and his *being-free*."[21] As freedom, then, human reality—being-for-itself—is ambiguous, metastable, open, fleeting consciousness (i.e., *bodily* consciousness), which is nothing outside of a "revealing intuition" of a "transcendent being,"

---

attendance was not recalled by many of the French "luminaries" who attended them (p. 8). It is also interesting—and perplexing—to note, here, that when asked by Orestes Pucciani, in the interview related to the Sartre volume of the *Library of Living Philosophers,* whether he had read Hegel during his École Normale days, Sartre responded: "No, I knew him through seminars and lectures, but I didn't study him until much later, around 1945." Paul Schilpp, ed., *The Philosophy of Jean-Paul Sartre* (La Salle, Ill.: Open Court, 1981), 9.

18. *BN* lxi (*EN* 28).
19. I base most of this summary account on Sartre's analysis in the introduction to *BN*.
20. *BN* lxv (*EN* 33).
21. *BN* 25 (*EN* 65); cf. also, e.g., *BN* 439 (*EN* 515–16).

that is, of "something other than itself."[22] In contrast to being-in-itself, which is *object*-being, being-for-itself is self-conscious *subject*-being.

This brief elucidation of Sartre's pivotal distinction between *being-in-itself* and *being-for-itself* paves the way for considering the ontological status of the Other and our *being-for-Others,* and for understanding the origin of the *conflict* that Sartre first attributes to the original for-itself/for-itself relationship.

For Sartre, "we *encounter* the Other; we do not constitute him"; the Other is not "a consequence which can derive from the ontological structure of the for-itself."[23] I encounter the Other when he "looks" at me. His "looking" at me makes me conscious of myself as an object of his look. The Other is the one who looks at me, the one who reveals my being as object "in the world," the one for whom I am an object, the one who renders me vulnerable because he makes me what I am "in the midst of the world." The Other's look is revelatory of another aspect of my being. Because the Other's look enables me to see myself as an in-itself, it may be said to give me a "nature," or "fixed" essence: "behold now I *am* somebody!" The Other gives my being a "foundation." The Other's look forces me to pass judgment on myself as an object.[24] It precipitates an immediate modification of my being and world. For instance, I react to the Other in shame, fear, or embarrassment. Why? Because the Other's look reveals me as a "looked at." It congeals me as an "object" in the world. I *recognize* that I am the object that the Other is looking at. I am this being, and do not for the moment "think of denying it: my shame is a confession." I am ashamed of *what* I am—an outside "nature" with which the Other has endowed me.[25] And my modified being does not reside in the Other: I am responsible for it.[26]

With the Other's look, then, "I *am no longer master of the situation.*"[27] In giving me a "nature," the Other decenters my world and restricts my possibilities. "I am a slave [this language immediately recalls Hegel's analysis] to the extent that my being is dependent within the bosom of a freedom that is not mine and that is even the condition of my being. . . . Through the

22. *BN* lxi, lxii.
23. *BN* 250 (*EN* 307), *BN* 297 (*EN* 358).
24. *BN* 261–63 (*EN* 319–21); also *BN* 268–71 (*EN* 327–30). For an earlier characterization of the Other, see, e.g., *BN* 230–31 (*EN* 285–86).
25. *BN* 261–62 (*EN* 319–21).
26. E.g., *BN* 221–23 (*EN* 275–77). As Sartre says later, "I am responsible for my being-for-Others, but I am not the foundation of it" (*BN* 364).
27. *BN* 265 (*EN* 323).

Other's look, I *live my life* as fixed [*figé*] in the midst of the world, as in danger, as irremediable."[28] I apprehend myself as an "unknown object of unknowable appraisals—in particular of value judgments" over which I do not have control. I become an "instrument of possibilities which are not my possibilities." My transcendence is denied in order to "make" me a "means to ends" of which I'm unaware. I become "a defenseless being for a freedom which is *not* my freedom."[29] I start to apprehend my possibilities from without. My possibilities are thus limited and alienated by the Other's "looking" at me. In this sense, I am *enslaved*—not by choice, one might say, as in Hegel's account of the "fight," but simply by being "looked at" by the Other. "My original fall is the existence of the Other."[30] The Other is a source of constant threat and danger to me. In the words of Garcin in Sartre's *No Exit*—and in keeping with that brilliant play's disturbing theme—"There's no need for red-hot pokers. Hell is—other people!"[31] The Other is watching me: I grasp the Other's look as the "solidification" of my possibilities.[32]

But the story is not over: there are two sides to it. Sartre makes it clear that the Other is given to us *not* as an object but as another freedom—presumably a subject—who abruptly challenges my being as the center of possibilities. For by fixing, objectifying, and alienating my possibilities, the Other reveals to me that I can be an object only for another freedom: I cannot be an object for myself. Moreover, I cannot be an object for another object; a material object or obstacle cannot restrict my possibilities or confer a "nature" on me; only another freedom can do that. Thus, the objectifying look of the Other "abandons me at the heart of the Other's freedom," causes me to experience the freedom of the Other.[33] "Consciousness can be limited only by consciousness."[34] The Other "looks" at me as he comes to the world and to me as a transcendence or freedom that is not mine. The Other, through whom I give my "objectness" and even the possibility of

28. *EN* 326–27, translation mine: "Je suis esclave dans la mesure où je suis dépendant dans mon être au sein d'une liberté qui n'est pas la mienne et qui est la condition même de mon être. . . . Par le regard d'autrui, je me *vis,* comme figé au milieu du monde, comme en danger, comme irrémédiable." See also *BN* 267–68.
29. *BN* 267–68 (*EN* 326), italics mine.
30. *BN* 263 (*EN* 321: "Ma chute originelle c'est l'existence de l'autre").
31. Jean-Paul Sartre, *No Exit,* in *No Exit and Three Other Plays,* trans. Stuart Gilbert (New York: Vintage Books, 1959), 47; in French, *Huis Clos,* available, e.g., in *Théâtre* (Paris: Gallimard, 1953), 167: "Pas besoin de gril, l'enfer c'est les Autres."
32. *BN* 263 (*EN* 321).
33. *BN* 270–71 (*EN* 328–29).
34. *BN* 286 (*EN* 346).

conceiving of myself in the objective mode, is thus given to me as pure, conscious subject, not as an object of my universe.[35]

But I must defend myself against this conferral of a nature on me, this assault on my freedom, this "death of my possibilities," this decentering of my world by the freedom of the Other who *looks* at me. By making me "be" irremediably an object for the Other, the Other *possesses* me. But I must refuse this objectification, this "possession." Although the Other holds the "secret of what I am," I must not, like a defenseless freedom, allow the Other to define who I am, to capture, imprison, or assimilate my freedom.[36] So I must try to recover myself as freedom. And as Sartre says at the beginning of his unsettling chapter "Concrete Relations with Others," "my project of recovering myself [as free for-itself] is fundamentally a project of absorbing the Other," and "my attitudes with respect to the object which I am for the Other" will "wholly govern" my concrete relations with the Other.[37] Sartre's descriptions of these (doomed) efforts at self-recovery are, as Arthur Danto has contended, among the most "psychologically rich" but relationally pessimistic pages in Sartre's writings.[38]

For Sartre, there are two main ways—equally unsuccessful—by which I can attempt to break the hold of the Other on me, to overcome his objectification[39] (*objectivation*) of me. Counterobjectification is one possibility. I can try to deny that being which the Other has conferred on me from the outside: if I can confer on the Other a "being-for-me," if I can constitute the Other as object, the Other's "objectness" will destroy my objectness, for, as we have seen, I cannot be an object for another object. In other words, by suppressing the freedom of the Other, by trapping him in his facticity, by giving him an object status, I can free myself from the consciousness through and for whom I've become an object, and from any subsequent danger that might come from it. In short, I can "transcend the Other's transcendence."[40] Violence would be one means by which I might try to accomplish this. On the other hand, to the extent that the freedom of the Other is the foundation of my being as object, of my being-in-itself, I might try to

35. *BN* 270 (*EN* 328).

36. *BN* 362, 364 (*EN* 429–30). Sartre says that the "What I am," the in-itself, that the Other confers on me "fixes me wholly in my very flight" (as For-itself) from the in-itself (*BN* 362).

37. *BN* 364, 363 (*EN* 431, 430).

38. Arthur Danto, *Jean-Paul Sartre* (New York: Viking Press, 1975), 175.

39. Hazel Barnes uses "objectivation" in this context as the literal translation of the same word in French. I prefer the ordinary-language English usage. See, e.g., *BN* 268 (*EN* 327).

40. *BN* 363 (*EN* 430); also *BN* 268 (*EN* 327).

recover and "possess" that freedom without destroying its character as freedom or transcendence, by, for example, trying to "incorporate" that freedom
within me and identifying with that freedom as the foundation of myself. In
this case, as Francis Jeanson so adroitly illustrates, I might try to seduce the
Other in her transcendence so as "to obtain [her] free choice of me as a lim-
itation of [her] freedom." I would strive to be loved by her: if successful, my
existence would be justified by my being given a "sort of supreme value" by
the Other.[41] For my beloved, then, I would not be *de trop,* that is to say, an
unjustifiable upsurge. But because love involves the mutual demand to be
loved freely by the Other, my acknowledgment of her freedom would, reci-
procally, call for her addressing her freedom to my own. The beloved, too,
shares the lover's project to be loved and also aims at seducing the lover's
freedom. For, as Sartre points out, "to the extent that the upsurge of being
is an upsurge in the presence of the Other, to the extent that I am both a
pursuing flight [*fuite poursuivante*] [toward the attainment of being] and a
pursued-pursuing [*poursuivant poursuivi*], I am, at the very root of my
being, a project of objectification and assimilation of the Other. That is the
original fact."[42] This is true for the Other as well as for me.

Here is not the place to recount the details of Sartre's meticulous but pessimistic accounts of many of the concrete relations with Others that illustrate the "primitive attitudes" and gestures by which I attempt to recover
my freedom from the Other's objectification of mine. For Sartre, each
attempt is opposed to the other, is the "death of the other," yet "motivates
the adoption of the Other" and "enriches the failure of the Other."[43] To use
Joseph Catalano's language, "Both projects fail because each implies the
other." If I constitute the Other as object, I can recognize in this freedom
made object the freedom of a subject (as in sadism, e.g.). If I try to appropriate and preserve the freedom of the Other, I run the risk of turning this
freedom into an object[44] and also the risk of further "objectification" by the
Other (as in the project of love). This means that my relations with the

41. Francis Jeanson, *Sartre and the Problem of Morality,* trans., with an introduction, by
Robert V. Stone (Bloomington: Indiana University Press, 1980), 167.
42. *BN* 363, translation altered (*EN* 430). The reader may note—or recall—that, for
Sartre, being-for-itself is both a flight (*fuite*) and a pursuit (*poursuite*); that is to say, it tries perpetually both to flee the in-itself and to pursue it (in order to complete itself, fill its emptiness).
BN 362 (*EN* 429).
43. *BN* 363 (*EN* 430).
44. Joseph S. Catalano, *A Commentary on Jean-Paul Sartre's Being and Nothingness*
(New York: Harper Torchbooks, 1974; reprint, Chicago: University of Chicago Press, 1980),
180.

Other are *circular,* not dialectical—as in Hegel—and neither of us can escape this circle of conflictual and doomed relations. "Everything which may be said of me in my relations with the Other applies to him as well. While I attempt to free myself from the hold of the Other, the Other is trying to free himself from mine; while I seek to enslave the Other, the Other seeks to enslave me." In a word, Sartre concludes, *"conflict is the original meaning of being-for-others,"*[45] and—at least in *Being and Nothingness*—there is no successful way out of it. To invoke Hegel's words, there is an "existential impasse" on each side of the relationship.

As dismal as this conclusion may be, it does not come as a surprise. Although Sartre has told us earlier in *Being and Nothingness* that we do not constitute the Other, but encounter him, he also tries, in these earlier pages, to provide an ontological foundation for our encounter with the Other. He tells us, for example, that "the Other exists for a consciousness only as a *refused self*"—and vice versa. The Other is the Not-me-not-object. And Sartre adds: "The Other whom I recognize in order to refuse to be him is before all else *the one for whom my For-itself is.* Not only do I make myself not-be this other being by denying that he is me, [but] I make myself not-be a being who is making himself not-be me."[46] As we have seen more concretely in "relations with Others," this double negation self-destructs. "Either I make myself not-be a certain being, and then he is an object for me and I lose my object-ness for him"—in which case "the Other ceases to be . . . the subject who makes me be an object by refusing to be me"—or "this being is indeed the Other and makes himself not-be me, in which case I become an object for him and he loses his own object-ness."[47] Either way, this double negation *fails,* and, as Klaus Hartmann has pointed out, our "being-for-others stands as a concrete foundation" of our *conflictual* encounter with the Other.[48] In other words, it grounds the incessant conflict that characterizes our concrete relations with Others. Although, as Sartre contends, our being-for-others is "not an ontological structure of the For-itself,"[49] *conflict* is indeed the core and "original meaning" of our being-for-others. (In passing, the reader may note that this becomes the basis for

45. *BN* 364 (*EN* 431: "le conflit est le sens originel de l'être-pour-autrui"), italics mine.
46. *BN* 284–85 (*EN* 344–45).
47. *BN* 285 (*EN* 345).
48. Klaus Hartmann, *Sartre's Ontology* (Evanston, Ill.: Northwestern University Press, 1966); see 114–24, esp. 114, 123–24. I am indebted to him for insights he has provided in this context.
49. See, again, *BN* 282, also 297 (*EN* 342, 358).

Merleau-Ponty's later contention, against Sartre, that a philosophy that fails to permit intersubjectivity must be in conflict with Marxism.)

The themes of struggle, domination, "enslavement" by the Other, pursuit of autonomy, and so forth, which we saw in Hegel's treatment of the Master-Slave relationship, have reappeared in Sartre's consideration of our being-for-Others. Without attempting a detailed comparison between the two, we may at least pause to observe a couple of contrasting points. Although there is no question that Sartre's analysis is, in many ways, a reconstruction of Hegel's analysis of the Master-Slave relationship in the "Lordship and Bondage" section of *Phenomenology of Spirit,* it seems similarly obvious that these two complex analyses exhibit differences. As Sartre points out, for Hegel "the relation 'Master-Slave' is *not* reciprocal":[50] it is, rather, the struggle between two *unequal* self-consciousnesses striving for "recognition"—indeed, "fighting to the death" for recognition. The reader will recall that in the fight the two consciousnesses "constitute" themselves as "unequals": although the Slave accords humanity to the dominating Master by recognizing him, the Master refuses to "recognize" the consciousness and dignity of the Slave-Other, who, for him, is *not* "essential," is not human, but is more like a thing. But, for Sartre, the relationship between being-for-itself and the Other *is* reciprocal: as we have seen above, "the Other exists for a consciousness only as a *refused self.*" Negation and counternegation are mutual; objectification and counter-objectification are reciprocal; "I make myself not-be a being who is himself making himself not-be me";[51] the Other negates my making him "be" as object, and I negate *his* making me "be" as object. Each negates his or her objectified, alienated Me-as-object, yet in doing so recognizes his or her "being-as-object" for the Other. In fact, in a strange way, for both Me and the Other, the "alienated and refused Me" becomes both the "symbol of our absolute separation" and our bond (*lien*) to the (i.e., each) Other.[52] Perhaps more important, my account above has also shown that, in Sartre, the Me-as-object effected by the Other's look leads to my awareness that an object *cannot* be an object for another object and, thus, that my "objectness" must have been given to me by the Other as *subject.* The situation is the same for the Other. This reciprocal acknowledgment of the Other as subject (or freedom) is precisely what leads to the incessant struggle of each side to

50. *BN* 240 (*EN* 296).
51. *BN* 284–85 (*EN* 344–45).
52. Ibid.

appropriate or recover the freedom she lost to the Other. Of course, it also provides a basis for hope in the possibility of authentic intersubjectivity, but Sartre does not take us there in *Being and Nothingness*.[53]

Despite the conflict and struggle that marks and pervades these two analyses of our original relation to the Other, there yet appears to be another related difference between these two accounts. However bleak the relationship between the Slave and Master, Hegel's account seems to offer an optimism that Sartre's does not share. Somewhat surprisingly, this optimism falls on the side of the Slave, not the Master. In spite of the Master's failure to "recognize" the Slave as anything but a thing (or animal), it is the Slave who, through the Master's domination, discovers his oppressed (or thingified) humanity, seeks his freedom, *works* to free himself from his oppression, dialectically overcomes his Master as Master and himself as Slave, and becomes the agent for making the human being more human in history. While the Master continues to fight, the Slave works and—unlike the Master—gains satisfaction and authenticity by overcoming slavery. For Hegel, even enslaved work in the service of Others is humanizing.[54] The Slave, unlike the Master, gains satisfaction through his self-expression in the product of his work. Although, to be sure, for Hegel as for Sartre, the Other may possess "the secret of what I am" (Sartre),[55] it is only for Hegel that the Slave as Other becomes the secret of change in history—assuming, of course, for the moment, that we are now restricting Sartre to his account in *Being and Nothingness*. Put another way, however much Sartre's analysis of our original relation to the Other may reflect Hegel's analysis of Master-Slave, it does not exhibit the same possibility of "overcoming" objectification, on the part of the Other or Me, that Hegel's account at least partially allows.[56]

53. This is clearly the topic for another work. I only intend to suggest this optimistic point here. In my judgment, a reciprocal acknowledging of the existence of the Other as subject whose look objectifies me might also become a step toward *transcending* the reciprocal objectification and perpetual conflict.

54. Kojève, *Introduction to the Reading of Hegel*, 20, 27–28, 42–43.

55. *BN* 364 (*EN* 431).

56. This is not intended to bypass or ignore Hegel's contention that "universal history, the history of the interaction between [human beings] and of their interaction with Nature, is the history of the interaction between war-like Masters and working Slaves." But—to go even further—Hegel also projects an end of history through a dialectical overcoming of both the Master and the Slave. Kojève, *Introduction to the Reading of Hegel*, 43–44. On the other hand, I must also point out that, in the *Notebooks*, Sartre challenges Hegel's view that conflict is inevitable for civilization.

The preceding summary and high points of Hegel's Slave-Master relationship and Sartre's *Being and Nothingness* version of our "existence-for-others" have made evident the constant threat represented by the Other, the root of conflict in our original relation to the Other, and, for Sartre, the genesis of our perennial failure—at least according to *Being and Nothingness*—to have authentic intersubjective rapport with Others. To say the *least,* human beings originally relate to one another concretely in an instrumental, adversarial manner that would have to be transcended for genuine intersubjectivity to be attained.

Now, to facilitate a transition to my book's basic project—namely, a study of Sartre's trajectory on violence—and to anticipate the language of violence that Sartre will use in his *Notebooks for and Ethics,* I must add in passing that Sartre's analysis in *Being and Nothingness* of the *conflict* at the heart my being-for-Others and all my "concrete relations" with Others can be viewed as an entry into his developing understanding of violence—and, perhaps also, its inevitability. The Other's original refusal of me, the Other's "looking" at me as object, the Other's "objectification" of me, and, conversely, my counterrefusal and counter-"objectification" of the Other *violate* me, as well as the Other, as *being-for-itself,* as free conscious being, as subject, as human reality, or—to repeat Sartre's idiomatic usage of the word—as *a freedom.* Although in *Being and Nothingness* Sartre does not employ the word "violence" to characterize my or the Other's attempts to "steal," absorb, assimilate, or recover my or the Other's freedom, it seems clear that these mutual violations have a claim to that word, for, etymologically, to violate (*violare*)—in this case, to violate free, conscious subjects—is at the root of the word "violence." (Readers might recall that one attitude toward and method of recovery of one's freedom even projects the "death" of the Other's freedom.) In fact, it is not, in my judgment, too extreme to suggest—if I may integrate two of Sartre's most unforgettable statements—that *violence* is at the core of my "original fall" and my original "being-for-others."[57] We shall do well to keep these observations in mind as we proceed to study and interrelate Sartre's explicit discussions of violence in selected but representative works, from the early *Notebooks for an Ethics* (1947–48) to the "final" published "conversations" (1979–80) in his brilliant but controversial philosophical oeuvre.

---

57. BN 263, 364 (*EN* 321, 431). I shall, of course, elucidate the meanings of violence for Sartre in subsequent chapters.

But, in proceeding, I want to reemphasize one qualifying point. The preceding analysis of conflict is based on Sartre's account in *Being and Nothingness*, but he later refers to this work as "an ontology before conversion" (*une ontologie d'avant la conversion*) that "takes for granted that conversion is necessary" (*suppose qu'une conversion est nécessaire*).[58] Even in a footnote in the latter part of *Being and Nothingness,* he tells us that his preceding analysis "does not exclude the possibility of an ethics of deliverance and salvation," which could come "only after a radical conversion that we cannot discuss here."[59] This means—as Thomas Anderson and others have also pointed out[60]—that conflict is the inevitable structure of relationships between people who are unconverted, that is, who are in natural bad faith and have not yet converted to an authentic way of being.[61] In support of this debated point, we may note Sartre's contention, early in the *Notebooks,* that the "struggle of consciousness" only makes sense "before conversion" and that, after authenticity has been achieved, "there is no ontological reason to stay on the level of struggle" (*le plan de la lutte*).[62] So we must bear this qualification in mind as we proceed, but should not be tempted to presume that conflict will disappear from Sartre's subsequent writings as a pervasive characteristic of interpersonal relationships. Such a presumption would invite an abrupt rethinking of Sartre's subsequent thought.

The preceding allows me to turn to Sartre's *Notebooks for an Ethics* and consider his first explicit and sustained effort to explore the issue of violence. In doing so, I begin a methodical presentation of the progression of Sartre's grappling with this issue at distinct points in his life and writing.

58. *NFE* 6 (*CPM* 13).
59. *BN* 412 (*EN* 484).
60. Thomas C. Anderson, "Sartre's Early Ethics and the Ontology of *Being and Nothingness,*" in *Sartre Alive,* ed. Ronald Aronson and Adrian van den Hoven (Detroit: Wayne State University Press, 1991), 195.
61. See Ronald E. Santoni, *Bad Faith, Good Faith, and Authenticity in Sartre's Early Philosophy* (Philadelphia: Temple University Press, 1995)—in particular, the final two chapters. There, I attempt to show the details of what I take to be a moral conversion from what Sartre calls a "natural attitude" of bad faith to an *authentic* mode of existing in which one affirms one's freedom and refuses one's natural "quest for being" (*la quête de l'être*).
62. *NFE* 20 (*CPM* 26).

"violence" in the *notebooks for an ethics* 2

Sartre's fundamental and pervasive distinction in *Being and Nothingness* between being-for-itself (*l'être-pour-soi*) and being-in-itself (*l'être-en-soi*), together with his view that there is constant potential for violence in the conflict that marks our ontological relation to the Other,[1] paves the way for his analysis of violence in the *Notebooks,* four or five years later. For Sartre here firmly situates violence ontologically as a "type of relation to the Other"[2] and as a relation that "affirms itself in terms of the destruction of the Other." It is "addressed to the freedom of the Other."[3]

Moreover, Sartre, in advance of contemporary analysts of violence such as Newton Garver,[4] begins by distinguishing *violence* from the concept of

---

1. Sartre, as I have indicated, says that "[c]onflict is the original meaning of being-for-others," though he insists that being-for-others is *not* part of the "ontological structure of the for-itself." He also says that "my original *fall* is the existence of the Other." BN 364, 282, 263. See my consideration of this issue in my introductory exposition.

2. *NFE* 215 (*CPM* 224).

3. *NFE* 178 (*CPM* 186).

4. See, e.g., Newton Garver, "New Reflections on Violence," in *Violence in America,* ed. Thomas Rose (New York: Vintage Books, 1969), 9–13.

force (*vis*), from which it is originally derived, and does so in terms of the consequences of each. Whereas force "brings about positive effects by acting in conformity with the nature of things" (*en agissant conformément à la nature des choses*) and conforms to some rule (*légalité*) or "internal laws of an object" (*lois internes de l'objet*), violence is negative, external to the law (*extérieure à la légalité*), destructive of a thing's nature, and is originally born of the inadequacy or "failure of using force" (*l'échec de la force*) ("If I uncork the bottle, it is force—if I break its neck, it is violence"). Hence, destruction of a thing's "nature" or "organic unity" or "internal laws" initially differentiates violence from force, and the choice of violence over force would "affirm the inessentialness of everything that exists in relation to me." From the outset, then, violence for Sartre presupposes the destructibility of "the form that is opposed to you" (*la forme qui vous êtes opposée*), and implies nihilism.[5] It is destructive of "chains of events and of natures."[6] It "is not just the refusal of making use of something, it is the destruction of the possibility of such use for everyone, the refusal of *all* lawfulness."[7] Lest one become preoccupied with what might seem to be Sartre's uncharacteristic concern for lawfulness, I need only point out that Sartre wants "lawfulness" here—as it relates to violence—to connote "laws of normal usage" that are "established by *wills*" (*les lois d'usage normal . . . établies par des "volontés"*).[8] And his apparent conjoining of these laws with "nature" becomes equally baffling alongside his statement, at the beginning of his appendix II, entitled "Revolutionary Violence," that "[v]iolence cannot be defined apart from some relation to the laws it violates (human or natural laws). It represents . . . a 'vacation from legality.'"[9] This is violation of *droit* in one sense of that word.

Let us note the importance of the French word *droit* in the present context. *Droit* in French can mean "law" as well as "right," and for Sartre both "force" and "violence" are closely connected to the word *droit*. Sartre's use of *droit* in the sense of law or legality is closely associated with "force," which, if it is to have the beneficial consequences it seeks, will involve "acting in conformity with the nature of things." Violence, on the other hand, involves a breaking with and violation of a thing's nature or "internal

---

5. All preceding quotations in this paragraph are from *NFE* 170–72, the French from *CPM* 178–80.
6. *NFE* 173 (*CPM* 181).
7. *NFE* 182 (*CPM* 190).
8. *NFE* 172 (*CPM* 180), italics mine.
9. *NFE* 561 (*CPM* 579).

laws"—hence, a violation of *droit* in this general sense of legality. But, more frequently, I think, Sartre uses *droit* in the sense of "right"—for example, the *right* of persons to be treated as human beings, not subhumans;[10] or the *right* of a child to be treated as an ontologically free being, not a "lesser freedom." To be sure, Sartre shows an initial preference for force (which does not violate a thing's nature or inner laws) over violence (which does),[11] but he also points to the "right" (*droit*) of a violated people (e.g., the oppressed) to resist, even fight, that violation. In turn, he refers to the (perceived?) right of a ruler (or "conqueror"), as a coequal moral agent, to *require* the oppressed, by force of law, *not* to resort to violence.[12] In short, the relationship between the two senses of *droit* (as "law" and as "right") is a complex but intimate one in which, as Bill McBride contends, the two senses sometimes "co-imply one another."[13] These all-too-brief observations should suffice to illuminate the closeness of that relation, and provide some guidance for following Sartre's extensive discussion of violence in the *Notebooks*.

Sartre tells us early in his *Notebooks* discussion that violence is "pure exercise of freedom," "unconditional affirmation of freedom," "pure non-being," "pure nihilating power," "pure consciousness," appropriating either the world or human being by *destruction*. As "pure freedom for himself," as "pure destructive consciousness," violent man is "man . . . when he destroys the given in itself in the world and . . . *thing* when he destroys man." Violent man wants the "ruin of the world," the disappearance of being, but he wants this related to a universe in which he is no longer "trapped," seized, or tied down by the "gaze," or "look," of the Other (note the influence of *Being and Nothingness*). Violence takes hold of the objects of the world as "pure densities to destroy," but what one destroys through them is the human being. The violent person "vacillates between a refusal of the world and a refusal of man," and she operates on the level of "pure right" (*droit pur*). The world ought not to have been; humans ought not to have been; I have a *right* (*droit*) to destroy them. "Pure violence" and

10. *CPM* 150 (*NFE* 142). Because I am dealing with the French word *droit,* I am deliberately citing the French first in this context.

11. *CPM* 179 (*NFE* 171). Sartre goes on to amplify, in subsequent pages of the *Notebooks,* the relation of the state and *droit* to *"Dieu et le droit"* (God and *rights*), for example (*CPM* 155 ff. [*NFE* 147 ff.]).

12. *CPM* 150 (*NFE* 142).

13. William McBride, *Sartre's Political Theory* (Bloomington: Indiana University Press, 1991), 67. I refer the reader to McBride's more complete account of Sartre's two senses of *droit* on pages 66–69. I owe much, here, to his account, and also to his recommendation that I include something about the two senses of this word in my present manuscript.

"pure right" are but one: "There has never been any violence on earth" that did not consist of "the affirmation of some right" against a "form" or "organization of the universe."[14] As Sartre says later, "Violence is a meta-morphosis of the universe such that violence becomes a right."[15] And because all violence "presents itself as the recuperation of a right," every right, in turn, contains within itself the seeds of violence. (Note: This con-nection hardly makes the two "one and the same" [*ne font qu'un*], as Sartre contends here.)[16] We shall need to come back to this important contention when we deal with Sartre's later (diverging) views on violence, but for now we must focus on the "contradiction" and "curious ambiguity" (*la curieuse ambiguïté*) to which Sartre has already alluded and which he proceeds to emphasize throughout his treatment of violence in the *Notebooks*.[17]

We have seen that pure nihilating freedom assumes the "divine right of the human person" to destroy the world.[18] "The contradiction is that the world is perpetually necessary as an obstacle to be nihilated"; the violent person depends on the richness of the world to support his destructions and provide new objects for destruction. But that is only one dimension of the "curious ambiguity." Violence is also a "demand on others."[19] To do vio-lence to Others, I have to consider myself "pure freedom," "the source of every right," but regard all other human beings as *inessential* to me. Yet, because violence demands to be recognized, I need the Other as freedom to recognize my violence as "legitimate" or "justified." "Destructive of the human world," violence requires the human world to acknowledge its destruction; it needs the freedom it negates. In doing violence to the Other, I treat the Other as both "essential and inessential": since I "require" her, I recognize her as free, while I simultaneously "declare" her to be "purely determined." I want both to "obligate" the freedom I address and to "destroy it."[20] This analysis echoes both Hegel's depiction of the Master's attitude in his demand for "recognition" from the Slave, and Sartre's own analysis in *Being and Nothingness* of the For-itself's attempt to absorb or destroy the freedom of the Other (who has "looked" at me) while simulta-

---

14. *NFE* 174–77 (*CPM* 183–85), for preceding quotes in this paragraph.
15. *NFE* 201 (*CPM* 209).
16. *NFE* 177 (*CPM* 185).
17. *NFE* 176 (*CPM* 184). See also, e.g., *NFE* 172, 173, 178, 193, 200, 204, 210, 211, 285, 400.
18. *NFE* 174, 177 (*CPM* 182, 185).
19. *NFE* 175, 177 (*CPM* 183, 185). Sartre analyzes the demand more fully in *NFE* 261 ff.
20. *NFE* 177–78 (*CPM* 184–85).

neously wanting to preserve her freedom to recognize or choose me—as in the case of sadism or love, for example. Indeed, for Sartre in the *Notebooks*, this is the deepest of violence's contradictions (*la contradiction la plus profonde*). Moreover, the violent person, given this duplicity, is in *bad faith* in this regard and others.[21]

To put the preceding point more sharply and see clearly its ontological significance, "In violence [for Sartre] one treats a freedom like a thing, all the while recognizing its nature [*sic*] as freedom."[22] The ambiguous double movement that Sartre applied to "concrete relations with others" in *Being and Nothingness*[23] returns to his analysis of violence in the *Notebooks*. As he defines it somewhat later: "Violence is an *ambiguous* notion: . . . [it is] to make use of the facticity of the other person and the objective from the outside to determine the subjective to turn itself into an inessential means of reaching the objective." This amounts to using a human being as a means to achieve a specific objective while retaining "the *value* of its having been chosen" by a subjective freedom.[24] In fact, the "impossible ideal of violence" is to "constrain the freedom of the Other [in order] to choose freely what I [as freedom] want."[25] With "force," of course, the freedom of the Other appears as a refusal of this constraint.

This inner tension, this curious ambiguity, of violence, now expressed blatantly in terms of freedom's thingification of freedom, virtually dominates Sartre's protracted analysis of violence in the *Notebooks*. In violence, I "deliberately transform a freedom into a thing":[26] as freedom, I want the freedom of the Other to "give way" to mine.[27] In the violence of rape, one possesses, negates, thingifies the other's freedom through destruction. For the auto-da-fé, whose inquisition deals death to the heretic, "freedom is something to destroy."[28] Even in the rearing of children—an example Sartre chooses to illustrate "violence in everyday life"[29]—the parent treats the

21. *NFE* 178 (*CPM* 185). For other aspects of the violent person's *bad faith*, see, e.g., *NFE* 175, 184, 189, 212, 220, 563. I do *not* intend, here, to focus on the bad faith of violence. But I should like to do so on another occasion.

22. *NFE* 193 (*CPM* 201).

23. *BN* 361–430.

24. *NFE* 204 (*CPM* 212), italicizing of "ambiguous" is mine.

25. *NFE* 204 (*CPM* 212: "c'est de contraindre la liberté de l'autre à vouloir librement ce que je veux").

26. *NFE* 200 (*CPM* 207).

27. *NFE* 178 (*CPM* 186).

28. *NFE* 185 (*CPM* 193).

29. *NFE* 189 (*CPM* 197).

child as a "lesser freedom." Moreover, in "limiting" or "minimizing" the child's freedom and issuing imperatives to her, parents make themselves "irremediable" by *means* of the freedom of the child as "lesser freedom" (*une liberté "mineure"*).[30] The child as lesser freedom is used as a means to her parents' end: limited in relation to her parents' freedom, the child is thing "to the extent that [she] is freedom."[31]

Similarly, "in lying to the Other, I address myself to the Other's freedom and demand . . . to be recognized as free."[32] But in the violence of lying I treat freedom, at once, as both means and end; I place the Other's freedom "in parentheses"; I treat the Other as free and not free at the same time; I "guarantee" myself against a free consciousness (*se garantir contre la conscience libre*) by "transforming it into a thing." And, at the same time, by wanting to be perceived by other people as pleasant (*agréable*)—indeed, I want to be recognized as being this certain way *permanently*—I try both to glue down my own freedom and to make the Other exercise his freedom in appreciating and valuing me as an amiable and praiseworthy being.[33] In short, in the lie, as another expression of violence, I make use of the freedom of the Other—specifically, his confidence in me—in order to destroy his freedom, but that also objectifies my freedom.[34] Violence, once more, turns out to be an ambiguous and thingifying enterprise—and as such a profoundly alienating experience that involves a "sectioning off" (*un sectionnement*) or "ungluing" (*un décollement*) of freedoms that need one another.[35] I "break off contact with the Other's freedom."[36] Moreover, even in covert defensive violence directed against nonviolent processes—when, for example, I refuse further discussion with the Other—I oppose the freedom of the Other with the limit of my facticity and thereby push him to confront his own facticity in a dehumanizing manner that breaks my "tacit contract" with him "by refusing the rules of the game" (e.g., to proceed in a specific manner).[37] In my "refusal of recognition," I refuse the Other as "pure valorizing freedom" and treat him as an "object," as an "alienated, distracted freedom." But this recalls to me the Other's freedom—for example,

30. *NFE* 190 (*CPM* 198).
31. *NFE* 193 (*CPM* 202: "Elle est chose précisément dans la mesure où elle est liberté").
32. *NFE* 195 (*CPM* 204).
33. *NFE* 198–99 (*CPM* 206–8).
34. *NFE* 200 (*CPM* 208).
35. *NFE* 202 (*CPM* 210), *CPM* 209 (*NFE* 200).
36. *NFE* 210 (*CPM* 219).
37. E.g., *NFE* 208, 230 (*CPM* 217, 240: "rupture des règles du jeu").

when the Other freely chooses to refuse my proposal—and refers me back to my own facticity, to my own objectifying and now "alienated" and "distracted" freedom.[38] This instantiates what Sartre calls the "principle of violence": the "enslaving of freedom gets posited" as a way of liberating this freedom.[39] Thus, ontological "contradiction" and thingification mark this quiet violence also, as does the key element of "refusal"—refusal of the not-me, refusal of persons, refusal of coexistence, refusal of rules, refusal of time, refusal of "the world."

Finally, the culminating illustration of violence is "violence against violence"—the type of violence that may bring to a head the double-edged, objectifying, negating patterns of violence. Here I can break "the system of rules" in order to "defend myself by all possible means."[40] Here, most clearly, freedom's choice of violence is, for Sartre, a choice to fall "into the world," to pass into "seriousness," to be "on the side of Being" (*du côté de l'Être*). Violence against violence seems to presuppose the Other's refusal—an obstinate refusal that is normally taken as a form of violence. In many cases, this negation of "interiority" is then transformed into exteriority: I *refuse* and negate the Other's freedom; I break off relations with him; "I make myself impenetrable and a pure for-itself over and against this freedom and do the same to it in relation to myself";[41] "I repel every means to make me change"; "I turn myself into a stone."[42] That is to say, the violent consciousness that negates and separates itself from the consciousness of Others also—as we've seen in other cases—negates and objectifies itself. This constitutes another instance of the ambiguity of "double negation." In the *obstinacy* of many types of counterviolence, I "withdraw from the community" of human beings; I negate the "essential relation of interdependence among freedoms"; I refuse to hear any appeal of the Other; I "affirm identity with myself"; I transform myself into pure *being*—"alongside others, with no connection to them."[43] In a word, violence against violence shows us not only that violence for Sartre is non-coexistential and, if you like, *destructively* noncommunitarian but also that it is manifestly self-objectifying, that it not only dehumanizes Others but is self-dehumanizing. This feature is repeated throughout his analysis of violence. The violent

38. *NFE* 207–9 (*CPM* 216–18).
39. *NFE* 211 (*CPM* 220).
40. *NFE* 213 (*CPM* 223).
41. *NFE* 209–10 (*CPM* 219).
42. *NFE* 214 (*CPM* 223).
43. Ibid.

man is a "pure man":[44] as "unconditioned [and "absolute"] affirmation of freedom" he becomes (Sartre quoting Hegel) "explicitly objective to himself";[45] he is "on the side of positivity";[46] he places himself "on the side of Being"; he "espouses the party of Being";[47] he "incarnates Being" and is "fundamentally identical with pure Being";[48] he is in-itself; he is "a thing when he [is destroying] man."[49] As I have said elsewhere,[50] violence for Sartre in the *Notebooks* not only ruptures and violates the ontological status, the ontological measure, of the Other as freedom, not only tears apart possibilities for human community (or, Sartre might say, the "system of rules"[51] for being authentically human), but turns the human into an *object*. Violence in all of its forms—even in prayer or in the *demand* of pity—exhibits a "negation of the negation,"[52] "double negation," a "doubly ambiguous existence":[53] it creates "two unconnected universes,"[54] two negated and self-negating freedoms, two freedoms/means mutually regarded and regarding as essential/inessential. Unlike force, violence does not *conduce* to constructive consequences for human reality or the human order: on the contrary, it destroys and severs it.

Before moving on to Sartre's position on violence in progressively later writings, we need to take note of two transitional considerations. First, for Sartre in the *Notebooks* violence connotes the deliberate choice to attain a specific end *"by any means whatsoever";* [55] what he calls the "maxim of violence" is plainly "the end justifies the means." By this maxim, any means that serves to bring about a specific end—and that end can change as the context changes—can be *justified,* in part because violence "creates a right."[56] But this must be viewed as an aspect of Sartre's phenomenological account

44. *NFE* 174 (*CPM* 182).
45. *NFE* 175 (*CPM* 183).
46. *NFE* 184 (*CPM* 193).
47. *NFE* 185 (*CPM* 193).
48. *NFE* 187 (*CPM* 196).
49. *NFE* 175–76 (*CPM* 183–84).
50. Ronald E. Santoni, "On the Existential Meaning of Violence," *Dialogue and Humanism,* no. 4 (1993): 146.
51. See, e.g., *NFE* 213 (*CPM* 283).
52. E.g., *NFE* 184 (*CPM* 192).
53. E.g., *NFE* 210, 217 (*CPM* 219, 227).
54. *NFE* 200 (*CPM* 208).
55. *NFE* 172 (*CPM* 180).
56. *NFE* 264–65 (*CPM* 275–76: "la violence crée le droit").

of violence:[57] it ought not to be taken as an endorsement of violence or the "maxim of violence." In fact, if anything, Sartre has often tried to show that the ambiguity of violence—the essential/inessential dialectic with respect to freedom—constitutes *bad faith*.[58] Yet one must concede in passing that, having stated that "the end of violence is to bring about the universe of violence," Sartre goes on to say that "the universe of violence is certainly one way of *affirming* man . . . [so] it is in no way . . . as is too often said . . . a return to bestiality."[59] Whether this also is part of Sartre's phenomenological description or is intended as a passing Sartrean contention or is another illustration of Sartrean "misspeak" is not entirely clear in the somewhat disordered context of the *Notebooks*. Yet it certainly bears some relevance to what he later affirms in his Preface to Fanon's *Wretched of the Earth*.

Second, the fact that I have not mentioned oppression with respect to violence should suggest neither that Sartre failed to deal with oppression in the *Notebooks* nor that Sartre does not intend an intimate connection between oppression—including class oppression—and violence. Although in appendix II he suggests a distinction between violence and oppression (violence always relates to "human or natural laws" that it violates, while oppression can be "institutional"),[60] the body of the *Notebooks* confirms oppression as a form of violence. (Even stupidity is viewed here as a form of oppression.) One might even say, as Thomas Anderson contends, that in the *Notebooks* Sartre views violence primarily in the context of oppression.[61] He devotes a large segment to a sustained, extensive analysis of oppression[62] and shows clearly that the features or conditions that he has attributed to violence apply to oppression. "Oppression comes from freedom," he says: It "can come to one freedom *only* through another freedom—only one freedom

57. After reading and commenting on an early, incomplete draft of this manuscript and noting my reference to Sartre's phenomenology of violence, Bill McBride referred me to his early article "Sartre and the Phenomenology of Social Violence." I later located and read it, and found it to be an insightful piece of work. I make reference to it later in this revised and completed book. See James M. Edie, ed., *New Essays in Phenomenology* (Chicago: Quadrangle Books, 1969), 290–313. In addition, I have subsequently noted McBride's repetition of this point in my rereading of his *Sartre's Political Theory*, e.g., 68.

58. E.g., *NFE* 178 (*CPM* 186). As I have already suggested, this is an issue for another study.

59. *NFE* 173 (*CPM* 181), italics mine.

60. *NFE* 561 (*CPM* 579).

61. Tom Anderson made this comment in response to my discussion here. See also Thomas C. Anderson, *Sartre's Two Ethics* (Chicago: Open Court, 1993), esp. chap. 5.

62. *NFE* 324 ff. (*CPM* 338 ff.). Note also that he earlier points out the "ambiguity" of oppression involved in class struggle; e.g., *NFE* 263 (*CPM* 274).

can limit another freedom"; it is "grounded in the ontological relation of freedoms to one another";[63] it is a "moment in the dialectic of freedoms."[64] That
is to say, "only a freedom can be oppressed," and freedom can be oppressed
only by another freedom "that recognizes it as freedom"; "if we pretend
that man is not free, the very idea of oppression loses all meaning."[65] There
is oppression "when *freedom* turns against itself," when it steals from
another freedom the "meaning" of her acts and the "unity of [her] life," when
one free being refuses to treat another human being as the free person she is.[66]
And there is a *"climate of oppression"* "when my free subjectivity gives
itself out as *inessential,* . . . when my activity is directed by the Other and
takes the Other as its end."[67] In the manner that Sartre has emphasized with
respect to violence, oppression—as freedom negating itself, or as freedom's
destructive act against freedom—is both dehumanizing and in *bad faith.*[68]
For to oppress a freedom—and thus *violate* it—one must both recognize the
freedom of the Other and treat it as an object. This is both a repetition of
one of Sartre's themes concerning our conflictual "concrete relations with
Others" in *Being and Nothingness* and a restatement of what he has said in
the *Notebooks* regarding *violence* to the Other.

    In this regard, it is of interest to note that Thomas Anderson, in *Sartre's
Two Ethics,*[69] rightly points out that, in both *Being and Nothingness* and the
Notebooks, to treat freedom as an end is to treat it as a thing, or, in the language of the *Notebooks,* to "reify" it, to "substantialize" it,[70] and thus to
alienate it as freedom. Objectification characterizes all forms of the violence
of oppression (e.g., Master-Slave, colonizer-colonized, forced labor). In fact,
objectification, or reification, is, for Sartre, the "ontological condition"
that makes oppression possible. In somewhat different language, Sartre,
later in the *Notebooks,* states that our original alienation (our original
presence to ourselves as *other*) "perpetuates oppression, and oppression perpetuates alienation."[71]

---

    63. *NFE* 325 (*CPM* 338).
    64. *NFE* 332 (*CPM* 345).
    65. *NFE* 326–28 (*CPM* 339–41).
    66. *NFE* 332 (*CPM* 345).
    67. *NFE* 366 (*CPM* 380), italics mine.
    68. E.g., *NFE* 328 (CPM 341).
    69. Anderson, *Sartre's Two Ethics,* 78–82. In what follows, I paraphrase and quote from
these pages, unless I indicate otherwise.
    70. Anderson takes these words from *NFE,* e.g., 169 and 468, respectively.
    71. *NFE* 384 (*CPM* 398).

In addition, Anderson contends that the discussion in the *Notebooks* moves significantly beyond "the exclusively psychological notions of oppression and conflict present in *Being and Nothingness*," arguing that Sartre in the *Notebooks* insists that oppression involves "more than just being the object of others." Citing references to Sartre that I have already invoked or discussed, he reminds the reader that oppression requires a free decision on the part of some (the oppressors) to deny or foreclose possibilities, projects, or opportunities to other free beings. Entire groups or classes of people may live in the oppressed conditions of poverty, segregation, or slavery because of the free *choices* and actions of others. It is these actions, not just objectification, that have brought about oppression.[72]

I think that Anderson is right in maintaining that the *Notebooks* extend Sartre's views of conflict, violence, and oppression from *Being and Nothingness* beyond what Anderson calls an "exclusively psychological" account into a wider one that begins to focus on social-material conditions and broadens the typology of violence and oppression. But I should qualify Anderson's contention in two ways. First, in the light of my preceding account of "conflict" in *Being and Nothingness*, I would caution Anderson about his labeling Sartre's account "exclusively psychological," rather than "ontological/psychological." The roots of our psychological moves and maneuverings (which Anderson describes) in our "concrete relations with Others" are ontological. And as Anderson so well knows, "conflict," for Sartre in *Being and Nothingness*, "is the original meaning of being-for-others." Second, I would maintain that even the extended view of oppression that Anderson sees in the *Notebooks* depends on the ontological framework that Sartre offers in *Being and Nothingness*. I believe that Anderson's statement that the *Notebooks* account entails *"not just . . . objectification"* indirectly acknowledges my point. Coincidentally, I should point out that Sartre's insistence in the *Notebooks* that the violence of "oppression requires a free decision on the part of some to oppress others" would be supported, not precluded, by *Being and Nothingness*. Even if in *Being and Nothingness* consciousness is originally and ontologically inclined toward an object (all consciousness "posits" or intends an object) and bad faith,[73] it does not follow that consciousness's objectification and/or oppression of the Other is

---

72. See, e.g., *NFE* 331 (*CPM* 345).
73. For a detailed discussion of bad faith and other modes of consciousness, I refer the reader to my *Bad Faith, Good Faith, and Authenticity in Sartre's Early Philosophy* (Philadelphia: Temple University Press, 1995).

not a free choice. In *Being and Nothingness,* consciousness, or human reality, has to be understood in terms of freedom, although, to be sure, free choices may be dominantly unreflective at the preconversion level.

Finally, in his perceptive attempt to show Sartre's "advance" in the *Notebooks,* Anderson contends that, here, to be an object of the Other "does not necessarily mean" to be oppressed or "to be degraded, reified, or enslaved" by the Other,[74] as it does in *Being and Nothingness.* Anderson mobilizes a good argument and pertinent quotations from the *Notebooks* to support the development in Sartre's position. His discussion of the *authentic* person's acceptance of her objective "transformation of herself" as a "gift" to the Other (as well as part of the human condition) is particularly to the point. But, again, I challenge part of the basis for Anderson's contention. In maintaining that in *Being and Nothingness* only subject-object relations are possible, Anderson seems to equate the epistemological subject-object relation (or consciousness's positing an object of knowledge) with the kind of objectification that goes on in the violence of oppression or the *praxis* of degradation. In my judgment, this constitutes, at minimum, an overinterpretation of consciousness's initial perceiving, or "knowing," the Other free for-itself as an object (of consciousness), or body in the world. To be sure, as I've suggested above, this intentionality of consciousness *predisposes* consciousness to negate the Other as freedom, but this intentional relationship should not be placed in the same category as the violent relationship of oppression that Sartre spells out in the *Notebooks.* This does not, however, repudiate Anderson's point that the bad faith of concrete relations with Others in *Being and Nothingness,* or the objectification that is part of oppression in the *Notebooks,* "may be transformed through conversion."[75] Unlike *Being and Nothingness, Notebooks for an Ethics* does provide the path to conversion to an authentic "way of being," in which genuine intersubjectivity can at least be a hope.[76]

---

74. Anderson, *Sartre's Two Ethics,* 79, 81.

75. *NFE* 499 (*CPM* 515: "peut se transformer par la conversion").

76. For a detailed discussion of authenticity, I again refer the reader to Santoni, *Bad Faith, Good Faith, and Authenticity,* esp. chap. 7.

"violence" in the *critique of dialectical reason*, volume 1

In order to suggest some continuity, and even a marked similarity, between positions that I intend to contrast, I begin with some telling observations from the final part of *Critique 1*.[1] One of Sartre's concluding statements about violence is that it "is *always* both a reciprocal recognition of freedom and a negation (either reciprocal or univocal) of this freedom through the intermediary of the inertia of exteriority." He also says in this context that the "only conceivable violence is that of freedom against freedom through the mediation of inorganic matter,"[2] and he refers to the violence of oppression—with which in the *Critique* he seems dominantly concerned—as a "pure and simple constraint exercised deliberately by men on men."[3] And

1. Jean-Paul Sartre, *Critique of Dialectical Reason,* vol. I, trans. Alan Sheridan-Smith (London: NLB, 1976); originally published as *Critique de la raison dialectique* (Paris: Éditions Gallimard, 1960). Subsequent footnote references to this work in translation (English) use the abbreviation *CDR* followed by the page number(s); the original French is cited as *CRD* followed by the page number(s). In cases where I prefer my own translation, I normally give only the *CRD* reference.
2. *CDR* I:736 (*CRD* I:689).
3. *CRD* I:679: "une pure et simple contrainte exercée délibérément par des hommes sur des hommes." I prefer my more literal translation here to Sheridan-Smith's in *CDR* I:724.

33

Sartre later refers to oppression as "pure violence."[4] But these core affinities must neither mislead nor distract us: we must put together at least a sketch of Sartre's overall view of violence in the *Critique* without pretending to do justice to that immensely rich and demanding work.[5]

If only two words were allowed to represent "violence" in the *Critique*, they would have to be "interiorized [or "internalized"] scarcity" (*rareté intériorisée*).[6] The material conditions of scarcity become the core consideration here. Scarcity is the environment and "milieu" of violence and, in turn, of our history.[7] As the "lived relation of a practical multiplicity to surrounding materiality,"[8] as a relation of individuals to their environment, it is "the basis for the possibility of human history,"[9] and it tyrannizes humanity. *"There is [simply] not enough for everybody"*: the resulting tensions between the human being and his environment and between "man and man" explain our "fundamental structures"—our "techniques and institutions"[10]—for, as William McBride and others have pointed out, our interactions with our fellow human beings are, for Sartre, the very "stuff of history." If there is not enough, the Other threatens me, threatens the fulfillment of my *need*. "Scarcity makes the passive totality of individuals within a collectivity into an impossibility of co-existence";[11] I see the Other as competing with me for a "particular natural substance" or "manufactured good";[12] I negate him and he negates me; human being becomes the enemy of human being; each, in the milieu of scarcity, appears as radically Other and carries the menace of death (*menace de mort*) to the Other; man, in facing "anti-man" (*contre homme*), becomes "nonhuman man" (*homme inhumain*),[13] and violence is thus in the making. So *"each and every man,"*

---

4. *CDR* I:749 (*CRD* I:700).

5. Raymond Aron has referred to the *Critique* as "a sort of baroque monument, overwhelming and almost monstrous . . . the work repulses some, seduces others and perhaps fascinates every reader." Aron, *History and the Dialectic of Violence*, trans. Barry Cooper (New York: Harper Torchbooks, 1976), xix.

6. *CDR* I, e.g., 132 (*CRD* I:208). Aron's translator, Barry Cooper, prefers the word "internalized."

7. *CDR* I:127 (*CRD* I:204).

8. *CDR* I:125 (*CRD* I:202).

9. *CDR* I:126–27 (*CRD* I:203–4).

10. *CDR* I:127–28 (*CRD* I:204).

11. *CDR* I:129 (*CRD* I:205: "la rareté réalise la totalité passive des individus d'une collectivité comme impossibilité de coexistence").

12. *CDR* I:128 (*CRD* I:204).

13. *CRD* I:208–9 (*CDR* I:132–33).

says Sartre, "will contain an inert structure of non-humanity," which is simply "material negation" that has been "interiorized." Everyone is a nonhuman human for all Others.[14]

But we must back up further. We already see that the "conflict" that marked "the original meaning" of our "being-for-others" in *Being and Nothingness*[15]—and that led Garcin in *No Exit* to exclaim, "*l'enfer c'est les autres*"—is translated into and exhibited in the sociohistorical, practical, and sociological context (and antagonisms) of the *Critique*. *Being-for-itself* and *being-in-itself* have not disappeared; they have reappeared, with new socialized and extended meanings in the material conditions of history, as *praxis* and *practico-inert*. *Praxis* is free, self-conscious, purposive, or active consciousness working on matter—that is, working in its material setting. In a way, labor is the paradigm of praxis and dialectical activity for Sartre (see, e.g., *CDR* I:559). In one place, he even refers to human labor as "the original praxis by which man produces and reproduces his life."[16] This surely reflects the influence of both Hegel and Marx. In other places, Sartre states that praxis is "a unifying and reorganizing transcendence of existing circumstances," and tells us that "there is a dialectical movement and a dialectical relation between action as the negation of matter . . . and matter . . . as the negation of action."[17] There is little question that "praxis," with freedom at its core, has primacy in the *Critique*.

The *practico-inert*, on the other hand, is the "worked matter," the "matter in which past praxis is embodied" (i.e., "worked upon inertia"),[18] sedimented praxis; it connotes passivity and what Sartre calls "counter-finality"—that is, results counter to those projected by praxis. To use Joe Catalano's phrasing, inverted praxis "can become engraved with matter."[19] At one point, Sartre even refers to the practico-inert field as a "caricature of the dialectic and its alienating objectification."[20] To use Sartre's own words, whereas praxis involves a "dialectic movement" between free action and matter, the practico-inert is

---

14. *CDR* I:130 (*CRD* I:206).
15. *BN* 364 (*EN* 431).
16. *CDR* I:90 (*CRD* I:174).
17. *CDR* I:310–11 n. 93, 159 (*CRD* I:230).
18. *CDR* I:829 (glossary). Sartre refers to it as "the realm of equivalence of alienated praxis and worked-upon inertia" (*CRD* I:159, translation mine). See also, e.g., *CDR* I:65–67 (*CRD* I:153–55).
19. Joseph Catalano, *A Commentary on Jean-Paul Sartre's Critique of Dialectical Reason*, vol. I (Chicago: University of Chicago Press, 1986), 125.
20. *CDR* I:556 (*CRD* I:547).

matter as the "negation of action."[21] Yet, as Tom Flynn points out, this worked matter still serves to "mediate" our "social and historical relations, even as it preserves the sediment of past praxis."[22]

Put another way, whereas praxis in the *Critique* is a "constituting" (or "constituent") dialectic, the practico-inert is viewed as "antidialectic," as the "objectification" and alienation of praxis within the conditions of materiality and what Sartre calls "seriality"—a term that connotes for him "alterity" and "reification" as well as "passivity."[23] And, in passing, it is important to note that even though scarcity leads to a "*reciprocity* of antagonism" and the "entrapment" of consciousness within the practico-inert—more specifically, within the "inertia of social beings"—consciousness, for Sartre, remains, ontologically, "constituting [or "constituent] praxis," free for-itself working on matter, if you like.[24]

"Reciprocity" in human relations deserves some elaboration. In the *Critique* Sartre passes from a conflictual binary, or dyadic, relationship with the Other (a relationship also seen in *Being and Nothingness*) to a ternary relationship that is *mediated* by the "Third" (*le tiers*), or what he calls the "Third Party," whose importance, both positive and negative, as a unifying and mediating factor in human interrelationships[25] and in "reciprocity" is unquestionable. But Sartre also makes it clear that the immediate binary relationship of human to human is "the necessary ground" of any ternary relation.[26] He refers to this ternary (or triadic) relation as "a free inter-individual reality." The "original structure" of "the Third," he adds, expresses "simply the practical power of his unifying any multiplicity [or collection of people] within his own field of action" by "totalizing" or gathering it "towards his own ends."[27] The Third, which is *praxis* first of all, unifies any

---

21. *CDR* I:159 (*CRD* I:230).

22. Thomas R. Flynn, *Sartre, Foucault, and Historical Reason*, vol. I (Chicago: University of Chicago Press, 1997), 121; similarly stated in his article "Sartre and the Poetics of History," in *The Cambridge Companion to Sartre*, ed. Christina Howells (Cambridge: Cambridge University Press, 1992), 241. See also *CDR* I:161 ("Matter as inverted praxis") (*CRD* I:231).

23. I borrow here from Raymond Aron, who makes the distinction well in *History and the Dialectic of Violence*, 37, 53, 92–94. See also, e.g., *CDR* I:66–67, 556. I am indebted here also to Thomas Flynn, from whose works I have gained much. Although his *Sartre, Foucault, and Historical Reason*, vol. I, appeared only after my first draft of this section, I have referred to it in my revisions. See, e.g., 121–27 of Flynn's book, and also my preceding note and acknowledgment. I highly recommend this book.

24. Aron, *History and the Dialectic of Violence*, 83, 91.

25. See, e.g., *CDR* I:100–109 (*CRD* I:182–89).

26. *CDR* I:109 (*CRD* I:189).

27. *CDR* I:368.

other two human beings by "observing or commanding them." In a group, as Sartre points out, each member is a Third, and each "totalizes the reciprocities of others."[28] As I can be a mediating Third for all the Others, each of the Others can be a mediating Third for the rest of us. The Third (or Third Party), who is *inside* the collective yet *outside* of it as "totalizer" and "unifier," can dissolve *seriality* by his or her free totalizing.

Put another way, each Third can synthesize the series into a developmental unity and thus provide mediation among others. And this new threefold relationship, as the mediation of human beings among human beings, is "the basis on which *reciprocity* becomes aware of it-self as a reciprocal connection."[29]

As Wilfred Desan has pointed out, *reciprocity* between human being and human being, human being and the world, the individual and the group, marks the dialectic or totalizing activity that, for Sartre, moves through history.[30] "Reciprocity," says Sartre, "becomes isolated as a human relation between individuals; it presents itself as a fundamental, concrete lived bond," always mediated by a Third. With respect to human interrelating in reciprocity, we both "transcend our being by producing ourselves as [human beings] among [human beings] . . . *and* allow ourselves to be integrated by everyone else to the [same] extent that they are to be integrated into our own project."[31] Reciprocity can be either positive or negative, and thus *human* relations, as reciprocal, can be positive or negative.[32] To be sure, there can be a cooperative or positive reciprocity that conduces to a group-in-fusion and, to use Flynn's words, "forms the counter-value to alienation."[33] But in "negative reciprocity" there is reciprocal refusal: "each refuses to serve the Other's end." Each reduces herself to her "materiality," to her instrumentality, in order to act on the Other, to use the materiality and instrumentality of the Other for her own ends. (Here, again, is the echo of the conflict and double negation already noted in Hegel, in *Being and Nothingness,* and in the *Notebooks.*) And this, precisely, is *struggle,* the origin of which is—again—scarcity.[34] Because of this scarcity, my relation to

---

28. *CDR* I:374. In this connection, see also Thomas R. Flynn, *Sartre and Marxist Existentialism* (Chicago: University of Chicago Press, 1984), 116–19.

29. *CDR* I:109 (*CRD* I:189: "le fond sur lequel la réciprocité se reconnaît elle-même comme liaison réciproque").

30. Wilfred Desan, *The Marxism of Jean-Paul Sartre* (Gloucester, Mass.: Peter Smith, 1974), 74.

31. *CDR* I:108–9 (*CRD* I:189).

32. *CDR* I:113, 131, 735 (*CRD* I:192, 207, 688).

33. Flynn, *Sartre, Foucault, and Historical Reason,* I:127.

34. *CDR* I:113 (*CRD* I:192); also *CDR* I:815 (*CRD* I:752).

the Other develops from matter and is one of "exteriority." Everyone's "reinteriorization" of scarcity "becomes meaningful in and through every-one" as the "negation of the Other in everyone."[35] Without the "human relation of reciprocity, the non-human relation of scarcity would not exist." But in reciprocity as *modified by scarcity*," "the Other than me," the "same man" of pure reciprocity, appears as "antihuman" (*contre-homme*), bent on destroying the human.[36] That is to say, in negative reciprocity *violent* strug-gle in the field of scarcity "engenders the Other as Other than [hu]man."[37] As long as scarcity exists—and for Sartre history is permanently modified by scarcity—"the permanent threat" will remain (as Catalano has pointed out) that "bonds of reciprocity between myself and others will degenerate" and we will perceive ourselves, as well as others, as "alien beings" struggling—nay, competing violently—for the limited resources of the same planet.[38] This is surely another version of the Sartrean "hell" of *Being and Nothingness*. "Interiorized materiality," "interiorized scarcity," makes "everyone *objec-tively dangerous* to the Other"; it objectively constitutes the human being as "nonhuman." This inhumanity "is expressed in *praxis* by taking *evil* as the structure of the Other."[39] And in perceiving the Other as evil (constituted inhumanity), Manichaeism—a central component in virtually any Sartrean ethical analysis during this period[40]—comes to the fore. "Alien freedom is a hostile force"; "evil *must* be destroyed."[41] The threatening praxis of the Other is what must be destroyed in him.[42] This means that in seeking to destroy evil—now seen as objectively constituted *nonhuman* or *inhuman* in man—I "pursue the liquidation of human beings."[43] But, given the context of scarcity, if I destroy "the inhumanity of the anti-human in my adversary," I cannot help but "destroy the humanity of [the human being] in him" and "realize in myself his inhumanity."[44] For, given the "interiorization of

35. *CDR* I:815 (*CRD* I:752).

36. *CDR* I:131–32 (*CRD* I:207–8).

37. *CDR* I:816 (*CRD* I:753).

38. Catalano, *A Commentary on Jean-Paul Sartre's Critique of Dialectical Reason*, I:115.

39. *CRD* I:208, translation mine ("se traduit dans la praxis par la saisie du mal comme structure de l'Autre").

40. Consider the centrality of Manichaeism in *Saint Genet: Actor and Martyr*, in Sartre's *Anti-Semite and Jew*, in his Preface to *The Wretched of the Earth*, and in portions of *Hope Now*, to give only a few examples. Sartre will say later that "Manichaeism is the primary deter-mination of morality" (*CDR* I:736).

41. *CDR* I:133 (*CRD* I:209).

42. *CDR* I:736 (*CRD* I:689).

43. *CRD* I:208 (in the third person, this appears as "poursuit la liquidation des hommes").

44. *CRD* I:209, translation mine.

scarcity" in the face of the threat of death—what Sartre now calls the "original relation between human beings through the mediation of matter"— free laboring praxis has, while attempting to transcend the material conditions of scarcity, "perceived [herself] in the Other as other freedom," as "antipraxis," to be destroyed. Although the Other is the same as I am, I see in her what I discover in myself: like me, she has the "permanent possibility of being anti-human."[45] So in seeking the destruction of freedom at this elementary level of a "struggle for life" (as in *Being and Nothingness,* the *Notebooks,* and, to a lesser extent, Hegel), I regard the Other's freedom not just as a "menacing object" (*un simple objet menaçant*) but as "a freedom recognized and condemned to its very root" (*jusque dans sa racine*).[46] The "matrix" of violence is a matrix of objectification, "reification," and destruction of human relations.[47] It is, in the language of *Being and Nothingness,* a matrix of bad faith.

What we observe in the preceding, then, is that, in the dual context of scarcity and human need, violence evolves as a "structure of human action under the sway of Manichaeism." To be more explicit—and to use Sartre's words again—"violence always presents itself as *counter-violence,*" that is to say, as "retaliation against the violence [or incipient violence] of the Other."[48] In all human beings there is a "universal motivation of counter-violence"—a process of "putting things back in order" (*processus de remise en ordre*) as a response to "broken reciprocity" (*réciprocité rompue*) and "provocation."[49] Evil comes to be "incarnated" in the Other (Manichaeism), violence evolves, and violence is then justified by its doer—as Catalano has pointed out—as a response to the threat of the Other's violence or the "passive presence" of radical evil or inhumanity in the situation.[50] The constituted inhumanity that has become part of our humanity seems to become a justification (excuse?) for our own violence. Even in *violent rebellion,* the oppressor recognizes "his own oppressive violence as an [enemy] force taking him, in turn, as object." Against his own violence *as Other,* he creates counterviolence in his effort to transcend the violence of the Other, which turns out to be "his own violence in the Other."[51] Violence, thus, presents itself as

45. *CDR* 1:736–37 (*CRD* 1:689–90).
46. *CDR* 1:736 (*CRD* 1:689), translation altered.
47. *CDR* 1:132 (*CRD* 1:208).
48. *CDR* 1:133 (*CRD* 1:209). See also, e.g., *CRD* 1:406 (*CRD* 1:429).
49. *CRD* 1:209, translation mine.
50. Catalano, *A Commentary on Jean-Paul Sartre's Critique of Dialectical Reason,* 1:114–15.
51. *CDR* 1:733 (*CRD* 1:687). I use "enemy" rather than "hostile" in the translated sentence above. See also *CDR* 1:720 (*CRD* 1:677).

"induced violence," as "counterviolence," as "legitimate defense," and as "self-justifying" (*se donnant sa propre justification*).[52]

To invoke a variant of what Sartre has said in the *Notebooks*, because the Other has violated the "system of rules" to serve his own interest, I now accept it as *legitimate* for me to abandon the rules and "*defend myself* by all possible means."[53]

Although I have not yet adequately represented Sartre's treatment of violence in *Critique I*, I have shown enough to observe that Sartre is here offering more of a descriptive account of the "evolution of violence"[54] within the human being's historical and material conditions of scarcity than either an ontology and definition of violence or an extended account of the existential consequences of violence for the human being.[55] William McBride is, I believe, right in insisting that Sartre's account in the *Critique* is not a "biological explanation" but a phenomenological description.[56] Nonetheless, it is clear that—*at least to this point*—his *Notebooks'* analysis of violence and his more indirect discussion of it in the *Critique* are similar. To be sure, the two are not entirely discontinuous. Although the *Critique* has less emphasis on violence as the violation of laws—human or natural—and less explicit mention of the "curious ambiguity" or "contradiction" of violence, Sartre seems to assume here that violence breaches or ruptures human measure (*mesure*) (the bonds of reciprocity are broken) and that, while affirming and addressing freedom-in-situation, the violent person attempts to use the Other's freedom as inessential and thus "deliberately transforms" freedom into a thing. In both works, violence seeks to appropriate the Other's freedom by *destruction,* and my freedom's violation and thingification of the Other's freedom manifests my own (self-)objectification—that is, the antihuman, or "evil," in me. In each case, violence is the exercise of freedom against freedom in order to get what one wants, and involves the reciprocal recognition and negation of the Other's freedom; that is to say, it involves "double

---

52. *CDR* 1:720 (*CRD* 1:677).

53. *NFE* 213 (*CPM* 223), italics mine.

54. *CDR* 1:720 (*CRD* 1:676).

55. This is not to say that he does not come close to defining it. For example, he says—agreeing with Engels—that "violence is not necessarily an act . . . [or] a characteristic of Nature [or] a hidden possibility. It is the constant inhumanity of human conducts . . . [as] scarcity interiorized" (*CRD* 1:221), translation mine.

56. William McBride, "Sartre and the Phenomenology of Social Violence," in *New Essays in Phenomenology,* ed. James M. Edie (Chicago: Quadrangle Books, 1969), 299–300. See note 57 to Chapter 2, in which I refer to McBride's article to confirm my own contention regarding Sartre's "phenomenological account of violence" in the *Notebooks*.

negation," "reciprocal refusal," "two negated freedoms." (To be sure, in the *Critique* Sartre explicitly qualifies this in terms of the mediation of "exteriority" and "inorganic matter," or "practico-inert.")[57] In both works, too, violence is *Manichaean:* its destructive impetus is rooted in seeing the Other as evil incarnate. In the form of oppression, for example, violence is exercised against an "anti-human species whose freedom is essentially the freedom to do evil."[58] Also, in both the *Notebooks* and the *Critique,* the violent man thus identifies with pure Being; he incarnates Being and incarnates the Other as Being. Further, in both works, Sartre sees violence, at least initially, as *alienating*—either because of ontological conflicts or because of the combination of need and material scarcity or because of both. And in effecting alienation violence usually appears, in both accounts, to prevent the possibility of genuine, mutually enhancing coexistence among human freedoms. In short, on both accounts so far, violence both recognizes and threatens to annihilate or constrain freedom, treats it as both essential and inessential (this, again, exemplifies what Sartre has called its "curious ambiguity"), purports to be self-justifying (the end justifies the means—what Sartre calls the "maxim of violence"),[59] sunders human community, and is rooted in an assumed conflictual relation with the Other, who is initially regarded as alien and hostile. Moreover, in both works, oppression, colonialism, and racism are taken as paradigmatic illustrations of violence.

But I have not yet even outlined the whole story regarding violence in the *Critique I.* And I cannot hope to do even partial justice to Sartre's view of it there unless I give some attention to his view of Terror in relation to the so-called pledged group, or, more specifically, in relation to the effort of the "group-in-fusion" to preserve and protect itself against dissolution. For his views in this regard are at the core of so much of the controversy aroused by the *Critique,* and of some of the harshest criticism leveled against it by such important figures as Raymond Aron[60] and, to a lesser extent, Wilfred Desan.

Perhaps the best way of introducing this controversial part of his account is by borrowing—out of sequence—an oft-quoted statement from the concluding part of *Critique I.* "Violence," says Sartre, "bears the name of *oppression* when it is exercised against one or more individuals and imposes on them

---

57. See, again, e.g., *CDR* I:736 (*CRD* I:689).
58. *CDR* I:747 (*CRD* I:698); see also, e.g., *NFE* 175 (*CPM* 182–83).
59. See, e.g., *NFE* 172 (*CPM* 180).
60. Aron, *History and the Dialectic of Violence;* see, e.g., 107 ff., where Aron refers to Sartre's humanism as one that "begins with rebellion and fraternity-terror." See also 160–96.

an untranscendable statute [or "status," *statut*][61] that is a function of [*en fonction de*] scarcity"; and "it is called *Terror* when it defines the bond of fraternity itself."[62] It is the latter part of this quotation that now commands our attention. In the *Critique*'s account of the dialectical movement from individual praxis and inert, passive seriality (e.g., the queue waiting for the *collective entity*, bus) to the common or group praxis of the "group-in-fusion" (e.g., the storming of the Bastille), the "fused group," one might recall, is born of revolt against "necessity" (i.e., the necessity of alienation); it dissolves seriality and resurrects human freedom. In short, this dialectic is one of freedom's tearing itself away from alienation[63] by joining together with other praxes in common action and a common project to obtain a shared goal—specifically, the overcoming of "frozen freedoms" and the "power of anti-praxis."[64] The constitution of "group-in-fusion" represents a kind of "apocalypse" of human rebellion against the antihuman, the coming-to-be of a new episode of genuine humanity—what Aron, using Sartre's expression from *Hauser*, sometimes labels a "perfect moment" or McBride refers to as a "crescendo." But, as Aron puts it—and here he follows Sartre's dynamic dialectic—"perfect moments do not last."[65] As Sartre says early in *Critique I*, "Alienation exists as a constant danger within the practical group. . . . The most lively and united group is always in danger of relapsing into the series from which it came."[66] Although lack of organization and absence of leadership may mark the limits of fusion, they do not give cohesion to the group or guarantee its continuation or permanence. The group must now become reflexive, must view itself as object, must continue to protect itself against external threat, must find a way of surviving permanently in unity while guaranteeing that the separate action of each of its members is in behalf of common action and reciprocity. Distribution of enforceable rights and duties must be organized. Organization and differentiation of individual projects must be set up, maintained, and mediated through the group's common project, or "constituted dialectic."

61. A statute (*statut*) is to be understood here (and elsewhere in *CDR*) as the condition of an individual (or "ensemble") insofar as it is "prescribed" or directed by the kind of collective of which it is a part. *CDR* I:829–30 (glossary), in the English translation only.

62. *CRD* I:689, translation and italicizing of "oppression" mine; also *CDR* I:737.

63. *CRD* I:425, translation mine ("s'arrache à l'aliénation"); also *CDR* I:402.

64. I borrow these apt expressions from Catalano, *A Commentary on Jean-Paul Sartre's Critique of Dialectical Reason*, 180. They are, of course, Sartrean expressions.

65. Aron, *History and the Dialectic of Violence*, 59.

66. *CDR* I:67 n. 29 (*CRD* I:154 n. 3).

My self-conscious dreadful freedom allows me to dread the possibility of my own infidelity and treason to the group, not to mention the Other's. A "practical device" (*invention pratique*) is needed to bind the group in unity and permanence.[67]

For Sartre, this practical device is the *oath,* or *pledge (le serment)*, and through it the potential for violence and its justification—presumably within the framework of a new humanity—emerges in full force. I can only bind myself—my own freedom—by swearing a transference to the group of my freedom of preservation and authorizing the group to castigate me in case of desertion or treason.[68] This pledge, or oath, is "mediated reciprocity."[69] In fact, the act of making a pledge can only be common: "I give my pledge to all third parties" (*tous les tiers*) insofar as it is "the group of which I am a part that guarantees the status of permanence to everyone." In the order "'Let us Swear'. . . I also make myself . . . a guarantee," for and in every Third Party, "that alterity cannot come to him through me."[70] "To swear is to give [to Others] what one does not possess in order that the Others shall give it to you so that one can keep one's word."[71] That is to say, the order "Let us Swear" is "a common decision to swear."[72] In swearing, each one gets an objective guarantee from the other Third that he will never become the Other.

But this is precisely where violence and the threat of Terror reenter. The oath (or pledge) turns out to be "the common production, through mediated reciprocity, of a statute of violence."[73] It finds its origin in fear and its strength and élan through violence and the threat of *Terror.* The pledge purports to guarantee the freedom of everyone against necessity—that is, against the force of antifreedom and antipraxis—even at the cost of one's life. "To swear is to say, as a common individual, I demand that you kill me if I secede [or betray the group]. And this demand has no other goal but to establish Terror in me against the fear of the enemy."[74] Common freedom "violates necessity" and thus "constitutes itself" as Terror.[75] The attempt to

---

67. CDR I:420 (CRD I:439). See also CDR I:736–37 (CRD I:689).
68. I acknowledge the influence of Aron here.
69. CDR I:419–21 (CRD I:439–41).
70. CDR I:421 (CRD I:441).
71. CDR I:427 (CRD I:445).
72. CDR I:428 (CRD I:446).
73. CDR I:431 (CRD I:448). On "statute," see note 61 to this chapter.
74. CRD I:448–49, translation mine. See also CDR I:431.
75. CDR I:430–31 (CRD I:448–49).

transcend individual alienation through the pledge by common freedom simply "reactualizes" violence and establishes a group over which "absolute violence" reigns. Terror becomes the "fundamental statute" of the "pledged [or sworn] group" (*groupe assermenté*),[76] the reciprocal "right" of everyone in the group over the life and death of every other member. This right is rooted in freedom's affirmation of itself as "justified violence" against the practico-inert and necessity. "Transcendence" is present in the pledged group as "the *absolute* right of all over every individual." And by the Terror that the "common right" has established in me, I grant everyone (including the Third Party) the "right" to eliminate me in case of my free betrayal.[77]

Again, as in the *Notebooks*, Sartre links rights (*les droits*) with violence[78] and—in this case—Terror. But, on this dialectical analysis, far from separating or sundering, Terror *unites*. Terror is the "primary unity" of the pledged group "in so far as it is the power of freedom over necessity in everyone." Although it is the "bearer of death," it unifies by guaranteeing "solicitude [i.e., uneasiness] for everyone." And through this "mortal solicitude," Sartre says, the human being as a "common individual" is created—for all Third Parties, or mediating Thirds, are fundamentally related by their having "created themselves together"[79]—and *fraternity* is born. Through the "creative act of the pledge"[80] and the statute of Terror, we have become brothers. "We fraternize because we have made the same pledge" (*nous avons prêté le même serment*); we have accepted everyone's *right* of violence over the Other in behalf of freedom, against alterity and the practico-inert, and for the sake of constraint.[81] That is to say, fraternity, having originated in violence, becomes "the most immediate and constant form of Terror."[82] Fraternity and Terror are twin brothers. In pledging constraint through a unity of common praxis at the risk of death to any treasonous member, I become a "common individual," and the group-in-fusion becomes a "group-in-constraint" (*groupe-en-contrainte*)—a constraining group—that turns the "positive violence" of fraternity into the "negative violence" of Terror.[83] To repeat,

---

76. *CDR* I:430, 433 (*CRD* I:448, 450).
77. *CDR* I:432–33 (*CRD* I:449–50).
78. William McBride develops such a point in *Sartre's Political Theory* (Bloomington: Indiana University Press, 1991), e.g., 67, 68, 69, and 152–53. See my brief discussion of this at the beginning of my consideration of Sartre's account of "violence" in the *Notebooks*.
79. *CDR* I:434–35 (*CRD* I:451).
80. *CDR* I:437 (*CRD* I:453).
81. *CDR* I:440 (*CRD* I:456).
82. Ibid.
83. Ibid.

violence bears "the name of *Terror* when it defines the bond of fraternity"[84] in opposition to group dissolution. A brotherhood at work is "Fraternity-Terror" (*une Fraternité-Terreur*),[85] and Terror is the new "statute of totalization" and "jurisdiction," that is, the new mode of relating (to the group) that will influence, if not determine, the manner in which each member of the group will incarnate, or "singularize," all the actions in the collective.[86] If my brother conducts himself as an Other and if my "constraining group" perceives him as threatening dissolution, the "violence of my fraternization" will be expressed in "either a lynching, *in its own name,* or in a merciless condemnation"—that is, extermination.[87] Yet, as paradoxical as it may seem, for Sartre "the *Sacred* constitutes the fundamental structure of Terror as juridical power" ("it is freedom returning to man as a superhuman petrified power"),[88] and Terror, as Catalano has pointed out, "creates the very context for all concrete forms of mediated reciprocities"—love and fraternity as well as hate.[89] "Through the mediation of all," Sartre says, "everyone consents with everyone else that the permanent foundation of every freedom should be the violent negation of necessity, that is to say, that the freedom in everyone, as a common structure, should be the *permanent violence* of the individual freedom of alienation."[90]

It is hardly surprising, given the above, that a critic might find in *Critique I* a dialectic that "transforms a philosophy of human liberation into a philosophy of violence,"[91] or might seriously question how Terror could ever be a vehicle for overcoming alienation and creating a new humanity. Although this is not a primary concern of my study, it is an important one, and I shall give attention to it in Part II of this book. But, for now, I must return to the issue of consistency and coherence in Sartre's trajectory on violence.

---

84. *CDR* I:737 (*CRD* I:689), italics mine.

85. Desan, *The Marxism of Jean-Paul Sartre,* 145.

86. *CDR* I:441 (*CRD* I:457). For Sartre, as we shall see in our discussion of *Critique II,* there is no ontological distinction between "totalization" and "incarnation." "Totalization" unifies in a singular process what appears to be disparate actions or events. A boxing match can incarnate, or totalize, all of boxing, as Stalin can all of bureaucracy.

87. *CRD* I:456, translation mine; or *CDR* I:440.

88. *CDR* I:442 (*CRD* I:457).

89. Catalano, *A Commentary on Jean-Paul Sartre's Critique of Dialectical Reason,* 186; *CDR* I:439.

90. *CRD* I:457, translation and italics mine ("Chacun consent à chacun par la médiation de tous que le fondement permanent de chaque liberté soit négation violente de la nécessite, c'est à dire que la liberté en chacun, en tant que structure commune, soit violence permanente de la liberté individuelle d'aliénation").

91. Aron, *History and the Dialectic of Violence,* 160.

I have already shown some of the core similarities between Sartre's account of violence in the *Notebooks* and his treatment of it in the *Critique*. To be sure, there are others, some of which we can note in passing. Just as in the *Notebooks* violence presents itself as a "recuperation of a right" and/or "creating a right,"[92] so in the *Critique* the violence of Terror is created as a "common" right (*droit*) and in turn creates and guarantees rights through the pledge, or oath. Similarly, in both works violence is said to present itself—without exception in the *Critique*[93]—as *counterviolence,* as retaliation against the violence or threatened violence of the Other, against broken reciprocity, or against the alienating power of the antipraxis, or antihuman, in our situation. And because of these latter points—that is, violence's creation of rights and its appearance as "counter" to the violation of freedom— violence in both accounts, but especially in the *Critique,* presents itself as *justified:* justified self-affirmation or justified affirmation of freedom against alien freedom, "evil," or whatever violates or degrades humanity.[94] In this way, often in the *Critique* and sometimes in the *Notebooks,* violence also presents itself as both cleansing and as a "process of restoration" or regeneration,[95] for "evil must be destroyed," the antipraxis must be eliminated.

Yet it is clear that, in spite of some core similarities—which must neither be overlooked nor forgotten—Sartre's considerations of violence in these two works are *not* at one. The differences are not simply in tone or between a dominantly ontological (or phenomenological-ontological) and a dominantly sociohistorical focus informed by ontology: they are, at least in part, differences that reflect Sartre's greater tolerance and acceptance of violence as he comes to understand human freedom and human relations more in respect to the concrete, material, practico-inert conditions of scarcity and "necessity." Despite his appendix II, on "revolutionary violence," it would be hard to imagine Sartre in the *Notebooks* conceiving and justifying a "pledged [or sworn] group" in which the "violent negation of necessity"[96] grounds every freedom as a way of liberating or consolidating a new humanity. And despite the "curious ambiguity" of violence that he emphasizes throughout the *Notebooks* and that his careful ontological analysis affords

92. *NFE* 177, 201, 264–65 (*CPM* 185, 209, 275–76). In fact, he says on page 177 that "pure violence and pure right are one and the same" (*la violence pure et le droit pur ne font qu'un* [*CPM* 185]).
93. E.g., *CDR* I:406, 720 (*CRD* I:428, 677).
94. E.g., *NFE* 172–74 (*CPM* 180–82), *CDR* I:432–33, 720 (*CRD* I:449–50, 677).
95. *NFE*, e.g., 186–88 (*CPM* 194–96), *CDR* I:133 (*CRD* I:209).
96. *CDR* I:441 (*CRD* I:457); also *CDR* I:430 (*CRD* I:448).

him, it would be difficult to think of him either analyzing, accounting for, or invoking "Fraternity-Terror" in the *Notebooks* without condemning it heartily. Given his clear delineation of the shattering anticommunitarian and antiexistential consequences of violence in the *Notebooks*, consistency would not allow him to suggest there, as he has in *Critique I*, that the oath of Terror can yield reciprocity among all Third Parties, and unity, cohesion, and permanence to the continuing group. On the contrary, violence in the *Notebooks* "creates violence" and ruptures existential unity, despite Sartre's acknowledgment of a sometime "communion among the violent."[97] In *Critique I*, unlike the *Notebooks*, violence does not seem *necessarily* to involve self-objectification and objectification of the Other or to "create . . . unconnected universes,"[98] even though Sartre seems to recognize clearly both that the group (or group function) becomes "essential" at the price of making individuals "inessential" (terms common to both works) and that the pledge, or oath, returns the group to inertia and the structures of the practico-inert. Treating another freedom as "inessential"—even though the Other's individual praxis is recognized and though it is done for the sake of liberating freedom as freedom—exhibits, in the *Notebooks*, the "principle of violence" and "negate[s] the essential relation of interdependence among freedoms."[99] To alter the issue but slightly, although Sartre concedes in *Critique I* that "freedom's ruthless destruction of freedom buried in the practico-inert constitutes itself *a priori* as violence," he contends, against "reactionary writers," that the "only contradiction" between "sovereign Freedom in everyone and Violence against the Other" is a "dialectical one."[100] Moreover, whereas in the *Notebooks* Sartre repeats emphatically that the violent person is in bad faith, and illustrates many manifestations of violence's bad faith,[101] he here—in spite of his commendable recognition of the power of the antidialectic, antipraxis, and practico-inert—seems to subordinate, as Catalano has pointed out,[102] his concern for bad and good faith to a repeated basic use of Manichaeism as a tool for understanding and analyzing the dominant forms of violence in individual and collective behavior (e.g., oppression,

---

97. *NFE* 188 (*CPM* 196). In *Critique I*, Sartre says, for example, "Violence is the very power of this lateral reciprocity of love" (430 [*CRD* 448]).

98. *NFE* 200 (*CPM* 208).

99. *NFE* 211, 214 (*CPM* 220, 223).

100. *CDR* I:406–7 (*CRD* I:429).

101. *NFE*, e.g., 175, 178, 184, 188–89, 202, 212, 562–72 (*CPM* 183, 186, 192, 196–97, 211, 221, etc.).

102. Catalano. *A Commentary on Jean-Paul Sartre's Critique of Dialectical Reason*, 114.

colonialism, slavery, class struggle, and racism).[103] But surely, for Sartre, Manichaeism is itself in bad faith. Not so, apparently, for although Sartre's concern with "alienation"—a concept that might itself be construed, in certain conditions (e.g., instituted praxis, exploitation), as social bad faith—pervades the *Critique*,[104] and although Sartre regards the perennial condition of material scarcity as allowing the institutionalizing of the group in "a violent negation of alienation" (and seriality),[105] he does not appear to view—for example—the collective Third Party's "stealing of freedom from me" as necessarily constituting bad faith. In the *Notebooks,* and doubtless in *Being and Nothingness,* the Oath-Terror, despite its intent to preserve freedom and positive reciprocity against the force of the practico-inert, would definitely be in bad faith insofar as the oath imposes an unsurpassable limit on the unlimited freedom of every individual in the group. Even though, one might contend, freedom continues to exist in the practico-inert that the pledge of Terror has reestablished in the group, freedom has now placed chains on itself. In the language of the *Notebooks,* "the contradiction [as well as, indeed, bad faith] lies in the fact that a man of whom it is affirmed that he cannot go beyond some limit is no longer a man but an object."[106] Sartre would hardly be able to make such a statement in the *Critique.* In the *Critique,* violence and "necessity" (of the practico-inert)—and thus alienation—are an inevitable part of history "until the elimination of scarcity" by human praxis.[107] In a bourgeois class society, violence seems to be inevitable, itself the only recourse against violence. (In a 1972 interview

---

103. E.g., *CDR* I:736, 739 (*CRD* I:689, 691). The central place of his "Manichaean" analysis may also be found in *Saint Genet, Anti-Semite and Jew,* and his Preface to *The Wretched of the Earth.* In the preceding reference, he calls it "the primary determination of morality."

104. E.g., *CDR* I:338–39, 665–68, 747 (*CRD* I:375–76, 632–35, 698). In Sartre's basic sense of "alienation" as *otherness* of human praxis, alienation appears to be ineliminable. Other forms of it associated more specifically with capitalism seem to be eliminable, as Marx would have it, and indeed to be in "bad faith," in Sartre's normal use of that term. See McBride, *Sartre's Political Theory,* 130. The evidence suggests that Sartre distinguishes sharply between "alienation" in *Being and Nothingness* and "alienation" as he uses it in the *Critique.* In a footnote, he says: "Fundamental alienation does not derive, as *Being and Nothingness* might mislead us into supposing, from some prenatal choice: it derives from the univocal relation of interiority, which unites man as a practical organism with his environment" (*CDR* I:228 [*CRD* I:286]).

105. *CDR* I:741 (*CRD* I:693).

106. *NFE* 571 (*CPM* 591). Of course, this should not be taken literally: the human being, as free, conscious being (for Sartre), can never literally become an object. Only at death, when the human being becomes a human corpse, can he or she literally become an in-itself, or object.

107. *CDR* I:736 (*CRD* I:689).

with Pierre Verstraeten, among other places, Sartre repeats this point: in condemning "capitalist society" as an evil, he concludes that "we have no choice
but violence.")[108] Given this perspective—and his continuing movement here
away from a theoretical, abstract, or "writer's ethics"[109] and toward a more
concrete and practical one—Sartre appears to be backing away from the
judgment of "bad faith" on violence and Fraternity-Terror.[110]

Given my attempt above to show that, in spite of some core similarities
(a number of which are rooted in Sartre's ontology of freedom), Sartre's
treatment of violence in the *Critique of Dialectical Reason,* volume I, is
notably different from that of the *Notebooks,* we are now in a position to
begin a gradual transition to his Preface to Fanon's *Wretched of the Earth.*
And this transition can best be made by taking note first—however
briefly—of some of Sartre's contentions in his concluding consideration of
"racism and colonialism" near the last part of book II of *Critique I.*[111]

Racism and Colonialism. In this section of *Critique I,* Sartre confronts both
the violence of the colonialist/racist and the counterviolence of the native.
Much of his earlier analysis comes to a head here. For Sartre, "violence as
bourgeois *exis,*" or practico-inert habit, exists in "the exploitation of the
proletariat as an inherited relation of dominant class to the dominated"; the
process of exploitation is always "against a background of scarcity" and
has a practico-inert characteristic; "the son of the colonialist and the son of
the Muslim," for instance, are both "the children of the objective violence
which defines the system itself as a practico-inert hell." Violence as *praxis*
of the bourgeois generation exists in colonization.[112] The "practical attitude" of the colonialist is that of a human being up against a "sly and
vicious beast" (e.g., the Muslim) created in his own image. This becomes

108. Pierre Verstraeten, "I Am No Longer a Realist: An Interview with Jean-Paul Sartre,"
in *Sartre Alive,* ed. Ronald Aronson and Adrian van den Hoven (Detroit: Wayne State University Press, 1991), 96.

109. See, e.g., *NFE* 17, 507 (*CPM* 24, 522), also Michel Contat and Michel Rybalka, eds.,
The Writings of Jean-Paul Sartre (Evanston, Ill.: Northwestern University Press, 1974), 58.

110. In a passage that William McBride finds rather "remarkable" (*Sartre's Political Theory,* 80), Sartre says: "All History must be understood as a function of this primitive alienation
from which man cannot get out. Alienation is not in fact oppression. It is the predominance of
the Other in the pair, of the Other and the Same, the priority of what is objective" (*CPM,* 429).
It is of interest to note that, even here in the *Notebooks,* although alienation, like bad faith in
Being and Nothingness, is primitive and initially appears to be inescapable, it is not said to
instantiate bad faith. And this does, as McBride points out, anticipate the *Critique.*

111. *CDR* I:716–34 (*CRD* I:673–88).

112. *CDR* I:718–19, 739 (*CRD* I:675–76, 691).

part of the structure of the Manichaean self-justification that we have seen. The colonial *praxis* is a praxis of oppression that "complements" a *process* of exploitation and "merges into it."[113] It is a praxis of violence that developed out of an earlier practico-inert and matrix of violence (e.g., feudalism) and continues this process of exploitation by establishing a new network of violence. That is to say, violence "renews itself" in the new colonial, capitalist system that has actualized the practico-inert relations of the past system of exploitation. Racism, as a form of Manichaean "Other-thought," is developed and practiced by the colonialist to *justify* his violence: the colonialist's activity aims at perpetuating the myth and condition of the native's "subhumanity." Manichaeism is, again, abundantly at work. The native experiences the exploitation and oppression as "straightforward deliberate constraint":[114] the violence against him aims to keep him at a subhuman level, "to deprive him of any possibility of reacting,"[115] even if the deprivation amounts to "pauperization" (i.e., destruction of the social structures of the native community), torture, or, ultimately, "mass extermination" of at least part of the population. All the practices of colonialism, all of its violences—its cheap labor, its "superexploitation," and its reduction of the native to the status of commodity for profit and, thus, subman (*sous-homme*)—conduce to a "climate of violence" in which organized "groups of violence" prepare to "unleash" counterviolence or, in turn, counterviolence against counterviolence, "at the slightest provocation."[116] Each side comes to view itself as Other-Being. To be human, the Muslim—or any other exploited native—"must be violent."[117] Rebellion is the only reasonable response to exploitation and alienation. The native must break the colonialist's hold on him, disrupt the colonial praxis, destroy "the anti-dialectical system of super-exploitation" that living human praxis has created.[118] In the Algerian rebellion "the African army was the violence of the colonialists . . . and the colonialists were for the army the legitimacy of this violence."[119] All the violence of the Algerian insurrection, with its despairing character, was simply a "negation of the impossible"—the impossibility of

113. *CDR* I:721 (*CRD* I:677).
114. *CDR* I:720–24, 734 (*CRD* I:676–81, 687). In the latter reference, please note that "exploitation must be inseparable from oppression."
115. *CDR* I:724 (*CRD* I:680–81).
116. *CDR* I:725–27 (*CRD* I:681–82).
117. I am influenced here by Catalano's formulation of the point. Catalano, *A Commentary on Jean-Paul Sartre's Critique of Dialectical Reason*, 242.
118. *CDR* I:729 (*CRD* I:683).
119. *CDR* I:730 (*CRD* I:684).

living (*l'impossibilité de vivre*) in oppression.[120] "The violence of the rebel *was* the violence of the colonialist; there was never any other."[121] The conflict between the oppressed and the oppressor was essentially the interiorization of the same exploitation and oppression (i.e., *"pure violence"*)[122] in which even the oppressor recognizes his own objectifying and oppressive violence but, in turn, prepares his own counterviolence. As Catalano has expressed it, "the inhumanity of the colonialists is their praxis as colonialists," and the oppressed natives "have no human option except individual violence."[123] As it was for the menaced group, it is necessary for the colonized group to try to destroy the menacing praxis of the colonialist oppressor. In this manner, Sartre excuses their violence: he sees it as necessary.

Hence, to restate the observation with which I opened this chapter: violence in *Critique I* "is *always* both a reciprocal recognition of freedom and a negation . . . of this freedom through the intermediary of the inertia of exteriority."[124] But in *Critique I*, in contrast to the *Notebooks*, violence, though sharing some of the ontological characteristics delineated in the *Notebooks*, is understood and situated in the milieu of life-threatening material scarcity—with its accompanying hostile forces and antagonisms— and is often presented as justified or self-justifying praxis against objectification, group dissolution, exploitation, oppression, "necessity," and other expressions of antidialectic and practico-inert hell. Given the dialectic of the practico-inert—the inertia to which the praxis of any threatened or sovereign group seems inevitably to lead—one might ask again, as one leaves *Critique I*, how violent rebellion can usher in a "new humanity" without violating its very possibility. This appears to be part of the *ambivalence* of Sartre's developing approach to violence, a theme to which I shall return with regularity.

120. *CRD* I:686 (*CDR* I:733).
121. *CDR* I:733 (*CRD* I:687).
122. *CDR* I:749 (*CRD* I:700).
123. Catalano, *A Commentary on Jean-Paul Sartre's Critique of Dialectical Reason*, 242.
124. *CDR* I:736 (*CRD* I:689).

"violence" in the *critique of dialectical reason*, volume 2

Likely written in the late 1950s (and perhaps very early 1960s) but kept hidden from the public and only published posthumously by Gallimard twenty-five years after its release of the first volume, *Critique II*[1] brings to a head Sartre's volume I analysis of violence in the context of his culminating discussion of totalization and conflict—more specifically, as part of his inquiry into whether history's unifying, or totalizing, movement can take place even at the core of conflict and struggle in a disunified society.[2]

1. Jean-Paul Sartre, *Critique of Dialectical Reason*, vol. II, ed. Arlette Elkaïm-Sartre, trans. Quintin Hoare (London: Verso, 1991); originally published as *Critique de la raison dialectique*, vol. II (Paris: Gallimard, 1985). All subsequent references to this work are abbreviated *CDR* II (English) or *CRD* II (French), or *Critique II* in the body of the text. The reader should note that, through his Verso editor, Perry Anderson, Ronald Aronson had access to the typescript of *Critique II* as early as December 1977. Sartrean scholarship is indebted to Aronson's early and very perceptive commentary on *Critique II*, entitled *Sartre's Second Critique* (Chicago: University of Chicago Press, 1987).
2. I shall say more about "totalization" later. For the time being, let me just say that, in the *Critique*, all historical praxis (i.e., purposive activity in social-material conditions) seems to direct itself to ongoing totalization and dialectical unification of unrelated human actions. This "process," like the For-itself's project to be God in *Being and Nothingness*, appears to be an

Although my present study is not the place for a detailed examination of Sartre's understanding of "totalization" and "history," for example, I want now to ascertain whether and how Sartre's focused discussion of violence in the early part of volume II, in particular, elucidates, expands, or qualifies the views I have brought together from volume I. I shall bypass the question of whether one can make legitimate inferences from a work whose author had chosen not to publish.[3] Given the continuity and emphasis here of many of the key terms in Sartre's analysis of violence in *Critique I,* as well as his progressive development of the issues and conclusions that he has generated in volume I, I do so without hesitation. *Critique II* is, without doubt, one of the most important of Sartre's posthumously published works.

In *Critique I* Sartre characterizes "the violence of matter" as the "'midwife of History'"[4] and presents history as a relentless human activity of struggle and conflict because of and against the material conditions of scarcity. Violence as "interiorized scarcity" leads to a "reciprocity of antagonism" in which, in the face of need, human beings are related by reciprocal negation of each Other. As "*everyone's* intelligible reinteriorization of the contingent fact of scarcity," this social violence, says Sartre, "becomes meaningful in and through everyone" as the reciprocal "negation of the Other in everyone."[5] Hence, as "negative reciprocity," violent struggle in the field of scarcity "engenders the Other" as antihuman.[6] Thus, McBride appropriately refers to Sartre's social violence as "inhuman human behavior."[7] Although violence always recognizes the freedom of the Other, it also negates this freedom through the mediation of scarcity or inorganic matter—what Sartre here calls the "intermediary of the inertia of exteriority"—resulting in a "mortal relation" between all human beings.[8] In this way, among the others that I have tried to show, violence for Sartre continues to be curiously ambiguous in *Critique I.*[9]

---

impossible ideal, always sought but never attainable. Tom Flynn makes this suggestion in *Sartre, Foucault, and Historical Reason,* vol. I (Chicago: University of Chicago Press, 1997), 108.

3. Andrew Dobson, for example, raises this issue in his concise and helpful work *Jean-Paul Sartre and the Politics of Reason* (Cambridge: Cambridge University Press, 1993), 95.

4. *CDR* I:181 (*CRD* I:248).

5. *CDR* I:815 (*CRD* I:752).

6. *CDR* I:816 (*CRD* I:753).

7. William McBride, "Sartre and the Phenomenology of Social Violence," in *New Essays in Phenomenology,* ed. James M. Edie (Chicago: Quadrangle Books, 1969), 306.

8. *CDR* I:736 (*CRD* I:689).

9. It bears repeating here that Sartre states that "the only conceivable violence is that of freedom against freedom through the mediation of inorganic matter" (*CDR* I:736).

Critique II basically accepts the terms and analysis of *Critique* I but offers a concentrated elucidation of it within Sartre's overarching concerns for the meaning and possibility of a *single* history, the intelligibility—if any—of struggle, and the relation between the individual and the universal. Wishing to show that the source of the dialectic, of social phenomena, and of the historical process is to be found in the *praxis* of individuals and not in the activity of a "hyperorganism,"[10] Sartre continues to construe violence in terms of purposive human activity aroused by conditions of material scarcity. All history for Sartre is qualified by scarcity. To show "synthetic unity" in a "society riven through and through," and to demonstrate that all "rifts," fights, and struggles are "totalizing and entailed by the totalizing movement of the whole,"[11] Sartre chooses the *boxing match* as a paradigmatic illustration. "What is certain," says Sartre, "is that, in every brawl, the deep source is always scarcity."[12] (In Hegel, the reader will recall, it was the search for recognition.) The "movement of the evening [for the boxers] replicates the movement and hierarchy of their lives; and the preceding bouts reproduce the history of their own fights." "Each fight is all of boxing." "*Boxing in its entirety* is present at every instant of the fight as a sport and as a technique."[13] "In every fight, boxing is *incarnated,* realized, and elapses as it is realized." *This* particular scrap *totalizes:* "Every fight retotalizes boxing and all other fights."[14] In other words—to bring this point to a head with only a hint of preliminary explanation—each boxing match "individuates," or "singularizes" (two other of Sartre's terms), boxing as a whole.[15] And to make the ready and obvious connection to violence, "every boxing match incarnates the whole of boxing as an incarnation of all fundamental violence."[16] But the reader now deserves some fleshing out and development of this skeletal preliminary outline.

First, a word or two about "totalization" and "incarnation." *Totalization,* if I may borrow from the glossary at the end of *Critique* I, is "the constantly developing process of understanding and making history."[17] Ronald Aronson characterizes it as well as anyone when, with reference to *Critique*

10. See, e.g., *CDR* II:66 (*CRD* II:76).
11. *CDR* II:16 (*CRD* II:25).
12. *CDR* II:23 (*CRD* II:32).
13. *CDR* II:20–21 (*CRD* II:29–30).
14. *CDR* II:22 (*CRD* II:31).
15. See, e.g., *CDR* II:28, 36, 47–48 (*CRD* II:37, 45, 57–58). Dobson restates this rather unambiguous point in *Jean-Paul Sartre and the Politics of Reason,* 100. See also, e.g., Ronald Aronson, *Sartre's Second Critique* (Chicago: University of Chicago Press, 1987), 60.
16. *CDR* II:27, also 48 (*CRD* II:36, also 57).
17. *CDR* I:830 (glossary).

I, he tells us that "to totalize . . . is to draw together into the 'developmental unity of a single process' what appear to be separate actions and entities."[18] But I submit, following Sartre's use of it in *Critique II* and Arlette Elkaïm-Sartre's glossary at the end of *Critique II*,[19] that this process can acquire additional clarity by viewing it as a continuing, living work of dialectical synthesizing and unifying in the individual context of "determined conditions" and specific objectives. Mark Poster also puts it well when he points out that while, "at any given moment, human actions [appear] to be isolated and unrelated," there is "within the intentionality of each action . . . an opposite movement of synthesizing the totality."[20] And "in so far as, in a synthetic unification, the part is a synthetic totalization of the whole (or of the overall totalization), *incarnation*," says Sartre, "is an individual form of totalization"; it is totalization "individuated."[21] Both Aronson, following Sartre, and Andrew Dobson, following Sartre and Aronson, use the helpful words "gather together" or simply "gather" to convey the activity of totalization and incarnation in this context.[22] Sartre himself tells us that the two boxers *"gather within themselves [ramassent en eux-mêmes]*, and re-exteriorize by the punches they swap, the ensemble of tensions and open or masked struggles that characterize the regime under which we live—and have made us violent even in the . . . gentlest of our caresses."[23] With this in mind, Sartre can say that "the boxers *incarnate* in a real and dated conflict both the [preexisting] fundamental [or original] violence and the right to violence," and that this incarnation "transforms the whole hall."[24] Even the crowd is unified—totalized or in the process of totalizing—by this single

18. Aronson, *Sartre's Second Critique*, 2.

19. *CDR* II:459 (glossary) (*CRD* II:462).

20. Mark Poster, *Existential Marxism in Postwar France* (Princeton: Princeton University Press, 1975), 275.

21. *CDR* II:27, 28 (*CRD* II:36–37). I do not mean to suggest that Sartre has not used "incarnation" before. He has used it earlier, in *Critique I*, and also in *Being and Nothingness* when discussing, for example, body and sexual desire (e.g., 390 ff.), as well as in *Notebooks for an Ethics* (e.g., 187–88). Here he speaks of the violent man as *incarnating* Being.

22. Aronson, *Sartre's Second Critique*, 58; Dobson, *Jean-Paul Sartre and the Politics of Reason*, 100.

23. *CDR* II:26 (*CRD* II:36), italics mine. See Sartre's additional usage of "gather" or "gathering" (*ramasser*) in *CDR* II:33, 49 (*CRD* II:42, 59), e.g. In his earlier *Communists and Peace*, trans. Irene Clephane (London: Hamish Hamilton, 1969), originally published in *Les temps modernes*, nos. 81, 84, 85, 89, 101 (1952–54), Sartre also uses—in connection with "concrete singular universals"—the appropriate expression "takes in." See *Les temps modernes*, no. 89 (April 1953): 227.

24. *CDR* II:27 (*CRD* II:36), italics mine.

incarnation that brings together the crowd's common malaise, its "innumerable rifts," its diverse preexisting forms of violence, and the social and economic conditions it has interiorized. It is in this sense that Sartre says that "the fight is everywhere" and that *this* fight "incarnates all of boxing" or is "all of boxing." He makes it clear that this match, this singularized, or "individuated," form of totalization, this *incarnation,* is *not* an expression, representation, "exemplification of a concept," "symbolic realization," or "transcending signification" of all boxing—or violence for that matter.[25] Rather, it is the *whole* of boxing gathered together (Sartre also uses "fused together," e.g., *CDR* II:32–33) and retotalized.[26] And, in this regard, Sartre emphasizes that there is "no ontological or logical difference" between totalization and incarnation. Incarnation, I repeat, is totalization *individuated.* As Aronson points out, "incarnation does not have a diminished ontological status: it *is* totalization."[27] Every *internal* totalization is brought about as the "praxis-process of incarnation," and the "positive content" of "every practical and concrete reality" (incarnation) must be the "totalized ensemble," or whole, of "all ongoing totalizations."[28] Thus, again, *this* match incarnates and singularizes the entirety of boxing, and, to put it as Sartre later does, the "world of boxing," through this single fight, is in fact totalized, or gathered up, "as a multiplicity of contests which, in each weight, pit each against all and each against the other, and can find a solution only in violence." This incarnation is unrealizable except as a totalization of everything that came together to produce this event.[29]

This returns us properly to the specific topic of violence, for it is to that issue, within the context of totalization, that Sartre's painstaking analysis of boxing is directed. Moreover, it is likely, as Aronson has suggested, that it is in his "pursuit of violence" that his study of boxing makes the most distinct contribution.[30]

As I have already mentioned, the fight, or boxing match, is not only the incarnation of all boxing but also the incarnation of *all violence.* Even the spectator is the "incarnation of violence": he cannot enjoy the blows without giving them through the fists of his favorite in the ring.[31] "The fight,"

25. *CDR* II:29, 31, 33.
26. *CDR* II:26–27 (*CRD* II:25–26). See also *CDR* II:45 (*CRD* II:54–55).
27. Aronson, *Sartre's Second Critique,* 62, italics mine.
28. *CDR* II:33 (*CRD* II:42).
29. *CDR* II:47–48 (*CRD* II:57–58).
30. Aronson, *Sartre's Second Critique,* 75.
31. *CDR* II:26 (*CRD* II:35).

Sartre says, "encloses the *fundamental* [or *original*] violence within itself."[32] It is mediated by and gathers up the scarcity and resulting antagonisms of a divisive, factionalized class society. The violence of the boxer is the "re-exteriorization of interiorized scarcity" and, in this way, is *all* of violence. And this scarcity, Sartre insists, is not an abstraction external to the social whole. At every moment, rather, it is a synthetic relation of all human beings to nonhuman materiality and, in turn, of their relation to one another based on their relation to this materiality—including, of course, the "ensemble" of means, techniques, and relations of production that give the relation unity.[33] So, as Aronson puts it, "any individual act of violence interiorizes the general, social violence."[34] Sartre's point here, of course, echoes what he has argued toward the end of *Critique 1*.[35] Moreover, as Hegel's Master-Slave "fight" eventually leads to the Slave's "revealing" the reality of his condition, so Sartre's boxer's fight can be said to "reveal" (by his or her "incarnation") all of violence in his or her society.

Further, for Sartre, "every violence-event is produced, lived, refused, accepted as the *absolute*." This is so for two reasons: first, because, at any given time, it actualizes what Sartre calls "the diffused and confused ensemble of the *multiple violences*" that have led me to be fundamentally violent; second, because it arises "absolutely" in the struggle for life and reveals that the life of each participant in violence "can be based on the death of the other" and defined in terms of the risk of death as "a non-transcendable and threatening term of every life." So neither life nor death is absolute: rather, the absolute is, first and foremost, the difference that separates life from death. The "climate of violence," as Sartre puts it, whether in the form of Fraternity-Terror or actual conflicts, "defines life as risk of death and mortal fate." And sounding even more like the Sartre of *Critique 1,* he draws his point poignantly to a head: "By conflict, life reveals itself in its precious uniqueness, in its irreversibility, in its fragility, and in its fierce assertion of itself, through the alternative: kill or be killed."[36] (Again, this recalls Hegel's original "fight.") Although, in this context, Sartre still keeps the boxer in mind to model his contentions, he is clearly trying to indicate not simply the plural incarnations of exploitative conditions that the boxer

32. CDR II:27 (CRD II:36–37), italics mine.
33. CDR II:28 (CRD II:37). See also CDR II:31–32 (CRD II:41–42) for a detailed expansion of this point.
34. Aronson, *Sartre's Second Critique,* 60.
35. E.g., CDR I:736 (CRD I:689).
36. CDR II:31 (CRD II:40). See also CDR I:406, 430–44 (CRD I:428, 448–59). The reader may note that Sartre also speaks of the "climate of violence" in CDR I:726–27 (CRD I:682).

individuates (e.g., the injustice of poverty in capitalist society) but the "fundamental," or "original," violence of life and death, which we all *live* as "the historical legacy of material scarcity."[37] In fact, as Thomas Flynn emphasizes, every move of the boxer in the fight "incarnates" the fundamental violence that runs through history in a "field of scarcity."[38]

Sartre also says of an act of violence that it "never has witnesses," that there are "no witnesses to violence, only participants."[39] So-called historical witnesses who claim to have observed an act of violence (e.g., a fight) without having had any part in it either misspeak or simply do not exist (*ces individus n'existent pas*).[40] These so-called witnesses have participated in it in some way: for example, they might have tried to stop it or for some reason, usually bad (e.g., cowardice), might simply have let it run its course. To invoke the language of *Being and Nothingness,* every witness to a particular act of violence makes it her "situation," makes it her own, becomes—with the facticity of the "given," or what Sartre might, in *Critique II,* call the "determined circumstances" or "ensemble of determinations"—part creator of the situation.[41] Just as there is no nonhuman situation in *Being and Nothingness,* there is no nonparticipatory observer in *Critique II.* Observing is also a praxis. Whatever the objective incident of violence, the observer of it is participating in a unifying praxis of totalization in which human intentionality is involved and history—indeed, with its conflicting human intentionalities—is being made.[42]

Furthermore, Sartre here, as in *Critique I* and his Preface to *The Wretched of the Earth,*[43] among other writings,[44] takes his stand in opposition to

---

37. Tom Flynn makes this point, in these words, in his probing and masterly book *Sartre, Foucault, and Historical Reason,* I:154. I *strongly* recommend this book to the reader's attention.

38. Ibid., 161.

39. *CDR* II:29, 30 (*CRD* II:39). "Donc, pas de témoins pour la violence; mais seulement des participants" (*CRD* II:39 [*CDR* II:31]).

40. *CDR* II:29 (*CRD* II:39).

41. See *BN* 48, 548–53, e.g. The reader may wish to note that in my earlier book on Sartre, *Bad Faith, Good Faith, and Authenticity in Sartre's Early Philosophy* (Philadelphia: Temple University Press, 1995), I discuss Sartre's broader use of "situation" in his later works—e.g., *Anti-Semite and Jew.* Tom Flynn also notes Sartre's "expanded" view of "situation" in *Sartre, Foucault, and Historical Reason,* I:152.

42. In this regard, I recommend Aronson, *Sartre's Second Critique,* 40–44, for additional detail and clarification.

43. Frantz Fanon, *The Wretched of the Earth,* trans. Constance Farrington (New York: Grove Press, 1968), 21, 25, e.g. I examine this work later in this study.

44. E.g., Jean-Paul Sartre, "Reply to Camus," in *Situations,* trans. Benita Eisler, (New York: George Braziller, 1965), 71–105; originally published as "Réponse à Albert Camus," *Les temps modernes,* no. 82 (August 1952): 334–53.

nonviolence. "Non-violence, . . . especially when it is erected into a watch-word, is the choice of complicity." The nonviolent person "makes himself an accomplice of" the oppressor—that is to say, of "the institutionalized, nor-malized violence that selects its victims." He "realizes" the act in its entirety, and no one can say *a priori* whether he is more or less guilty than the one whose hands actually commit the crime.[45] But it is clear that for Sartre, here, commitment to nonviolence spells profound naïveté concerning the praxis-process of history—a point he makes forcefully in *Critique I*[46]—and that, as he'll say later in his Preface to Fanon's *Wretched of the Earth,* nonviolence amounts to passivity, and passivity in this context is a contribution to oppression[47] (i.e., freedom turning against itself, the exploitation of human being by human being),[48] which he has earlier called "pure violence." To recall the terms and analysis of *Critique I,* then, nonviolence for Sartre comes close to being a form of violence, given his account of violence and, now, of "incarnation." I shall not here offer a critique of Sartre's indictment of "nonviolence," but, in passing, I cannot resist mentioning that Sartre himself exhibits naïveté—indeed, philosophical naïveté—when he affirms that because "most legislative systems" provide sanctions "against persons guilty of non-assistance," it necessarily follows that nonviolence amounts to complicity.[49] And it is baffling to find Sartre appealing to the oppressor's law to confirm his point, especially in the light of his repudiation of middle-class, bourgeois law in *The Communists and Peace,* for example.[50] To say the least, his concept of "proof" (the word he uses) here can hardly be called robust.

45. *CDR* II:30 (*CRD* II:39). Jeanson makes a similar point in his review of Camus's *Rebel,* "Albert Camus ou l'âme révolté," *Les temps modernes,* no. 79 (May 1952): 2070–90. See also the next footnote.

46. E.g., *CDR* I:736 (*CRD* I:689).

47. I expect to show later in this work that, although Camus is not a complete pacifist, Sartre and Jeanson accuse him of rejecting history or refusing to enter history because of his condemnation of revolutionary murder, for example. See also Camus's counteraccusation in his reply to Jeanson/Sartre, i.e., in his "Lettre au directeur des 'Temps modernes'" *Les temps mod-ernes,* no. 82 (August 1952): 317–33. See also Jeanson's rejoinder in "Pour tout vous dire," *Les temps modernes,* no. 82 (August 1952): 354–83, esp. 365–67. Following Sartre, he suggests that nonviolence doesn't belong to history and represents a form of complicity. Of course, we shall see later in my study that Camus himself would agree that "in the world today only a phi-losophy of eternity could justify non-violence" (*The Rebel,* trans. Anthony Bower [New York: Alfred Knopf, Vintage, 1956], 287).

48. *NFE,* e.g., 332, 562.

49. *CDR* II:29–30 (*CRD* II:39).

50. E.g., *The Communists and Peace,* 44–46.

In choosing the boxing match as the incarnation of all violence, Sartre is able to exhibit and elucidate much about—and, of course, to corroborate—his earlier characterization (in *Critique I*) of violence as "interiorized scarcity" mediated by the structures, the practico-inert, the antidialectic, of bourgeois society. From the beginning to the end of his analysis Sartre struggles to show the relationship between the violence the boxing match singularizes and the violence embedded in the socioeconomic conditions and human-made structures of society. This point cannot be overstressed. Most young boxers, "formed by the violence to which they have been subjected, are well suited to subject others to violence. . . . They incarnate in their fights . . . the same violence that the ruling class exerts against the labouring classes." Since birth they have suffered the violence of oppression and exploitation, which later they have progressively interiorized.[51] But having interiorized that violence and being unable to establish solidarity with the workers, they try to escape their oppression by venting their built-up rage against members of their own class[52]—specifically workers/boxers, "other loners" (*solitaires*)—whose "combat group" (*groupe de combat*) has not yet been found.

Because the boxer's violence is "an ever fruitless spasm to struggle free from poverty and his milieu," the boxer agrees to make it "an instrument" for his elevation to a higher class. He sells his violence, his strength, his agility, his rage. But for the most part this effort fails. In selling his violence to the promoter,[53] he remains exploited and, on the boxing market, experiences the same "harshness of competition" and conflicts that workers confront on the labor market.[54] But while workers have at least reduced antagonisms and established some class solidarity, the boxer produces further competition, subjects himself to it and "lives it" in every one of his fights. He must prove his worth by waging a "brilliant battle" against his adversary; his violence becomes a very painful and dangerous work; it is no longer a "wild and liberating passion." Alienated, the oppressed individual's aggression is transformed into a competitive antagonism."[55] That is to say,

51. *CDR* II:36 (*CRD* II:45–46). The reader will immediately recognize this case as parallel to Sartre's contention in *Critique I* that "[t]he violence of the *rebel* was the violence of the colonialist" and that "the African army was the violence of the colonialists" (*CDR* I:730–33).
52. Frantz Fanon picks up this theme in *The Wretched of the Earth* (as does Sartre in his Preface).
53. Note that Sartre talks of the alienated worker's *selling* himself and becoming a *commodity* in, e.g., *CDR* I:741 (*CRD* I:693).
54. *CDR* II:36, 44 (*CRD* II:46, 53–54).
55. *CDR* II:43–44 (*CRD* II:53–54).

in fighting his "enemy brother," a "transformation of violence"—as Aronson has put it[56]—occurs. The violence that in every fight seizes him (*s'empare de lui*) and "hurls him against his enemy brother" is, in its origin, the same violence that moves from the oppressor to the oppressed and back.[57] (I remind the reader again of the parallel Sartre draws here to his analysis in *Critique I* of the colonized native's violence against the colonialist.) This opposition, this "exchange of violences,"[58] as Tom Flynn calls it, singularizes class struggle and incarnates violence as the "interiorization of scarcity." By buying this violence the promotional bourgeoisie has recovered it, but the potentially liberating violence of the oppressed has been alienated even further. In fact, the alienation is "total": the "promoted," commercialized boxer can no longer even find his own freedom and his value in his violence.[59] He becomes a paradigm of alienation—a human "commodity"—bought and sold in the marketplace.

In viewing this boxing match, spectators also take part in the "public alienation of free actions" and participate in fundamental violence and a "localization of that violence." And the participants in the match produce and realize their own alienation—an alienation "of the whole [human being] down to the root of his [or her] freedom and the reality of emancipatory violence." But this liberating violence (*violence libératrice*) moves against alienation only to alienate itself all the more. This event—what Sartre calls this "temporalization"—*incarnates* a perennially true aspect of "all oppressive and exploitative systems," all systems or "statutes" that "know no outlets" or general "decompressive explosions." In short, it incarnates and singularizes the "alienation of the violence of the oppressed,"[60] or what Sartre also calls the boxers' "emancipatory power" (*pouvoir libérateur*). Thus, the conflict in society, the violence of the oppressed, is not resolved through fighting of this kind. Although unleashed, this violence is simultaneously "de-realized." The match, this "deliberately mutilated violence," becomes a show (*parade*) that yet incarnates the "total violence" and "radical powerlessness" of the oppressed.[61] To repeat Sartre's repeated point, fundamental, or original, violence has interiorized itself and then reexteriorized itself through bourgeois marketing. The exploitation by capitalist

---

56. Aronson, *Sartre's Second Critique*, 69.
57. *CDR* II:44 (*CRD* II:54).
58. Flynn, *Sartre, Foucault, and Historical Reason*, I:154.
59. *CDR* II:43 (*CRD* II:53).
60. *CDR* II:45 (*CRD* II:55).
61. *CDR* II:46 (*CRD* II:56).

society has spawned a competition among human beings as commodities:[62] even their bodies have been marketed. And though members of different classes and milieux produce the same event with many "incompatible meanings," "*all* our violences are there, supported by the fundamental violence" in which they are rooted; everything occurs in the "insupportable tension of scarcity."[63] They are joined in what Sartre calls an "enveloping totalization"—a term that is unique to *Critique II*. By this, he seems to mean a unifying totalization that both gathers together (in the sense I have indicated) and is gathered together through a praxis-process. Arlette Elkaïm-Sartre notes that Sartre sometimes uses "enveloping totalization" as though it connoted a "system" (see *CDR* II:183 n), but in the segment with which we are dealing, Sartre says that every singular totalization is both "*enveloping* as a totalization" and "*enveloped* as a singularity."[64] In this way, enveloping totalization can be viewed as a unifying process that historicizes praxis-process by integrating our individual praxes temporally into a dynamic whole. In *The Communists and Peace,* Sartre has said that, in a society based on oppression, violence is, by a crowning injustice, first of all a result of the fact of oppression.[65] And now, having confronted early in *Critique II* the question of the intelligibility of struggle alongside the issue of the unity and intelligibility of history, he can drive home his point more forcefully— and dramatically: "Everything is given in the least punch: from the history of the one who delivers it to the material and collective circumstances of that history; from the general indictment of capitalist society to the singular determination of that indictment by the boxing promoters; from the fundamental violence of the oppressed to the singular and alienating objectification of that violence in and through each of its participants."[66]

In short, then, according to *Critique II,* every concrete struggle or instance of violence, every rift, incarnates all others, as well as the fundamental scarcity and the diverse forms that contemporary society gives to

62. *CDR* II:47 (*CRD* II:57). In an interview twenty years later with Pierre Verstraeten, Sartre is no less firm: "Capitalist society is an evil, . . . it is not made for men but for profits." Ronald Aronson and Adrian van den Hoven, eds. *Sartre Alive* (Detroit: Wayne State University Press, 1991), 96.
63. *CDR* II:48 (*CRD* II:57–58).
64. *CDR* II:49 (*CRD* II:59). For additional clarification of this notion of "enveloping totalization," or "totalization-of-envelopment," I recommend Thomas Flynn's discussion of its varied meanings in *Sartre, Foucault, and Historical Reason,* e.g., I:156–60, to which I am indebted here.
65. Sartre, *The Communists and Peace,* 45.
66. *CDR* II:48 (*CRD* II:58).

that scarcity.[67] A particular conflict, involving as it does the active participation of all concerned, is, for example, an incarnation and singularization of class struggle as it unfolds in contemporary forms of capitalism. *All* violence is "gathered in, clarified and made explicit" in, the single conflict or act of violence. And, as Aronson goes on to say, "all of history is the real meaning of each fight" or conflict.[68] In this way, Sartre believes, violence and conflict—and, of course, History, the main focus of *Critique II*—can be rendered dialectically intelligible. Totalization must be able to take place within violence and actual struggle if History is to be intelligible.[69]

To be sure, much more might be said here about Sartre's search for intelligibility and "synchronic totalization," as he puts it, "in the thick of battle."[70] And, of course, given my account of the "pledged group" of *Critique I*, I could develop Sartre's contention that, granted conflict between subgroups, "the group tends to reinforce its *unity* by violence, and [thus] 'fraternity-terror' is actualized."[71] But my task in this section has not been to establish Sartre's "go" at historical totalization and intelligibility or to show whether Sartre has succeeded in demonstrating dialectical unity in a "society cut up by class struggles."[72] Rather, I have tried to observe how Sartre's discussion of violence in *Critique II* fits into his trajectory of violence, and how, if at all, it elucidates and expands his account of violence in *Critique I*.

Accordingly, I have shown that Sartre's focus on the boxing match or fight in the early part of *Critique II* was not intended to amuse or entertain, however incompatible Sartre and boxing may initially seem to a reader. (The reader may be reminded that Sartre, while teaching in a lycée at Le Havre, had co-organized a boxing club for his students and closely followed boxing during its golden years in France; in short, the young Sartre was close to boxing and took it seriously.) His intent, rather, was to show how the "fight," or "match," incarnates and individuates (or "singularizes") not only all of boxing but all of violence, all of the *interiorized scarcity* and

67. CDR II:50 (CRD II:60).
68. Aronson, *Sartre's Second Critique*, 75.
69. CDR II:50 (CRD II:60). In this context, Andrew Dobson indicts Sartre for being more interested in historical intelligibility than in passing moral judgment on extreme violence and, for example, Stalinism. Camus, as we shall see later, would likely agree. See Dobson, "Sartre and Stalin: *Critique of Dialectical Reason*, Volume 2," *Sartre Studies International* 3, no. 1 (1997), 1–15, and Ronald Aronson's reply in the same issue.
70. CDR II:50 (CRD II:60).
71. CDR II:66 (CRD II:77).
72. CDR II:50 (CRD II:60: "une société tronçonnée par les luttes de classes").

original, or fundamental, violence—that is to say, the violence of life and death—that is mediated by the socioeconomic conditions of bourgeois society. Again in *Critique II*, as in *Critique I*, Sartre is more concerned with the socio-material genesis, evolution, and intelligibility of violence than with the definition and differentiae of violence. As bourgeois *exis*, violence still exists in "the exploitation of the proletariat as an inherited relation of the dominant class to the dominated class."[73] His distinct contribution here, with respect to violence, is his detailed elaboration of how interiorized scarcity is reexteriorized in, say, the violence of the boxer, which, in itself, totalizes and "gathers in" the ensemble of multiple violences that combine to bring it about.[74] But, on the whole, Sartre's understanding of and contentions about violence in *Critique II* do not diverge from those in *Critique I*. Sartre's representative themes on violence are either assumed or stated here. The "double negation," an aspect of the "curious ambiguity" of violence so prominent (and formative) in *Notebooks for an Ethics* as well as in *Critique I*, emerges less directly but just as emphatically here, in, for example, his analysis of the boxers as two negated freedoms trying in turn to negate each other. And given the practico-inert—the antidialectic of scarcity that he reaffirms in this volume—the Other's freedom is regarded as menacing; the individual perceives herself as radically "threatened by the violence of counter-men" and (thus) as "having to respond with counter-violence." Once again, violence for Sartre presents itself as "induced," "defensive," or "counter"-violence, and material scarcity leads to a Manichaeism in which one sees the Other as radically Other, as antihuman, as an "evil" to be destroyed.[75] As was the case in *Critique I*, given the social determinations that individuals interiorize in a society in which human beings are used for profit and are pitted against one another, violence (for the exploited boxer, for example, as for the colonized native) appears to be the *only* defense against violence; in short, violence seems not only understandable but both liberating and necessary. This is a point that Sartre draws to a head in his Preface to Fanon's *Wretched of the Earth*, to which I shall soon turn. So long as scarcity exists, the human being will be violent, and counterviolence will be his outlet. In fact, "it is [even] the violence of the majority's need that is the rich man's necessity for counter-violence."[76]

73. *CDR* I:719 (*CRD* I:676).
74. See, e.g., *CDR* II:26–27 (*CRD* II:36–37).
75. *CDR* II:24–25 (*CRD* II:33–34). See also *CDR* I:736–39 (*CRD* I:689–92), e.g.
76. *CDR* II:423 (*CRD* II:432).

Further, I have noted that in *Critique II*, far from disowning the pledged group and Fraternity-Terror, Sartre has offered further insight both into how groups emerge from social antagonisms and contradictions and into how subgroups, threatening to incarnate the group by themselves, use violence and "actualize" Fraternity-Terror in a contest to maintain or reaffirm the group's unity. *Critique II*—as Aronson has also intimated[77]—nurtures once more a curious ambiguity in Sartre's approach to freedom and violence: while Sartre sees freedom against freedom as necessary in bourgeois society, he also wants—as he did in his *Notebooks for an Ethics*[78]—to deplore any action that demeans the freedom of another, most particularly the violence of the dominant, or exploiting, class. Indeed, even in Sartre's most cohesive "sworn," or "pledged," group of Fraternity-Terror, members respect the freedom and autonomy of its members by subordinating ontological otherness to "free alterity" in pursuit of a common project.[79] I shall continue to address this tension in my examination of some of Sartre's subsequent writings on violence.

Hence—and this comes as no surprise—Sartre's treatment of violence in *Critique II* simply extends the analysis of it that he offers in *Critique I*. Moreover, his accounts in *Critique I* and the *Notebooks for an Ethics,* and the comparisons I have drawn between the two, are reinforced, not challenged, by volume II. In addition, the focus on the violence of colonialism, as it is detailed in book II of *Critique I*, stands as important preparation for a consideration of Sartre's approach to violence in his Preface to Fanon's *Wretched of the Earth.*

77. Aronson, *Sartre's Second Critique,* 181–82.
78. I do not suggest that this constitutes the earliest evidence. Sartre surely also deplores any degradation of freedom in, for example, *Being and Nothingness* (1943).
79. Flynn makes this point in *Sartre, Foucault, and Historical Reason,* I:259. It is repeated in the "Rome Lecture," which I discuss in Part II.

"violence" in sartre's preface to *the wretched of the earth*

5

Sartre's early thinking had a profound impact on the development and thought of the Martinique-born psychiatrist and intellectual revolutionary Frantz Fanon (1925–60). In his first book, *Peau noir, masques blancs* (1952) (translated as *Black Skin, White Masks* [1967]),[1] in which he offers, among other contributions, a discerning diagnosis of the alienation of the "black man" in a white world, together with an outline of his own philosophical anthropology, Fanon gives early evidence of the influence of *Being and Nothingness* (1943), *Anti-Semite and Jew* (1945–46), and "Materialism and Revolution" (1946) on his development. Toward the middle of this work, he specifically invokes "Sartre's masterful study of the problem of anti-Semitism" to help explain racism and "Negrophobia."[2] In his concluding pages, he makes clear his view of the ontological freedom of the human being: "No attempt must be made to encase man; for it is his destiny to be set free"; and sounding a theme from both *Being and Nothingness* and *The*

1. Frantz Fanon, *Peau noir, masques blancs* (Paris: Éditions de Seuil, 1952); translated as *Black Skin, White Masks*, by Charles Lam Markmann (New York: Grove Press, 1967).
2. Fanon, *Black Skin, White Masks*, 160.

Flies, he says, "I find myself suddenly in the world . . . [with] one duty alone: That of not renouncing my freedom through my choices."[3] The very words in the first part of this sentence are close to Sartre's; and Sartre could easily have uttered the second, also. Moreover, in a manner that integrates his emphasis on freedom and his stand against determinism, as brought out in *Being and Nothingness, Existentialism and Humanism* (*L'existentialisme est un humanisme*, 1946), *The Flies* (1943), and "Materialism and Revolution," he concludes: "The body of history does not determine a single one of my actions. I am my own foundation" (i.e., the free creator of my own "essence").[4] Fanon clearly, following Sartre, understands human reality as freedom, affirms freedom at both an ontological and an existential/social level as human reality's highest value,[5] and regards racism, colonialism, or any *oppression* of human freedom as blatant *violence*—that is, as in the early Sartre, *violation* of human reality as freedom.

Fanon, however, was not an uncritical disciple of Sartre. To mention only one disagreement—one to which Emmanuel Hansen and Lewis Gordon also refer—Fanon vehemently denounced, albeit with later qualification, Sartre's characterization (in *Black Orpheus*, for instance) of negritude as "anti-racist racism" and just a "fleeting moment of the dialectic."[6] "Without a Negro past, without a Negro future," Fanon replies, "it was impossible for

3. Ibid., 230, 229. In this regard, see, e.g., *BN* 555–56 and *The Flies*, in *No Exit and Three Other Plays*, trans. Stuart Gilbert (New York: Vintage Books, 1959), esp. 108, 115, 120–22. Fanon's affirmations have an "Oresteian" ring to them.

4. Fanon, *Black Skin, White Masks*, 231. In this connection, see, e.g., *BN* 25: "Human freedom precedes essence in man and makes it possible: the essence of the human being is suspended in his freedom." See also Jean-Paul Sartre, "Cartesian Freedom," in *Literary and Philosophical Essays*, trans. Annette Michelson (New York: Collier Books, 1962), 197: "The sole foundation of being is freedom."

5. Although Emmanuel Hansen, in one of the first books in English on Fanon, makes a similar point, I do not think he makes the right Sartrean distinction regarding types of freedom. The distinction should not be between "existential freedom" and "social freedom," as Hansen suggests, but between "ontological freedom," the freedom to which we are abandoned (our *facticity of freedom*), and "existential," or "practical," freedom, that is, the manner in which we "exist" or "practice" or "live" the (ontological) freedom that we *are*. The latter includes "social" and "political" freedom. Hansen's otherwise good, informative, and instructive study occasionally lacks, I believe, philosophical sophistication regarding Sartre's views. See Emmanuel Hansen, *Frantz Fanon: Social and Political Thought* (Columbus: Ohio State University Press, 1977). In this regard, see pages 62–68, for example. Hansen's "Frantz Fanon: Portrait of a Revolutionary Intellectual," *Transition* (Kampala, Uganda) 46 (October–December, 1974): 25–36, is a good synopsis of what Hansen says later in his book, and presents a strong case for why Africans (and, may I add, all of us) should be concerned with Fanon.

6. Hansen, *Frantz Fanon: Social and Political Thought*, 34. I owe these two short quotes, also, to Hansen.

me to live my Negrohood." Jean-Paul Sartre "was reminding me that my blackness was only a *minor* term." He "had forgotten that the Negro suffers in his body quite differently from the white man."[7]

Furthermore, it is evident that Fanon's thinking also had some impact on Sartre's: this was not a one-way intellectual or ideological street. Simone de Beauvoir confirms that Fanon was "passionately interested" in *Critique de la raison dialectique* (*Critique of Dialectical Reason*), but also acknowledges the impression Fanon made on her ("one of the most remarkable personalities of our time") and Sartre. She also refers to the explosive role he played at the 1958 All-African People's Conference in Accra, where, two years prior to Sartre's publication of the *Critique*, Fanon—invoking Hegel—argued *against* Nkrumah's pacifist views and *for* the necessity of violence for decolonization.[8] She goes on to tell us that Sartre, while in Cuba, "had realized the truth of what Fanon was [then] saying," namely, that "it is only in violence that the oppressed can attain their human status" and be liberated from their thingification in colonialism. Now in accord with Fanon on this point, Sartre "agreed gladly to do a preface" for *The Wretched of the Earth*—"an extreme . . . incendiary book" that was at the same time a "complex and subtle manifesto of the 'Rest of the World.'"[9] In fact, if we

---

7. Fanon, *Black Skin, White Masks,* 138, italics mine.

8. Simone de Beauvoir, *The Force of Circumstances,* trans. Richard Howard (New York: G. P. Putnam's Sons, 1964–65), 583; originally published as *La force des choses* (Paris: Gallimard, 1963). As Emmanuel Hansen points out, Fanon "quotes Hegel with relish to substantiate his contention for the necessity of revolutionary violence" ("Frantz Fanon: Portrait of a Revolutionary Intellectual," 32). Indeed, in *Black Skins, White Masks,* Fanon devotes a subsection of chapter 7 to "the Negro and Hegel," in which, among similar statements, he says, "Human reality in-itself-for-itself can be achieved only through conflict and through the risk conflict implies" (218). For an interesting article on this topic, see Lou Turner's "On the Difference Between the Hegelian and Fanonian Dialectic of Lordship and Bondage," in *Fanon: A Critical Reader,* ed. Lewis R. Gordon, T. Denean Sharpley-Whiting, and Renée T. White (Oxford: Blackwell Publishers, 1996), 134–50. Yet, in this context, it is imperative to note that Hansen, like Aimé Césaire, Peter Worsley, Barbara Deming, and other interpreters of Fanon, regards it a "travesty" of Fanon's position to view him as an "apostle of violence." (See, e.g., Hansen's "Frantz Fanon: A Bibliographic Essay," *Pan-African Journal* 5 [winter 1972]: 390). Even in *Black Skin, White Masks* (e.g., p. 11), Fanon acknowledges, as does Sartre in places (e.g., *What Is Literature?* trans. Bernard Frechtman [London: Methuen, 1950], 406), the negative human consequences of violence. But this is not necessarily to endorse Barbara Deming's suggestion that "violence" in Fanon's writing can be interpreted simply as "radical and uncompromising action." I don't believe that a close examination of Fanon's text warrants such a blanket statement.

Hansen confirms Fanon's stand at the Accra Conference. See, e.g., *Frantz Fanon: Social and Political Thought,* 45.

9. De Beauvoir, *The Force of Circumstances,* 591. For her more complete account of the Sartre-Fanon relationship, see 583–97.

may rely on de Beauvior's account, the opportunity given Sartre to write a preface for this "exceptional man" helped Sartre "recompose" himself after his own blind but exhausting struggle against death in the late 1950s, while he was rushing to complete his *Critique*.[10]

Fanon's powerful and stirring *Wretched of the Earth* (*Les damnés de la terre*), published only one year after Sartre's *Critique of Dialectical Reason*, volume 1, strongly exhibits the influence of Sartre's thinking in the *Critique*. References to Manichaeism pervade Fanon's analysis,[11] and his account of the colonial world seems to borrow and/or reformulate the essential points of Sartre's analysis. The colonial world is a *tragic* world: the colonized masses live in violence; the colonizer faces the threat of intense countervio-lence.[12] "The colonial world is a Manichean world," "a world divided into compartments": "the settler paints the native as a sort of quintessence of evil"[13] and orders and rules over the colonized world with violence.[14] The "intuition of the colonized masses" is that "their liberation must, and can only, be achieved by force."[15] "Decolonization," a "process of replacing a certain species of [human] beings by another," is "always a violent phenom-enon."[16] The colonized native "finds his freedom in and through violence."[17] "The violence of the colonial régime and the counter-violence of the native counter-balance each other and respond to each other in extraordinary reci-procal homogeneity." "Terror, counter-terror, violence, counter-violence: that is what observers bitterly record when they describe the circle of hate."[18] Violence can be regarded—given Fanon's attraction to Hegel's analysis in the *Phenomenology*—as a dialectical necessity. (In *Black Skins, White Masks*, he makes clear his points of agreement with Hegel.) But whereas the vio-lence of the colonialist is "separatist," the native's violence frees, cleanses,

10. De Beauvoir, *The Force of Circumstances*, 596–607.
11. Frantz Fanon, *The Wretched of the Earth*, trans. Constance Farrington (New York: Grove Press, 1968), e.g., 41–42, 50, 51, 84, 93.
12. Lewis R. Gordon skillfully elaborates the tragic aspect of Fanon's revolutionary posi-tion in *Fanon and the Crisis of European Man* (New York: Routledge, 1995), chap. 4. See also Gordon, "Fanon's Tragic Revolutionary Violence"—essentially the same piece—in *Fanon: A Critical Reader*, 297–307. I am glad that a reader, after examining the first draft of my manu-script, referred me to Gordon's work on Fanon. Gordon's work challenged my perspective on Fanon.
13. Fanon, *The Wretched of the Earth*, 41, 51, 84.
14. Ibid., 40.
15. Ibid., 73.
16. Ibid., 35.
17. Ibid., 86.
18. Ibid., 88, 89.

and unifies the people; it "binds them together as a whole"; it delivers them from "despair and inaction," and "restores" their "self-respect."[19] Nonetheless, even in this "emancipatory" action, as Lewis Gordon suggests, the tragic element cannot be ignored. Here, too, violence "takes the path of someone's being dragged 'downward': the human being tragically emerges out of a violent situation of 'gods' and the 'damned.'"[20] The tragic also, I must add, exhibits "ambiguity."

Given the strong Sartrean flavor to Fanon's analysis here, and in turn the clear influence that, by Sartre's admission, the close association and discussion with Fanon had on Sartre's "mode of expression" at the time,[21] it is not surprising that Sartre's Preface contains a ringing endorsement of both Fanon's vehement indictment of colonialism and his unequivocal defense of the natives' anticolonialist violence. "Have the courage to read this book," Sartre challenges; "Fanon is the first since Engels to bring the processes of history into the clear light of day."[22] Violence in the colonies "seeks to dehumanize" the "enslaved men." Here, too, Sartre reaffirms the position that Fanon affirms and that he himself has taken in the *Critique:* colonialism is a structure of oppression governed by violence. At first the only violence is the violence of colonialists, but soon the natives "will make it their own, . . . the same violence is thrown back upon us as when our reflection comes forward to meet us when we go toward a mirror."[23] The natives stubbornly refuse the "animal condition" to which they have been reduced. The colonial aggression—in this case, in Algeria—"turns inward in a current of terror among the natives." The terror of the natives, Sartre (supporting Fanon) is reaffirming here, is the dehumanizing violence of the colonialists. If the "suppressed fury" of the oppressed natives does not find an outlet, the natives themselves will be devastated by it. Their mad "boomerang" violence is the "last refuge" of the native's humanity;[24] it is "the proof of his humanity." And as with the "fused group" storming the Bastille, the native's violent rebellion against counterhumanity constitutes the human being "recreating

19. Ibid., 93–94.
20. Gordon, "Fanon's Tragic Revolutionary Violence," 303; see also Gordon, *Fanon and the Crisis of European Man.*
21. Jean-Paul Sartre and Benny Lévy, *Hope Now: The 1980 Interviews,* trans. Adrian van den Hoven, with an introduction by Ronald Aronson (Chicago: University of Chicago Press, 1996), 94. See also Simone de Beauvoir, *The Force of Circumstances,* 591, 583–97.
22. Jean-Paul Sartre, Preface to *The Wretched of the Earth,* 14.
23. Ibid., 15, 17.
24. Ibid., 17–18.

himself."[25] In this way, the native "cures himself of his colonial neurosis." A child of violence, he draws from violence his own humanity and begins life as this "new man" at the end of it, for he now views himself as a "potential corpse." He finds his humanity "beyond torture and death."[26] His violence, though it may come back on both himself and the colonialist, is an instrument for both his and our (the colonialists') humanization.

Faced again with the practico-inert hell of exploitative and oppressive colonialism—this time as depicted by Fanon—Sartre has no place here for nonviolence. Sounding like the Sartre of the *Critique,* who saw violence as part of all history,[27] he says mockingly—and with a clear slap at Camus: "A fine sight . . . the believers in non-violence, saying that they are neither executioners nor victims. . . . Try to understand this . . . : if violence began this very evening and if exploitation and oppression had never existed on earth, perhaps [then] the slogans of non-violence might end the quarrel. But if the whole regime . . . [is] conditioned by a thousand-year-old oppression, your passivity serves only to place you in the ranks of the oppressors."[28] No gentleness can eradicate the "marks of violence"; only violence can do that.[29] And although, as in the *Critique,* he is fully aware of the dialectical internalization of violence by the colonialist as well as the colonized, he is here more explicit and unequivocal in his defense and justification of the native's violence against oppressive colonialists. If nonviolence against oppression equals passivity, as Sartre states, and passivity in this historical context places one in the "ranks of the oppressors," then clearly (Sartre is saying) counterviolence against the oppressors is morally justified as well as liberating and humanizing.

To be sure, following his own intricate analysis in the *Critique,* Sartre accepts Fanon's contention that, "on the logical plane, the Manicheism of the settler produces a Manicheism of the native," and the colonialist/settler's theory of the "absolute evil" of the native is answered with the native's violence against the "absolute evil" of the colonialist. But Sartre applauds Fanon's creative characterization of the colonized people's "great organism of violence" that has "surged upwards" against the settler's violence and

25. Ibid., 21–22.
26. Ibid., 21–24.
27. *CDR* I:736 (*CRD* I:689).
28. Sartre, Preface to *The Wretched of the Earth,* 25.
29. Ibid., 21. The reader may note that Martin Luther King Jr. turned this around and contended that only nonviolence could put an end to violence.

given the native new life and freedom.[30] This violence is a "cleansing force" that frees the native from his "inferiority complex" and transforms him from subman into man,[31] that "rehabilitates humankind"[32] and generates a higher level of human being. Despite its hurt, despite the destruction it does to human freedoms, this regenerative violence, "like Achilles' lance, can heal the wounds that it has inflicted."[33] In this manner, I believe, Sartre is *justifying* violence: violence can be emancipatory, purgative, curative, restorative, creative, unifying, and humanizing. This is the Sartre of the *Critique*,[34] still, I think, assuming that "the reign of scarcity" in history[35] has reduced the human being to the level of "antihuman," but more focused on Fanon's context and reinterpretation and more willing to *justify*, rather than only *describe*, the native's (counter)violence against the colonialist.[36] Within the framework of colonialism, Sartre's views on the genesis and process of violence, as expressed in the *Critique* and in the Preface, are essentially at one. Yet unlike the Sartre of the *Notebooks* and, to a lesser extent, the *Critique*, Sartre in the Preface does not offer a theoretical analysis or definition of violence. The more limited focus of his discussion and polemical nature of his support of Fanon virtually preclude his doing so. Sartre seems simply to adopt here the outline of what he has contended earlier in the *Critique*.

Granted the closeness, if not identity, between Sartre's views in his Preface and his related observations and contentions in the *Critique*, it would be redundant to compare or contrast what he says in the Preface to his views on violence in the *Notebooks*. But given Sartre's emphasis in the Preface on

---

30. Fanon, *The Wretched of the Earth*, 93, 94.
31. Ibid., 94.
32. Ibid., 106.
33. Sartre, Preface to *The Wretched of the Earth*, 30.
34. *CDR* I:133. It is to be noted again that in the *Notebooks* (188), also, Sartre speaks— within a specific "morality"—of a "cleansing," or "purifying," function of violence.
35. *CDR* I:130.
36. In this general connection, it is of interest to note that in *The Ethics of Ambiguity* Simone de Beauvoir not only shares Sartre's view of violence but, even prior to the *Critique*, offers a justification of it. She says, for example, "A freedom which is occupied in denying freedom is itself so outrageous that the outrageousness of the violence which one practices against it is almost cancelled out" (97). See also, e.g., 135–38, 147–50. In other places, she employs words like "legitimation" and "justify." She seems much more willing than Sartre to use words of "justification" in a *moral*, not simply a descriptive or phenomenological, sense. (I don't mean to suggest that de Beauvoir, here, is not aware of negative consequences of violence.) I give further attention to this matter in Part II of this study.

a unifying as well as restorative role for the violence of the colonized, it is hard to pass up the opportunity to point out how radically different this emphasis is from his contention, for example, in the *Notebooks* that "violence does not know how to put things together."[37] To be sure, Sartre in the Preface seems aware of the nihilism, the human-destroying intent, the anti-coexistential consequences, the "broken reciprocities," the severing effects, the backfiring internalizations of violence in the Other's consciousness, which he saw earlier as part of the matrix of violence. But it is clear in the Preface, as in the *Critique*, that for the oppressed, colonized native, counterviolence "puts things together": violence is the assertion of his or her ontological freedom against degradation, alienation, "necessity," and subhumanity. Violent rebellion creates and gives cohesion to a new group and re-creates their humanity. This counterviolence—according to Sartre— will "heal the wounds it has inflicted" and pave the way for a new "full-grown" humankind that will define itself not as "the sum total of the world's inhabitants" but as "the infinite unity of their mutual needs."[38] Although Sartre's Preface appears to share the *Notebooks'* view that counterviolence *presents* itself as a "recuperation of a right" and is a "demand on Others," it seems to allow, in the name of re-creating human self-respect and bringing about a new higher-level humanity, a counterviolence by the oppressed that—at least temporarily—can transcend the antidialectical, non-coexistential, anticommunitarian dimensions of violence.[39] In this regard, among others, it is at a considerable distance from the *Notebooks*. Although the Preface presupposes some of the root analysis of oppression and violence that the *Critique*, in places, shares with the *Notebooks*, it is the logical, and perhaps overstated, sequel to the *Critique*, not the *Notebooks*, with respect to both the subhumanizing and violent nature of practico-inert colonialism *and* the role of (counter)violence in overturning it.

37. *NFE* 173.
38. Sartre, Preface to *The Wretched of the Earth*, 27.
39. The reader may recall that I develop this point about the non-coexistential nature of violence in "On the Existential Meaning of Violence," *Dialogue and Humanism*, no. 4 (1993): 139–50.

"violence" in *hope now: the 1980 interviews*

Having remarked basic lines of continuity as well as basic differences and tensions within the trajectory of Sartre's developing views on violence from the *Notebooks* through the *Critique* and his Preface to Fanon's *Wretched of the Earth,* I return now to the "conversations" that prompted my book's inquiry and generated the concerns with which it began (see my Introduction). In proceeding to examine Sartre's views on violence in *Hope Now,*[1] the 1980 "interviews" between Benny Lévy and Sartre, I intend for the most part to stay away from the continuing controversy surrounding Lévy's dominating role in these "interviews" or the reliability of Sartre's statements in reply to Lévy's questions and challenges. I proceed on the assumption that even if Lévy had ulterior motives, Sartre's views here ought to be taken seriously and represent the continuing and, as it turned out, concluding

1. Jean-Paul Sartre and Benny Lévy, *Hope Now: The 1980 Interviews,* trans. Adrian van den Hoven, with an introduction by Ronald Aronson (Chicago: University of Chicago Press, 1996). The original French, from which this translation comes, is *L'espoir maintenant: Les entretiens de 1980* (Lagrasse: Verdier, 1991). In what follows, I offer French page references only when I give French quotations or when I deem reference to the French text clarifying and/or important.

evolution of his thinking on violence. Although not so well thought out and argued as Sartre's writing at his best, his statements must not be dismissed abruptly as the Lévy-manipulated views of a man in his dotage. Sartre, in fact, held his own with Lévy: he checked, countered, and challenged Lévy at important points in their exchange. In addition, Lévy's incisive mind, though sometimes domineering, at other times drew out of Sartre some noteworthy revisions in his views. For that, Sartre scholars should express gratitude, not disdain.

The issue of "fraternity" is again a prelude to Sartre's reconsideration of violence in *Hope Now*. Midway through the interviews, he tells Lévy: "if I were to consider society as I viewed it in the *Critique of Dialectical Reason,* I would observe that fraternity has little place in it" (*je constate que la fraternité y a peu de place*).[2] We must recall that, in the *Critique*, fraternity (of the "pledged group") was understood as "*the right of all* through everyone and over everyone" (*le droit de tous à travers chacun sur chacun*) and that it "originated in violence" and "is violence affirming itself as a bond [lien] of immanence through positive reciprocities."[3] But now prompted by Lévy's wish to have him break the necessary connection between fraternity and Terror—the connection that Sartre made in the *Critique* but began to suspend in his earlier interview with Michel Sicard in 1978[4]—Sartre says he sees "society" as a "bond among people that's more basic than politics," and regards *fraternity* as a "relationship of being born of the same mother," call her "mother-humanity" or "mother-earth." "To belong to the same species is, in a way, to have the same parents. In that sense, we are brothers." This relationship is a "family relationship" (*rapport familiale*) and constitutes the "primary relationship" (*rapport premier*) of society.[5] The "common origin" and "common end" of all human beings as "neighbors" reflect their fraternity and fraternal possibilities.[6] In response to Lévy's adamant suggestion that he is invoking "mythology," Sartre replies: "There is no longer any need to appeal to mythology. . . . All human beings will be in a state of fraternity when they can say of themselves, through all our history,

2. Sartre and Lévy, *Hope Now,* 86 (*L'espoir maintenant,* 56).
3. *CDR* 1:438 (*CRD* 1:454).
4. Jean-Paul Sartre and Michel Sicard, "Entretien," in *Sartre* (*Obliques: Numéro spécial* 18–19), ed. Michel Sicard (Paris: Obliques, [1979]), 9–29. I provide more details about this point later in this study.
5. Sartre and Lévy, *Hope Now,* 86–87, 90 (*L'espoir maintenant,* 56–57, 60).
6. Sartre and Lévy, *Hope Now,* 90.

that they are . . . bound to each other in feeling and in action." This allows the sketching and enacting of new principles of common action based on materiality and scarcity: "what I have is yours; what you have is mine; if I am in need, you give to me, and if you are in need, I give to you."[7] For Sartre, this is the "future of ethics," of which he offers only intimations toward the end of the *Critique* but greater details in his unpublished 1964 "Rome Lecture" and his "notes" for his undelivered 1965 Cornell lectures, the former of which I discuss in Part II of this book.

It is precisely at this point in their dialogue that Lévy challenges Sartre pointedly—and I think deservedly—regarding his statements on violence in the *Critique* and in his Preface to *The Wretched of the Earth.* "Struggle against scarcity" is the cause of violence in the *Critique,* Lévy says. And "speaking of colonized man, . . . [y]ou didn't write 'son of the mother' but 'son of violence.' Violence is the midwife here."[8] Lévy not only presses Sartre to confront and account for what appears to be a basic shift or inconsistency in his position but adds another question that seems entirely on target: "Can humanity be generated thus through violence?"[9] He makes it clear that he is not asking whether, on certain occasions, violence is necessary, but whether violence can ever have "the redemptive role" (*rôle rédempteur*)[10] that Sartre assigned to it in his Preface to *The Wretched of the Earth.* And when Sartre responds by pointing to the necessity of violence in Algeria, for instance—the position he took both in the *Critique* and his Preface—Lévy focuses in even more sharply: "Does the experience of fraternity appear through the activity of killing one's enemy? . . . why the exaltation of violence in your [Preface] to *The Wretched of the Earth?*"[11]

Placed on the defensive, Sartre continues to articulate an important shift in his position. To be sure, "violence is not going to speed up the pace of history and draw humanity together." At best, it serves to "break up" a "certain state of enslavement" that prevents colonized people from becoming full human beings. Fraternity and fraternal love do *not* come from the violence and Terror of killing: violence and fraternity are no longer "twin

7. Ibid., 91.
8. Ibid.
9. Sartre and Lévy, *L'espoir maintenant,* 62, translation mine ("Est-ce que l'humanité peut s'engendrer ainsi dans la violence?").
10. Sartre and Lévy, *Hope Now,* 92 (*L'espoir maintenant,* 62).
11. Sartre and Lévy, *Hope Now,* 93 (*L'espoir maintenant,* 64), translation altered.

brothers"; in fact, *"violence . . . is precisely the opposite of fraternity."*[12] To say the least, this major point of concession is a far cry from the statements in the *Critique* in which Sartre defined fraternity in terms of violence and referred to it as "the most immediate and constant form of Terror."[13]

Yet Sartre is still, by his own admission, unsettled in his view of the relationship between violence and fraternity. On the one hand, he maintains that, for ethics to be possible, one must "extend the idea of fraternity . . . until it becomes the manifest, unique relationship among all human beings."[14] If so, violent rebellion, the "creative act of the pledge," and the "statute of terror"[15]—which played such important parts in the process of fraternization in the *Critique*—can no longer constitute us as "brothers," or effect "fraternity." Yet, on the other hand, Sartre continues to confess his approval of the violent "struggle of those tortured [Algerian] people against the French."[16] And preferring to stay with the issue of "necessary violence" or "necessary evil"—the question that Lévy initially wanted to exclude—Sartre answers Lévy's "exaltation of violence" charge with a point that he developed in the *Critique* and brought to a head in his Preface to *The Wretched of the Earth:* "The *only* way I saw to get out of colonialism was violence. This violence that we could call *just,* which was of the colonized against the colonizer."[17] Sartre is still acknowledging past anticolonialist violence as both necessary and just. But to Lévy's question about the possible redemptive or regenerative role of violence, Sartre does not add much to what he has already said here. Sidetracking the issue of *why* he had failed to develop an ethics of "regenerative violence" at the time of the occupation, he simply states—in a rather uncharacteristic Sartrean tone—that the French bombings and murders and so forth during this period were "something we were *forced* to do [*qu'on nous forçait à faire*], almost as a necessary evil."[18] It is true that Sartre lends general, if seemingly halfhearted and provisional, agreement to Lévy's account of "the three phases in which violence appears," and, in the end, does not challenge Lévy's indictment of violence as the means of sustaining fraternity or "human unification."[19] (How could he, given what he

12. Sartre and Lévy, *L'espoir maintenant,* 63–64, translation and italics mine.
13. *CDR* I:440 (*CRD* I:456).
14. Sartre and Lévy, *Hope Now,* 93.
15. *CDR* I:437 (*CRD* I:453).
16. Sartre and Lévy, *Hope Now,* 95.
17. Sartre and Lévy, *L'espoir maintenant,* 64, translation and italics mine.
18. Sartre and Lévy, *Hope Now,* 95 (*L'espoir maintenant,* 66), italics mine.
19. Sartre and Lévy, *Hope Now,* 96–99.

has stated earlier in the dialogue about the inability of violence to "draw humanity together"?) Nonetheless, by the end of these 1980 interviews, despite the change in his views from those of both the *Critique* and the Preface, Sartre's overall position on violence remains somewhat *ambivalent*. On the one hand, he now appears to see Fraternity-Terror as a contradiction in terms and violence as anti-coexistential and destructive of human community. On the other hand, he appears to sympathize with the position he took in the Preface—a position generated by his analysis in the *Critique* and his intolerance of intense oppression—that violence in certain circumstances is both necessary and justified. And in response to Lévy's persistent probing about whether violence can ever be redemptive or regenerative for humanity, Sartre tends to be ambivalent as well as evasive: he answers neither explicitly nor directly. While affirming that violence is "the very opposite of fraternity" and cannot heal humanity, he suggests that the violence of the oppressed colonized against the "pure violence" (oppression) of the colonialists was *restorative* for the natives: to echo words of Sartre I quoted earlier, it ruptured the enslavement that "makes it impossible . . . to become human beings."[20] In the case of Algeria, for example, "a non-violent solution was never in the cards," given the proposed solution of the settlers. Only "violence brought about the expulsion [*renvoi*] of the settlers and their return to France," allowing the conditions for the rehumanization of colonized "submen" (*sous-hommes*).[21] Moreover, Sartre makes a distinction that seems to support this remaining ambivalence, a distinction between two existential "attitudes" that we must endeavor to sustain at the same time: the ethical/fraternal one in which we attempt to "engender" humanity, and the attitude that characterizes our "struggle against scarcity" (*la lutte contre rareté*).[22] Unfortunately, he does not, here, draw out sufficiently the implications of this important distinction for the crucial issue in question.

Yet the unsettledness and ambivalence in these interviews of 1980—just weeks before his death—should not be taken to suggest that, over the period of his writing on violence, Sartre has been unwavering or thoroughly consistent in his views on violence. His distinctly different view of "society"—or, more specifically, "fraternity"—occasioned by his critical rethinking of his earlier ontology, has led him to a perspective on violence that

20. Sartre and Lévy, *Hope Now*, 92 (*L'espoir maintenant*, 63: "un certain état d'esclavage qui ne permettait pas de devenir un homme").

21. Sartre and Lévy, *Hope Now*, 92 (*L'espoir maintenant*, 62).

22. Sartre and Lévy, *L'espoir maintenant*, 62 (*Hope Now*, 91).

differs markedly from many of the views he expressed in both the *Critique* and his Preface to Fanon. As Bill McBride has pointed out, Sartre, in his 1978 interview with Michel Sicard, confesses that the ethical position he is working out is premised on a reconsidered ontology that permits the "interpenetration of consciousness" and intersubjectivity.[23] Robert Stone and Elizabeth Bowman have also mentioned Sartre's acknowledgment, in the late 1970s, that he was taping with Benny Lévy a "third ethics" that would proffer a morality of the "WE" of "intersecting consciousnesses."[24] All human beings—as we have observed—are "brothers" (and, may I add, sisters) "in as much as they are born of the same [mother]" and share a "common origin and end."[25] Violence violates that common bond, that "womb-like unity," which human beings share beyond the depths of scarcity and production.[26] Gone is Sartre's notion in the *Critique* that "we are brothers in so far as, following the creative act of the pledge, we *are our own sons, our common creation.*"[27] Fraternity, the group-in-fusion of the *Critique*, can no longer be sustained by the threat of Terror/violence. Genuine fraternity can no longer be directed by "positive violence."[28] The "pledged group" can no longer be the "origin of humanity." Although violence may still be understood as "deliberate constraint of men by men"[29] and the exercise of freedom against the recognized freedom of the Other—a view shared by both the *Notebooks* and the *Critique*—it is clear that Sartre in *Hope Now* no longer views violence only as a function of material scarcity in relation to human need. Economic problems "are *not* the essential problems,"[30] Sartre now contends. He sees "fraternity" as rooted in an ontological bond and as a "primary" "ethical relationship" in which human beings live *for*

23.   William McBride, *Sartre's Political Theory* (Bloomington: Indiana University Press, 1991), 206. I assume that McBride is referring to Sartre's response to Sicard's question regarding what is fundamentally different about Sartre's "second ethics." Sartre mentions that there are here "entre les consciences, les pénétrations" ("Entretien," *Obliques*, 18–19:15). It must be noted, however, that as early as 1947–48, when discussing violence and "appeal" in *Notebooks for an Ethics*, Sartre mentions the possibility of bringing about a certain kind of "interpenetration of freedoms" (i.e., of consciousnesses). NFE 290.

24.   Robert V. Stone and Elizabeth Bowman, "Dialectical Ethics: A First Look at Sartre's Unpublished 1964 Roman Lecture Notes," *Social Text*, nos. 13/14 (winter/spring 1986): 196. I shall be engaged intensively with this work in Part II of this book.

25.   Sartre and Lévy, *Hope Now*, 89, 90.

26.   Ibid., 88, 86.

27.   CDR I:437 (CRD I:453).

28.   CDR I:737 (CRD I:689).

29.   CDR I:724 (CRD I:679).

30.   Sartre and Lévy, *Hope Now*, 107, italics mine.

one another. He is unwilling to permit a justification in terms of "solidarity," or "unity," which he invokes in his Preface to *The Wretched* and which, in the *Notebooks,* he describes, but does not endorse, as the "goal and final justification of violence."[31] Here, it is our common humanity that gives us unity. And although still allowing that the "violence of the colonized" against the colonialist oppressors "could be called just," Sartre would not maintain now, as he did in his Preface to *The Wretched,* that the colonized "have become men" because of the settlers' wanting "to make beasts of burden of them," or that hatred was the natives' "only wealth."[32] If "Humanity" is the common end that all human beings have within them (*la fin que tous les hommes ont en eux*),[33] Sartre can only, *with* reservation—not "without reservation," as he provisionally states—allow violence as one "facet" of the fraternal experience."[34] Unfortunately, his deteriorating health and impending death prevented him from subjecting Lévy's analysis to more stringent scrutiny. Had he done so, and had he remained strictly with his stated view of the radical opposition between violence and fraternity, he might well have adopted—especially given the maturing of his ethics—a more unambiguous stand against revolutionary violence as a "midwife" (Lévy's word) for the reunification of humanity.[35] For, as Thomas Anderson has pointed out, we find in *Hope Now* the beginnings of what might be called Sartre's "third ethics," an ethics of an intersubjective humanity.[36]

Lévy, at any rate, has detected a tension, even a conflict, in some of Sartre's stated views regarding violence over the course of his writings. Lévy is right to have pointed out the marked differences between Sartre's views and perspectives on violence in the *Critique* and his Preface to *The Wretched of the Earth* of the late 1950s and early 1960s and those of his *Hope Now* interviews approximately twenty years later. But I have attempted to show, as I have moved from one representative work to another in the trajectory of Sartre's writing, that core similarities may also be found in the seemingly disparate stages of Sartre's thought. Further, in the case of the 1980

31. *NFE* 186 (*CPM* 194). I realize that my point runs somewhat against what Lévy is saying in his outline of the three "phases" of violence. But one must note that Sartre's agreement with him is qualified by "I will keep my reservations until later." Unfortunately, his death intervened. See Sartre and Lévy, *Hope Now,* 99.

32. Sartre, Preface to *The Wretched of the Earth,* 17. Note also that Sartre, in *Hope Now,* acknowledges "fraternal love" as the "opposite of hatred" (92).

33. Sartre and Lévy, *L'espoir maintenant,* 60.

34. Sartre and Lévy, *Hope Now,* 99.

35. Ibid., e.g., 91, 106–7.

36. Thomas C. Anderson, *Sartre's Two Ethics* (Chicago: Open Court, 1993), e.g., 171–72.

interviews, I have tried to indicate that Sartre's reticence and ambivalence with respect to regenerative or redemptive violence, combined with his apparent "justification" of the violence of the colonized against their oppressors, permit a line of continuity—somewhat forced, to be sure—between *Hope Now* on the one hand and the *Critique* and the Preface on the other. For these reasons alone, I would hesitate to call Sartre's overall position on violence incoherent. Moreover, the fact that there are demonstrable tensions or conflicts between Sartre's views from one work to another—for example, from the *Notebooks* to the *Critique,* or from the *Critique* or the Preface to *Hope Now*—does not logically entail, as Lévy's sharp questioning and counterpoints sometimes suggest, that his overall position on violence is incoherent. Thinkers are entitled to shifts in their positions. And Sartre's shifts regarding violence are usually a function of his major shifts in philosophical orientation and concerns—in brief, from a dominantly ontological analysis in *Being and Nothingness* to an increasingly sociohistorical portrayal of the human being in the material conditions of history in the *Critique* and finally to the progressive development of a concrete ethics and sketch of an authentic, ethical Fraternity/Humanity, or "city of ends," in *Hope Now.* Sartre's acknowledged and well-known tendency to think against himself, both *within* some works and, more definitely, *from* one work to another, should certainly allow him conflicts in his views that do not necessarily spell incoherence or inconsistency.

Of course, this pattern of doing philosophy does not permit him the luxury of maintaining, without resolution, the kind of internal conflict in views that the 1980 interviews seem to generate. The mutual exclusivity he affirms here between violence and his altered view of fraternity makes virtually untenable the combination of his *Hope Now* position on violence[37] with his partial acceptance of the regenerative function of violence that he developed in the *Critique* and the Preface. If violence is destructive of the Other, is non-coexistential, antifraternal, and nondialogic—as I have found in the *Notebooks*[38] and to some degree even in the *Critique*—it cannot readily be said to regenerate or reunify humanity. The *prima facie* case against it is very strong. And assuming the "fraternal" relationship into which human beings, as children of the same mother, are born, and the prospects for a "messianic" community that Sartre projects with greater optimism in *Hope*

37. Sartre and Lévy, *Hope Now,* 92.
38. For a development of this point, see Ronald E. Santoni, "On the Existential Meaning of Violence," *Dialogue and Humanism,* no. 4 (1993): 139–50.

Now, it would seem to follow that if violence can have no regenerative function for human beings, it is without justification.

To return to the beginning of my inquiry, I submit that the spirit of what Sartre says about violence in his final 1980 interviews is more akin to his mood and thinking in the *Notebooks* than to his approach to it in the *Critique* and the Preface. While *Hope Now* still reflects aspects of the "curious ambiguity" of violence, which Sartre emphasizes in the *Notebooks* and details variously in both the *Critique* and the Preface, it shares with the *Notebooks* Sartre's strongest indictment of violence. In proposing and commending the "future of ethics" in which we human beings share the common goal of Humanity and treat one another as members of the same family—and, of course, in affirming the incompatibility of violence and fraternity—Sartre here seems to exhibit the same antipathy to violence that he showed in parts of the *Notebooks*. Without explicitly saying so, he seems to take for granted the *destructive* thrust and impetus of violence. Although he does not speak of violence as destructive of "laws" or "natures," as he does in the *Notebooks,* he seems clearly to see it—to use the language of the *Notebooks* (and *Being and Nothingness*)—as freedom against freedom, the "negation of the Other's freedom," the attempt to appropriate the Other's freedom by destruction, or by what in the *Critique* he calls the "antihuman." And in spite of his retrospective reference to the "violence of the colonized" as "just," his embrace of nonviolent "fraternity" recalls his contention in the *Notebooks* that violence "unglues" and "sections off" freedoms from each other and "negates the essential relation of interdependence among freedoms."[39] In short, *Hope Now* shares with the *Notebooks* Sartre's view that violence is destructive both in its intent and its alienating, anticommunitarian consequences. I am quick to add that although Sartre moves increasingly in the *Critique* and the Preface toward the justification of what might be called *restorative fraternal violence,* he exhibits in them, too, a lucid awareness and articulation of the freedom-destroying capacities of violence. Yet, whereas in the *Critique* and the Preface he seems able to view certain eruptions of violence more positively as a necessary step toward human cohesion and liberation, in the *Notebooks* and *Hope Now*—even when he refers to counterviolence against oppression as that which "can be called just"[40]—he winces at it. Although Sartre may still understand and

39. *NFE* 200, 214.
40. Sartre and Lévy, *Hope Now,* 93.

condone the "evolution" of the natives' anticolonialist violence, he views it
as a "necessary evil" or perhaps the "recuperation of a right" (*Notebooks*),
not as the way to a socialist Humanity in which all human freedoms live for
one another. But neither in the *Notebooks* nor in *Hope Now* is the violent
breaking away from enslavement a "return to bestiality." On the contrary,
it is, as defended in the *Critique* and the Preface and *described* in the *Notebooks,* a way of "affirming man."[41] And although there are intimations of
a "city [or "kingdom"] of ends" in works as early as *Existentialism and
Humanism* and the *Notebooks*[42] (here he speaks, for instance, of what
"forbids the city of ends from being the only goal that must be pursued")[43]
and, later, in the *Critique,* there is in *Hope Now* a pronounced emphasis
on this Kantian ideal, according to which every person treats the Other as
an end, never as a means, and all live with respect for, and in unity with,
the Other's freedom. There is also, in *Hope Now,* a stronger hope in the
possibility of achieving this "city": it takes the form of Sartre's projected
fraternal community. Although, as Ronald Aronson has pointed out,
Marxism in *Hope Now* is no longer "the philosophy of our time," Sartre
here continues his commitment to "the [revolutionary] project of social
transformation"[44]—a commitment that permeates his work and life. Far
from suggesting violence as the instrument for reuniting fractured humanity, Sartre, in these 1980 interviews, appears to be returning to his *Notebooks* conception of *authentic* human interrelating. Rather than see the
Other as menacing, each of us, on that view, is summoned to will and adopt
each Other's end as his or her own, not because it is unconditioned but
because the Other wants it (i.e., is in need), because the Other "posits" it as
an end. Each of us is now to recognize and will the "legitimacy of each
other's free ends." This willing of each Other's end as the "only authentic
form of willing"[45] prefigures a moral "ought"[46] and provides a basis, I submit, for the more mature ethical community (or "city of ends") that Sartre at
least begins to develop in *Hope Now.* The latter turns out to be Sartre's final
expression of hope against both despair and the hell of interpersonal conflict
and alienation.

41. *NFE* 173 (*CPM* 181).
42. E.g., *NFE* 277–81, esp. 279–80 (*CPM* 288–92, esp. 290–91).
43. *NFE* 170 (*CPM* 178).
44. Aronson, introduction to *Hope Now,* 26.
45. *NFE* 279 (*CPM* 290).
46. I describe this point further in Santoni, *Bad Faith, Good Faith, and Authenticity in
Sartre's Early Philosophy* (Philadelphia: Temple University Press, 1995), 166–71, in which I
also cite relevant textual support. See also Sartre and Lévy, *Hope Now,* 91.

conclusion to part I

As I stated at the beginning, I fully realize that my study is selective and does not cover all of the works, philosophical or literary,[1] in which Sartre deals with violence. And I also recognize that I have knowingly conflated—as has Sartre—distinct subtopics of the issue of violence that might better have been systematically separated and treated in separate categories. But with respect to such separation, the progression of Sartre's writing on violence—focusing on different aspects of the topic (e.g., the nature and definition of violence, the evolution of violence, the function of violence, the justification of violence) in different works at different stages of his oeuvre—virtually precluded that possibility. Nonetheless, I have attempted to deal with particular issues separately *within* the specific topical context that his

1. E.g., *On a raison de se révolter, Le diable et le Bon Dieu* (*The Devil and the Good Lord*), *Le Fontôme de Stalin* (*The Ghost of Stalin*), and "Les Communistes et la paix" (*The Communist and Peace*). But I shall discuss additional works by Sartre that exhibit his views on violence and revolution in Part II of the present work. They will include "Materialism and Revolution" and "The 1964 Rome Lecture Notes." The latter extensive "notes" are often referred to simply as the "Rome Lecture Notes" or the "Rome Lecture." I use these references here interchangeable.

individual works suggested. And within that framework I have also attempted to make comparisons, interconnections, and contrasts in Sartre's trajectory, as his writing and my inquiry have progressively allowed. With respect to my first admission above, let me say that although I have not examined all of Sartre's relevant works, I believe that I have examined some of the dominant and most representative ones. (I have reserved others for Part II of this study.) In short, I have discussed works that have exhibited both the pattern of his thinking on violence, with its shifts, modifications, and differences in emphasis, and a line of minimal continuity concerning the "curious ambiguity"—that is, the freedom-affirming/freedom-destroying tension—at the ontological heart of all violence. In addition, I believe my study has been broad enough to show Sartre's residual ambivalence regarding the possible restorative function of violence. This ambivalence began rather mildly in the *Notebooks,* mounted in the *Critique,* gained relief in the Preface to *The Wretched of the Earth* (where Sartre appears to justify some violence unequivocally), and served, finally, to tantalize the Lévy-driven 1980 interviews entitled *Hope Now.*

If my inquiry thus far has succeeded, it has helped us understand both Sartre's sensitivity to the dehumanizing dimensions of violence and his grounds for the role he allows for violence in the *Critique* and the Preface, as well as in other works that I have not yet examined. To be sure, his analysis of the "pure violence" of oppression and the corollary evils of colonialism permits us to comprehend better the excesses of his passionate endorsement of Fanon's analysis and manifesto in *The Wretched of the Earth.* Further, I submit that my study allows us the indirect benefit of understanding better, in the context of his treatment of violence in the *Critique,* Sartre's vehement break with Camus over the latter's position on violence and revolution in *The Rebel.* But that is the topic for Part II of my present work.

In concluding this part of my inquiry, I return, once more, to my starting place. Benny Lévy's challenge in *Hope Now* has given us the opportunity to pursue and, indeed, locate basic tensions and shifts within Sartre's discussion of violence. But these shifts have not meant radical incoherence. They have, rather, signified the evolution of his thinking on violence. Sartre's position in his Preface to Fanon is the logical outcome of his analysis in the *Critique,* reinforced by Fanon's vehement position and his own subsequent argument in the unpublished "Rome Lecture" of 1964, which I shall discuss in Part II. His statements in *Hope Now* suggest a major turn in his position—this time away from violence and back to the implied or explicit denunciation of it that he offered in his *Notebooks for an Ethics* in 1947–48. But that turn has not eliminated the curious ambivalence in his overall position on violence. He has *not* come full circle, but he *has,* both in his earliest extended discussion of violence in *Notebooks for an Ethics* and in his last statements about it in *Hope Now,* placed violence at a pronounced distance from his ethical goal *for* and *of* Humanity. The latter "end" does not make way for violence.

part II the sartre-camus confrontation: violence and its limits

introduction

Having examined some of Sartre's most representative philosophical writings on violence, and having attempted to show the main moves in his trajectory on violence, I now plan to consider the intense and acrimonious debate between him and Camus in 1952. The bitter confrontation between two of the intellectual giants of the twentieth century was a tragedy of contemporary thought. But that is not my main concern here. I wish, rather, to exhibit some of the philosophical roots of their vehement dispute within the context of my present study of Sartre's overall position on violence. Although the two had other diverging philosophical views (e.g., on freedom, Marxism, the Communist Party, the genesis of rebellion) that contribute to the intensity of the exchange, I believe that it is their differing perspectives on violence, related, to be sure, to their differing approaches to oppression and history, that account most for their *philosophical* separation. Hence, I shall show how my preceding analysis of Sartre's evolving views on violence elucidates the bases for his philosophical—though not his personal—attack on Camus. I recognize that a number of the works I have covered in my foregoing study were written after the 1952 controversy, but that recognition does not deter me. For by 1952 Sartre had already written, for example,

"Materialism and Revolution" and *Les mains sales (Dirty Hands)*[1]—a play dealing with revolutionary ideals and violence—and his thinking was already reflecting the impact and influence of Merleau-Ponty's *Humanism and Terror*.[2] (With respect to the latter, Sartre said in his eulogy to Merleau-Ponty: "This small dense book revealed to me the method and object. It gave me the push that I needed. . . . It was Merleau who converted me."[3] He seemed clearly to mean that he now understood Marxism in relation to its historical reality.)[4] And during the period that he was engaged in his untempered, sometimes vitriolic, dispute with Camus, he was publishing, in *Les temps modernes,* his first installment of *Les Communistes et la paix (The Communists and Peace),* the completed text of which was published later by Gallimard in *Situations* VI and VII.[5] In these works, Sartre was developing his analysis of the economic base of society, class struggle, history, revolution, historical intelligibility, and violence as interiorized scarcity— topics he would later bring to fruition in the first volume of the *Critique of Dialectical Reason* and expand and fine-tune in the second volume. In short, by the time of his response to Camus, Sartre had already ceased to be predominantly an ontologist of individual freedom and had become instead a political philosopher passionately engaged with historical reality, the violence of bourgeois oppression, and the adequacy of Marxism,[6] Stalinism, and the Communist Party. Thus, I hope that my examination of the vehement Sartre-Camus exchange will illuminate Sartre's progressive understanding and "justification" of violence, just as Sartre's cumulative account of violence through *Critique II* and the "Rome Lecture" helps us to understand, but

1. Jean-Paul Sartre, *Dirty Hands,* in *No Exit and Three Other Plays,* trans. Stuart Gilbert (New York: Vintage, 1959); originally published as *Les mains sales* (Paris: Gallimard, 1948).
2. Maurice Merleau-Ponty, *Humanism and Terror,* trans. John O'Neill (Boston: Beacon Press, 1969); originally published as *Humanisme et terreur* (Paris: Gallimard, 1947).
3. Jean-Paul Sartre, "Merleau-Ponty," in *Situations,* trans. Benita Eisler (New York: George Braziller, 1965), 253, 255; published previously, in French, in *Situations* IV (Paris: Gallimard, 1964); originally published in *Les temps modernes,* October 1961.
4. Ronald Aronson makes this point in *Sartre's Second Critique* (Chicago: University of Chicago Press, 1987), 7.
5. See *Les temps modernes,* no. 81 (July 1952). His "Reply to Camus" ("Réponse à Albert Camus") appeared in the following issue, no. 82 (August 1952). The first English translation, by Irene Clephane, appeared in 1969 (London: Hamish Hamilton). *Situations* VI and VII were published respectively in 1964 and 1965 by Gallimard.
6. See Jean-Paul Sartre, "Materialism and Revolution," in *Literary and Philosophical Essays,* trans. Annette Michelson (New York: Collier Books, 1962). In what follows, I give page references to this Michelson translation unless elucidation calls for citation of the French original.

hardly condone, his unmeasured denunciation of Camus's views on meta-physical rebellion and revolutionary killing. Sartre's "Reply to Camus"—and, I might add, his "Answer to Claude Lefort" the following year (1953),[7] written with the same vehemence—brings to a head the widening differ-ences since 1945 between Sartre and Camus on the matter of combating violence, class exploitation, and oppression. But to background material that will help us understand this heated confrontation, I now turn.

---

7. Jean-Paul Sartre, "An Answer to Claude Lefort," in *The Communists and Peace*, trans. Irene Clephane (London: Hamish Hamilton, 1969), 207–64; originally published in *Les temps modernes*, no. 89 (April 1953). Lefort had criticized Sartre for contending that "the Party" was "the only subject of praxis" (in the preceding, March issue of *Les temps modernes*). He strongly criticized the bureaucracy of Stalinism, of which he took Sartre to be indi-rectly approving. Sartre struck back in an intemperate tone similar to that of his reply to Camus—as we shall see.

background to the confrontation

"Materialism and Revolution"

Although "Materialism and Revolution"[1] (1946) is sometimes viewed as
an immature, somewhat unsophisticated attack on dialectical materialism
and on a Stalin-infected Marxism,[2] Sartre devotes more than half of its
pages to the "philosophy of revolution"—more specifically, to revolution,
the revolutionary, and revolutionary violence. Hence, a brief consideration
of it will likely unearth early roots of the bitter disagreement that focuses
on the legitimacy of revolutionary violence. Moreover, it will doubtless
make evident the relation between Sartre's earliest sustained writing on

1. Jean-Paul Sartre, "Materialism and Revolution," in *Literary and Philosophical
Essays,* trans. Annette Michelson (New York: Collier Books, 1962); originally published as
"Matérialisme et révolution," *Les temps modernes,* no. 9 (June 1946): 1537–63, and no. 10
(July 1946): 1–32, and subsequently published by Gallimard in *Situations* III in 1949.
2. According to Contat and Rybalka, Simone de Beauvoir was of this judgment. See
Michel Contat and Michel Rybalka, eds., *The Writings of Jean-Paul Sartre,* vol. 1, *A Biblio-
graphical Life,* trans. Richard McCleary (Evanston, Ill.: Northwestern University Press, 1974),
154.

revolution and the positions we have seen him advance later in both the *Critique of Dialectical Reason* and his Preface to *The Wretched of the Earth,* for example.

For Sartre, in this essay, revolution occurs "when a change in institutions is accompanied by a profound modification in the property system." Though more focused on property, this view anticipates his later view that revolution involves replacing the present society with a more just society in which human beings care for one another.[3] "Revolutionary thinking is *a thinking within a situation;* it is the thinking of the oppressed in so far as they rebel together against oppression."[4] The oppressed person feels like a "native"; that is to say, he feels "colonized"; in his situation he cannot share in the privileges of his oppressor: "Each single event in his life repeats to him that he has not the right to exist."[5] The oppressed worker-revolutionary wants a "going beyond," a "surpassing" of his situation, and the only way he can do it is by destroying the class that is oppressing him. This observation immediately recalls Fanon's view—endorsed by Sartre—that "the intuition of the colonized masses [is] that their liberation must, and can only, be achieved by force."[6] The revolutionary wants to go beyond his situation in order to change it, not just for himself but for "his whole class." He wants to liberate himself and all other humans from the values and rules of behavior that the dominant—and dominating—ruling class has created, fostered, and lived by.[7] "We, too, are human beings" is the cry at the heart of any revolution. The revolutionary's cause is the human cause, and his philosophy "ought to express the truth about the [human being]." Although he will struggle to break the yoke of his oppressors and do violence to them for the sake of human liberation, he recognizes that his oppressors are also human beings, and will thus attempt to minimize their destruction.[8] (We must keep this point in mind when we get to the heart of the Sartre-Camus confronta-

---

3. Sartre, "Materialism and Revolution," 224. Here he follows the view of Albert Mathiez. See also Sartre's later expression in Jean-Paul Sartre and Benny Lévy, *Hope Now: The 1980 Interviews,* trans. Adrian van den Hoven, with an introduction by Ronald Aronson (Chicago: University of Chicago Press, 1996), 107.

4. Sartre, "Materialism and Revolution," 227. This is at least partly in line with what Sartre says in *Portrait of the Anti-Semite,* or *Anti-Semite and Jew,* which was initially published in French in 1945–46.

5. Ibid., 230.

6. Frantz Fanon, *The Wretched of the Earth,* trans. Constance Farrington (New York: Grove Press, 1968), 73. He clearly seems to see force as "violence" (in Sartre's sense) here.

7. Sartre, "Materialism and Revolution," 231.

8. Ibid., 232, 254.

tion: Is Sartre, in 1946, calling for the *mesure* on which Camus, against Sartre, will later insist?) His rebellion calls for the "unification" of all human beings and "posits human freedom, metaphysical and entire." To be sure, the revolutionary attitude beckons a theory of violence as a response to oppression (the oppressed want to free themselves from the "tyranny" of their Masters), but what the revolutionary demands most is the possibility for the human being to invent her own law—in short, to be autonomous,[9] that is, to be self-determining in the sense that Sartre has specified in *Being and Nothingness* and *The Flies*,[10] for instance. It is for the recognition of this freedom that the oppressed revolutionary struggles—for himself and all human beings. So, already in this early essay, as in his early *L'existentialisme est un humanisme* (1946; trans. *Existentialism and Humanism*) and *Notebooks for an Ethics*, which he wrote in 1947–48, Sartre is projecting a "community of ends" and a "new humanity" (and what, in the "Rome Lecture," he will call "integral humanity") and allows violence as a means to attain liberation. In fact, in a telling—though now repeated—theme early in this essay, Sartre says, "It is precisely in becoming revolutionaries . . . that slaves best manifest their freedom. Oppression leaves them no choice [but] resignation or revolution."[11]

The premises of Sartre's philosophy of freedom, then, enunciated meticulously in *Being and Nothingness* and summarized here, ground and generate Sartre's "philosophy of revolution" in this essay. As Sartre puts it, "if man is not originally free, we cannot even conceive what his liberation might be." Freedom is a "structure of human action":[12] freedom oppresses and freedom liberates, or, as Sartre might have put it, free being oppresses and free being liberates, for human reality *is* freedom.[13] Indeed, among Sartre's central aims in this essay is to formulate his arguments against both determinism and dialectical materialism—or what he calls the "materialist myth."[14] "The

---

9. Ibid., 250, 253.

10. See, in particular, *BN* 483. In this passage Sartre identifies freedom with "autonomy of choice" and self-determination.

Orestes in *The Flies* (*Les mouches*), 1943, powerfully dramatizes the movement to one's *realization* and affirmation of one's awesome metaphysical freedom (and accompanying responsibility)—to which human reality (for-itself) is condemned. "Neither slave nor master," he concludes, "I *am* my freedom."

11. Sartre, "Materialism and Revolution," 245.

12. Ibid., 244, also 251.

13. See *BN* 25, e.g.: "There is no difference between the being of a man and his *being-free*" (Il n'y a pas de différence entre l'être de l'homme et son *être-libre* [*EN* 61]).

14. Sartre, "Materialism and Revolution," 248.

possibility of rising above a situation in order to get a perspective on it," he says in a likely overstatement here, "is precisely what we call freedom." What he means, of course, as he later explains, is that the movement of *transcendence* required for becoming a revolutionary *cannot* be explained in terms of material conditions alone.[15]

Thus, in this essay Sartre sees both the revolutionary and revolution in terms of free human action against the violation of human freedom by the oppressors. Violence by the oppressed against the oppressors of freedom for the sake of bringing about a new human order, a new "solidarity in freedom,"[16] seems clearly to be *justified,* provided it also recognizes the humanity of the oppressor. Although Sartre does not say it explicitly, oppression here seems to qualify for what, in *Critique I,* he calls "pure violence."[17] Along this line, it is also of interest to note that Sartre here states that "one never oppresses anything but a freedom."[18] This surely anticipates his views in the *Notebooks* that "only a freedom can be oppressed," that "oppression can come to one freedom [i.e., human reality] *only* through another freedom,"[19] that oppression is freedom turning against itself, for to oppress a freedom one has to *recognize* it, and only a "freedom can *recognize* freedom in another."[20] Of course, this position is rooted in Sartre's analysis, in *Being and Nothingness,* of our conflictual "being-for-Others," in which he maintains that freedom can be limited only by freedom, that only a free consciousness can limit or violate another free consciousness.[21]

Thus, borrowing from *Being and Nothingness,* Sartre's views on violence and the justifiability of revolutionary violence in "Materialism and Revolution" prefigure central points that he makes about violence in his *Notebooks* and about some of the conditions that warrant revolutionary violence in the *Critique.* In short, violence is the "unconditional affirmation of freedom," is always addressed to freedom, and always needs to be recognized by the freedom(s) against which it is affirmed (i.e., it wants its adversary activity to be *acknowledged*).[22] Moreover, the violence of oppression involves both a

---

15. Ibid., 235.
16. *NFE* 325 (*CPM* 338).
17. *CDR* I:749.
18. Sartre, "Materialism and Revolution," 251.
19. *NFE* 327, 325 (*CPM* 341, 338).
20. *NFE* 328 (*CPM* 341); also *NFE* 332 (*CPM* 345).
21. See, e.g., *BN* 286 (*EN* 346). This point is, of course, repeated in *NFE* 325 (*CPM* 332).
22. *NFE* 175–78 (*CPM* 183–86).

"reciprocal recognition" of freedom and a negation of that freedom, and all "counterrevolutionary activity" is—to use his subsequent language from the *Notebooks* and *Being and Nothingness*—a "negation of a negation."[23] Once more, we recognize Hegel's definite influence on Sartre—an influence we also noted with regard to Fanon. Hence, even before the *Notebooks*, Sartre has shown in this essay what he went on to call the "curious ambiguity" and "contradiction" of violence. His analysis provides an explicit intimation of it when he here delineates the "double character" of freedom[24]—specifically, the capacity of freedoms to treat other freedoms as objects.

Finally, with regard to the justifiability of violent revolution, that is to say, of the use of violence to effect a radical transformation and replacement of a social system that oppresses, Sartre's answer here appears to be unequivocal. Insofar as domination and inhumanity are the *praxis* of the oppressor—to invoke the terminology he uses in the *Critique*—the oppressed have no realistic option except destructive counterviolence; and in these circumstances this alternative is not only justifiable but *affirming* of the human being. (This surely anticipates his endorsement of Fanon's position in *The Wretched of the Earth*.) Put another way, revolutionary action, for Sartre, albeit violent, involves the "affirmation of human freedom in and through history."[25] Rooted in oppression, it surpasses oppression in behalf of freedom and the socialist goal of a "new humanity."

Coincidentally, let me remind the reader that Sartre, in the *Notebooks*, stated emphatically that "all violence presents itself as the recuperation of a right."[26] Here, in this background essay, although he acknowledges that the oppressed revolutionary takes action against the oppressor's denial of his "right to exist," Sartre depicts the revolutionary as one who, far from demanding rights, "destroys the very idea of rights"[27]—especially when they are the enforced customary rights of the oppressors. This tension may have consequences for the hostile confrontation between Sartre and Camus.

In any event, some of the views Sartre expressed in "Materialism and Revolution" doubtless unsettled Camus, while nurturing the reformulated position that Sartre adopts six years later in denouncing Camus's position in *The Rebel*.

23. *NFE* 164 (*CPM* 172). To be sure, this is a key notion in *Being and Nothingness*. See, for example, my discussion of *conflict* in *Being and Nothingness* in Part I of this book.
24. Sartre, "Materialism and Revolution," 251. I have said much about this in Part I.
25. Ibid., 253.
26. *NFE* 177 (*CPM*, 185).
27. Sartre, "Materialism and Revolution," 232.

The Rebel and Related Background

As most students of Sartre and Camus know well, it was the publication of Camus's extraordinary book *L'homme révolté* (*The Rebel*),[28] in 1951, that occasioned the discussion that quickly became polemical and hostile rather than dialogic, an exchange, involving Camus on the one side and Sartre and Francis Jeanson on the other, that began with Jeanson's harsh critical review in *Les temps modernes*.[29]

Nine years earlier, in the *Myth of Sisyphus* (1942), Camus had presented, as the fundamental issue for philosophy, the question whether life is worth living, and had pondered whether suicide is an acceptable response to the "absurd"—that is, to the "confrontation" or "divorce" between the human's longing for rational clarity or meaning and the universe's silent indifference.[30] He concludes in this work that revolt is "one of the only coherent philosophical positions"—for "only revolt gives life its value"—and he rejects suicide, physical or philosophical, as an inauthentic form of escape that "settles the absurd." Vis-à-vis life's absurdity, suicide cannot be justified: "living is keeping the absurd alive."[31]

In *The Rebel*, Camus proposes to pursue this "train of thought." But *murder*, he says, is the problem of our time—a horrific time in which millions of people have been systematically killed. If we repudiate suicide in the face of life's meaninglessness and the silence of the universe, what are we to do with murder? Initial awareness of the absurd seems to make murder a matter of indifference. If God does not exist, as Dostoyevsky would put it, is everything permissible? The "absurdist attitude" prepares us "to commit murder."[32] The nihilism that "accepts suicide as legitimate leads, even more easily, to logical murder." If our age has its justifications for murder—it has offered many "justifications" for allegedly "just" causes—it is because of its indifference to life, the differentiating mark of nihilism. But murder, Camus is quick to affirm, cannot be rendered coherent if suicide cannot be viewed

---

28. Albert Camus, *The Rebel*, trans. Anthony Bower (New York: Alfred Knopf, Vintage, 1956); originally published as *L'homme révolté* (Paris: Gallimard, 1951).

29. Francis Jeanson, "Albert Camus ou l'âme révolté," *Les temps modernes*, no. 79 (May 1952): 2070–90.

30. Albert Camus, *The Myth of Sisyphus and Other Essays*, trans. Justin O'Brien (New York: Vintage Books, 1955), 16, 21, 22; originally published as *Le mythe de Sisyphe* (Paris: Gallimard, 1942).

31. Camus, *The Myth of Sisyphus*, 40. See also *The Rebel*, 6, for his later formulation.

32. Camus, *The Rebel*, 5.

as coherent.[33] "If we deny that there are reasons for suicide, we cannot claim that there are grounds [i.e., justifiable grounds, given the absurd] for murder." Suicide and murder are two parts of a "single system."[34] The moment we recognize that "absolute negation" is impossible—"merely to be alive is to recognize this"—the right of others to live, he contends, cannot be denied. Thus, the absurd itself is self-contradictory: in wishing to continue life, it excludes all value judgments, but living is, in itself, a value judgment.[35] Considered as a "rule of life"—as Camus is wont to say—the absurd is also contradictory. So what are we to do? "Deprived of all knowledge, incited to murder or to consent to murder, all I have at my disposal is this single piece of evidence, which is only reaffirmed by the anguish I suffer. Rebellion is born of the spectacle of irrationality confronted with an unjust and incomprehensible condition."[36] As in the *Myth of Sisyphus,* rebellion seems to be the only coherent response and the "single piece of evidence." But it spawns precisely the actions that it is asked to legitimate, without knowing whether such actions (e.g., murder) are legitimate. So by undertaking an intense analysis of metaphysical and historical rebellion, Camus resolves to discover whether all rebellion has to end in the "justification of universal murder"[37] or, put more narrowly, whether rebellion, which follows directly from the absurd, can ever legitimate murder. Alternatively, he wants to find out whether an analysis of it might yield a "principle of reasonable culpability."

Only selected highlights of Camus's brilliant and controversial analysis can have a place here. And even before considering Jeanson's or Sartre's response, one can anticipate Sartre's unease with Camus's analysis. "In every act of rebellion," Camus says, "the rebel simultaneously experiences a feeling of revulsion at the infringement of his rights and a complete and spontaneous loyalty to certain aspects of himself. Thus he implicitly brings into play a *standard of values* . . . that he is prepared to support . . . no matter what the risks."[38] While acknowledging that there is a limit beyond which one must not go, the rebel is affirming a "yes" about himself and the human being as well as a "no"; he is acting on behalf of values that he takes to be common to all human beings. Against the "postulates of contemporary thought"—certainly some of the early Sartre's—he is rebelling on the

33. Ibid., 6.
34. Ibid., 7.
35. Ibid., 7–8.
36. Ibid., 10.
37. Ibid., 11.
38. Ibid., 14, italics mine.

presumption that "a *human nature does exist*," that there is something in oneself and all human beings that is worth preserving.[39] If human beings cannot refer to a common value that they recognize as existing in everyone, then "man is incomprehensible to man."[40] So rebellion for Camus is "profoundly positive" to the extent that it reveals the dimension of the human being that needs always to be defended.[41] Moreover, rebellion is never alone. The rebel rebels "in the name of the identity of man with man."[42] "I rebel—therefore we exist."[43] In exhibiting one of the "essential dimensions" of the human being, rebellion both discloses human integrity and points toward human solidarity, in which it finds its justification. "Rebellion lures the individual from [her] solitude." It even places total human freedom on trial.[44] That is to say, human solidarity is founded upon rebellion, and rebellion in turn justifies itself on that solidarity. Because of this reciprocal relationship, one can justifiably conclude that any rebellion that "claims the right to deny or destroy" human solidarity "loses the right to be called rebellion and . . . becomes [instead] an acquiescence in murder." Thus, in order to exist, the human being has to rebel, but rebellion "must respect the *limit* it discovers in itself."[45]

Thus, Camus—in implicit opposition to Sartre—suggests a basis for a human nature and a standard of values and repudiates any view of absolute freedom. (He'll later say that "absolute freedom mocks at justice," although it is not clear that he understands Sartre's view of complete freedom.) But, though basic, these are not the decisive issues for understanding the painful confrontation between Sartre and Camus. Rather, it is the relationship between rebellion and murder that is at the center of their developing feud. So in order to focus on the emerging and decisive role of radical violence in the debate, we must attend to this relationship, which hinges on the distinction Camus draws between "metaphysical" and "historical" rebellion.

"Metaphysical rebellion" is, as we have already partially observed, the dynamic in which the human being protests against his "incomprehensible condition" and the whole of creation. Although, in the history of ideas, it

39. Ibid., 16, italics mine.
40. Ibid., 23.
41. Ibid., 19.
42. Ibid., 281.
43. Ibid., 22. See also, e.g., 104, 250.
44. Ibid., 284.
45. Ibid., 22, italics mine.

does not appear in coherent form until the end of the eighteenth century, its consequences, Camus contends, have shaped the history of our times. The metaphysical rebel protests against a shattered and disunified world, against life's suffering and death, against evil, against the "incompleteness" (because of death) and "wastefulness" (because of evil) of the human situation, against our universal condemnation to death ("a mass death sentence," "a universal death penalty").[46] He does not suppress God; he, rather, like Sisyphus, denounces God "as the father of death and as the supreme outrage." Like Ivan in *The Brothers Karamazov*, the rebel rebels against a murderous God. He rejects "divine coherence." But from the moment he begins to "rationalize his rebellion," he begins to allow for the legitimacy of murder.[47] To kill God is acceptable. Human rebellion ends in metaphysical *revolution*. Although the rebel hates the death penalty—for him it is the "image" of the deplorable human condition—he is yet drawn to crime.[48] Having overturned the "throne of God" ("he drove him from his heaven"), the metaphysical rebel takes on the responsibility of creating an order of justice and unity that he sought in vain within his own condition. He wants to take hold of all of creation. But, like Ivan, he is willing to do so at the price of crime and a new dominion (or domination) by man. He deifies man. Already metaphysical rebellion is joining hands with revolutionary movements.[49] If that is the case, what has happened to the "positive content" of rebellion—for example, the human solidarity, the standard of values, the affirmation of limits—to which, explicitly or implicitly, rebellion, on analysis, has given testimony and evidence and which metaphysical insurrection, in its first stages, shares with the slave's rebellion?[50] If the rebel "obstinately confronts a world condemned to death . . . with his demand for life and absolute clarity," and if the rebellion against death is tantamount to claiming that life has a meaning,[51] how can human insurrection in the form of murder ever be legitimated? Does the "killing of God," or subsequently that of creation, to which it might in turn lead, retain the right to be called "rebellion"? For the time being, the question is manifestly rhetorical. But the move from "metaphysical" rebellion to revolutionary violence is, for Camus, straightforwardly the move from *metaphysical* rebellion to *historical* rebellion that has taken the form of revolution.

46. Ibid., 24–25, 100.
47. Ibid., 58.
48. Ibid., 61.
49. Ibid., 103.
50. Ibid., 25.
51. Ibid., 101.

To bring the distinction to a head, we must get a clearer grasp of Camus's view of *historical* rebellion and take note of the nihilism to which, historically, it has led. ("Nihilism," he tells us rather early, "smothers the force of creation.")[52] By doing so, we shall be able to understand better both Camus's denunciation of revolutionary killing and the Jeanson/Sartre observation that, with Camus's "transformation" of metaphysical rebellion into *historical* rebellion, "everything starts to go sour" (*tout commence à se gâter*) for him.[53] And here we get closer to the core of the bitter controversy.

For Camus, to put it now somewhat differently, "every act of rebellion expresses a nostalgia for innocence and an appeal to the essence of being." But one day this nostalgia assumes the "responsibility of total guilt," "takes up arms," and "adopts murder and violence"—all in the name of affirming human dignity in defiance of that which offends or negates its existence. In history, violent revolution seems to be the logical consequence of metaphysical rebellion: it is the form in which historical rebellion has expressed itself. The revolutionary spirit, in defending that part of the human being which draws its limits and refuses to submit to the level of subhumanity, replaces God with history through "an apparently inevitable logic."[54] But to choose history alone is to choose nihilism (for history "is not a source of values but . . . of nihilism"),[55] and nihilism builds "the temple of Caesar." Man wants to be God. Servile rebellions, regicide revolutions, and the revolutions of the twentieth century have all moved to violent revolt. Nihilism, with no respect for values, illuminates the last century. Like Kierkegaard and Heidegger before him, Camus sees nihilism as the crucial issue of our time. Twentieth-century revolution has, in fact, consecrated historical nihilism. Moral nihilism has generated cynicism and justified the revolutionary means employed by both Nazism and Communism. Europe became in the 1940s "a land of inhumanity."[56] To be sure, "when confronted with death, man from the very depths

52. Ibid., 103, 104.

53. Jeanson, "Albert Camus ou l'âme révolté," 2075. Unless otherwise indicated, I make use of the Sprintzen/van den Hoven translation of all the original materials that constitute the Sartre-Camus "confrontation" (*Contested Terrain: The Sartre-Camus Confrontation*, ed. David Sprintzen and Adrian van den Hoven, forthcoming). I express my profound appreciation to David Sprintzen for placing all of his relevant translated materials at my disposal. This is additional testimony to his trust and to his open, nonpossessive approach to scholarship. As a longtime friend, I have become accustomed to that. I hope that some of my suggestions—especially with regard to translation—have in some way assisted him in his work.

54. Camus, *The Rebel*, 105–6.

55. Ibid., 249.

56. Ibid., 102, 105, 246–48.

of his soul cries out for justice."[57] But when expressed in history, rebellion
has repeatedly forsaken values and turned to revolution, violence, murder.
In so doing, Camus asserts, historical rebellion has "turned against its rebel
origins,"[58] violated its creative affirmation of the human spirit. In short,
rebellion has been "cynically travestied."[59] But human rebellion refuses to be
limited to historical terms alone. That is not to imply that the revolutionary
is not a rebel. Indeed, if he is not simultaneously a rebel, he is "a policeman
or bureaucrat." But, indeed, if he is a rebel, he ends up "taking sides against
the revolution; so much so that there is absolutely no progress from one attitude to the other, but coexistence and endlessly increasing contradiction."[60]
For, as we have seen, rebellion is an affirmation of a nature common to *all*
human beings—a nature that is not to be humiliated but insists on human
dignity and points to shared human solidarity, unity, and values. Rebellion,
in its original expression, makes known the limits of freedom and exhibits a
value by which to judge history.[61] The violent revolution into which rebellion
is transformed in history is a betrayal of rebellion: it is rebellion gone astray.
Authentic rebellion seeks unity—even of the oppressor and the oppressed;
historical revolution wants totality. Rebellion is creative in its aspiration;
violent revolution is nihilist in its deeds and in its refusal to recognize any
moral demands.[62] For Camus, authentic rebellion and revolutionary murder
are contradictory.[63] Rebellion is not a demand for "total freedom." The freedom to kill, the most extreme expression of freedom, is not compatible with
the genuine spirit of rebellion. Claiming the unity and universality of *la condition humaine,* rebellion is a "force of life," not death; of creation, not
destruction. When rebellion moves into destruction, it is illogical. For the
rebel to justify violence, destruction, and murder in historical rebellion
would be—as I affirmed in my introductory summary for this section—to
renounce the reasons for his initial insurrection, to violate the roots of rebellion. To rebel against the violence, destruction, and injustice of the world by
adding more to it makes neither logical nor moral sense.[64] Like Kaliayev in
The Just Assassins, the rebel refuses to add to what he takes to be the "living

57. Ibid., 303.
58. Ibid., 247.
59. Ibid., 280.
60. Ibid., 249. I have altered the punctuation in this quotation.
61. Ibid., 249–50.
62. Ibid., 251.
63. Ibid., 281.
64. Ibid., 283–85.

injustice" all around him.[65] The "logic of the rebel" is to serve justice. As a consequence of his rebellion, the rebel refuses "to legitimize murder."[66] Rebellion intends freedom and dignity for *all* human beings. Historical, violent revolution, especially of our time, tramples on freedom and—here Camus virtually echoes what Sartre has said in his *Notebooks for an Ethics*—destroys the promise of community and dialogue, the very goals of rebellion. In protesting the violence of his condition, the rebel cannot accept revolutionary murder as a response that is faithful to his rebellion. Despite an understandable motivation for revolutionary violence (e.g., "If men kill one another, it is because they reject mortality, and seek immortality for all men"; "terror and concentration camps" are "drastic means" by which man affirms himself in order to "escape solitude"), rebellion—if it is to exist—requires for survival a "strange form of love."[67] If I give up on the project of human identity and community, I give way to oppression. (This is not unlike Sartre's claim that when freedom turns against itself, there is *oppression*.) Justice and freedom must set limits for each other. Justice, far from affording more killing, is a "living thing."[68]

However, although Camus speaks clearly here against revolutionary murder and violence, it is evident that he is not advocating total nonviolence or pacifism. I repeat: "In the world today, only a philosophy of eternity could justify non-violence," and the rebel cannot ignore history or the world without forsaking "the very principle of his rebellion."[69] Camus later adds that though systematic violence does "rupture" human communication—once more his words are virtually identical to Sartre's in the *Notebooks*[70]—absolute nonviolence is the "negative basis of slavery and its acts of violence." Violence must only be "an extreme limit which combats another form of violence," and genuine acts of rebellion must only serve to *limit* violence.[71] Rebellion always draws a line.

65. Albert Camus, *The Just Assassins,* in *Caligula and 3 Other Plays,* trans. Stuart Gilbert (New York: Vintage Books, 1958), 260; originally published as *Les justes* (Paris: Gallimard, 1950). All subsequent references give pagination from the English publication. See also Camus, *The Rebel,* 285.

66. Camus, *The Rebel,* 285.

67. Ibid., 304, 247. See also page 104 for revolution as the "logical consequence of metaphysical rebellion."

68. Ibid., 306.

69. Ibid., 287.

70. See my discussion, earlier in this study, of Sartre's consideration of violence in the *Notebooks for an Ethics.* See also Ronald E. Santoni, "On the Existential Meaning of Violence," *Dialogue and Humanism,* no. 4 (1993): 139–50.

71. Camus, *The Rebel,* 292.

Indeed, a year before the publication of *The Rebel*, Camus rehearsed the position he was formulating in it on the violence/nonviolence "contradiction," and tried to anticipate the later objections from his critics. In one of his responses to Emmanuel d'Astier de la Vigerie, he said:

> I preach neither nonviolence . . . nor, as the jokers [*farceurs*] say, saintliness. . . . Violence is inevitable and at the same time unjustifiable. . . . I shall not say that we must do away with all violence, which would be desirable but is, in effect, utopian. I say only that we must refuse all legitimization of violence. . . . I think we should set a limit to violence, restrict it to certain quarters when it is inevitable, [and] muffle its terrifying effects by preventing it from going to the limit of its fury. I loathe comfortable violence.[72]

Although this statement of his position seems somewhat less idealistic than his position in *The Rebel*, it confirms his declaration of disagreement with pacifism and his recognition of the inseparability of violence from history—issues crucial to any consideration of the justifiability of Sartre's later attack. In spite of what appear to be counterstatements in *The Rebel*—some of which I've quoted above—the Camus scholar David A. Sprintzen is unambiguous in stating: "No essential conflict between rebellion and revolution need exist for Camus."[73] "Nor is there any requirement that revolutions always be nonviolent. Violence is always an internal diremption of the potential human community. But nonviolence is often only the acquiescence in the oppressive violence of the Other. A necessary misfortune, violence . . . can be a legitimate instrument of individual or collective self-defense, though never a morally defensible vehicle of revenge."[74]

72. Albert Camus, "Première réponse," in *Actuelles I: Chroniques, 1944–1948* (Paris: Gallimard, 1950), 184 ("à Emmanuel d'Astier de la Vigerie"), translation mine. I express appreciation to Peter Royle, whose work on this topic led me to Camus's "Première réponse." I have taken the liberty of changing the order of sentences in one or two places in this passage.
73. I am less persuaded than Sprintzen is on this point—especially given what Camus has said in his overall argument in *The Rebel*. But I understand that a number of texts would support Sprintzen's point. See, e.g., *The Rebel*, 288. Certainly some statements in Camus's "Défense de *L'homme révolté*," which I discuss later in this part, lend additional support to Sprintzen's contention, despite Camus's insistence there that each—rebellion and revolution—"is the limit of the other" ("Chacune est la limite de l'autre") (in *Essais*, Bibliothèque de la Pléiade, 183 [Paris: Gallimard, 1965], 1709). I remind the reader of the quotation to which I have alluded earlier: "Logically, one should reply that murder and rebellion are contradictory." *The Rebel*, 281.
74. David A. Sprintzen, preface to *Contested Terrain: The Sartre-Camus Confrontation*. Again, I express my appreciation to Prof. Sprintzen for sharing his materials with me in 1999, in advance of publication or even completion of his own book.

We have already seen enough to observe that Camus's position against violence and revolution, though often sounding unequivocal in *The Rebel,* is qualified, not absolute. I am tempted to say that, given the above, his position seems, if not equivocal, "curiously ambiguous"—if I may resort to Sartre's early characterization of violence, which I, in turn, have used to describe segments of his own trajectory. But, for the time being at least, I'm willing to proceed on the assumption that the statements above from Camus and Sprintzen accurately represent Camus's overall position with regard to pacifism and nonviolence. From that perspective, the vehemence with which both Sartre and Jeanson repudiate Camus's *Rebel* becomes more baffling and less philosophically comprehensible. To support what is now only a suggestion, I remind the reader, in passing, of what Sartre said in *What Is Literature?* twelve years *before* the publication of his *Critique of Dialectical Reason,* volume I, in which he declares violence to be an inevitable part of history:[75] "I recognize that violence under whatever form it may manifest itself is a *setback.* But it is an inevitable setback because we are in a universe of violence; and if it is true that recourse to violence risks perpetuating it, it is also true that it is the only means of bringing an end to it."[76] And we may note again Sartre's statement in the *Notebooks* that terrorist violence may be viewed as a *"dead end [une voie sans issue]* . . . an experience that can benefit no one [*qui ne peut profiter à personne*]."[77] Camus, both in his reply to d'Astier de la Vigerie and in *The Rebel,* appears to share certain important features of Sartre's perspective on violence—in particular the inevitability of violence (and "necessary violence") in human history. Camus, like Sartre, is somewhat ambivalent on this topic.

Dirty Hands and The Just Assassins

But I can do justice neither to my inquiry nor to my background to the Sartre-Camus skirmish without giving some detailed attention to Camus's *Just Assassins (Les justes),* mentioned above, which was likely written (in

75. *CDR* I:736.
76. Jean-Paul Sartre, *What Is Literature?* trans. Bernard Frechtman (London: Methuen, 1950), 214; originally published in book form as *Qu'est-ce que la littérature?* (Paris: Gallimard, 1948), 347.
77. *NFE* 406 (*CPM* 420). The statement reads: "We need not see in terrorist violence, in a Hegelian manner, a passage towards liberation, but . . . *a dead end.* This is an experience that can benefit no one. [And] . . . it does not suppress slavery and alienation" (italics mine).

1949) as a prelude to *The Rebel*, and—I should contend—with Sartre's *Dirty Hands* (*Les mains sales*, 1948) in mind. If nothing else, *The Just Assassins* represents Camus's painstaking attempt to work out, in the context of a play,[78] the human complexities and consequences related to revolutionary killing. In my judgment, it stands out as a model for any probing, sensitive dialogue on violence, its justifiability, and the revolutionary dilemma.

Dirty Hands (*Les mains sales*). For purposes of comparison, I must first offer a brief account of Sartre's *Dirty Hands,* a masterful play that anticipates the issues between Sartre and Camus. In this powerful drama, Sartre places Hoederer, a seasoned general secretary of the Communist Party and revolutionary realist who is willing to compromise, in dialectical opposition to Hugo, a young revolutionary idealist, who shares Hoederer's goal of eliminating classes and class oppression but insists on maintaining his bourgeois-rooted sense of purity. As a consequence, he vehemently resists any compromise with the fascist government of the regent. Says Hugo: "The party has one program: the realization of a socialist economy, and one method of achieving it: the class struggle."[79] Hoederer, who acknowledges that he has "dirty hands . . . plunged in filth and blood" and asserts that "purity is an idea for a yogi or a monk," accuses Hugo of not loving human beings but "only principles" (which we would be well advised to bear in mind when confronting Sartre's later denunciation of Camus). To Hugo's insistence that he is interested in human beings not for what they are but for what they can *become,* Hoederer responds, "I love them for what they *are*. With all their filth and all their vices." And he adds pointedly: "You are a destroyer. . . . Your purity resembles death. . . . You're all alike. An intellectual is never a real revolutionary; just good enough to make an assassin."[80] And facing Hugo during Hugo's first assassination attempt on him for compromising with the regent government, Hoederer adds, "I prefer people who fear the death of others: it shows they know how to live."[81] A little later, Hugo, having caught Hoederer in a compromising romantic situation with his wife, Jessica, and concluding that Hoederer had had an ulterior motive for sparing him earlier, shoots him dead—but not without Hoederer's last words, "What a god-damn waste!" After two years in prison, Hugo acknowledges

78. *Les justes* was presented for the first time at the Théatre Hébertot in Paris on December 15, 1949.
79. Jean-Paul Sartre, *Dirty Hands,* in *No Exit and Three Other Plays,* trans. Stuart Gilbert (New York: Vintage, 1959), 221.
80. Ibid., 223–25, italics mine.

that he loved Hoederer "more than I ever loved anyone in the world," and that it is not the crime that tortures him but "the fact that [Hoederer] is dead."[82] This statement is similar to the emotional confession of Scipio to Camus's Caligula: "When all is ended, remember that I loved you."[83]

Finally, refusing to renounce either his ambiguous crime or his party's would-be cover-up of it, and disgusted with his party's renewed acceptance of Hoederer's compromise with the program of the regent party, he symbolically kills Hoederer for the wrongness of his policy of compromise by confronting the angry party members at his door and killing himself in front of them. This way, Hugo gives Hoederer "the death he deserves."[84] The tension between purity or principle and compromise in behalf of a better humanity (violence is often regarded as such) comes to the fore here. And it will assume an important place in the Sartre-Camus quarrel.

Camus says in *The Rebel*: "The rebel has only one way of reconciling himself with his act of murder if he allows himself to be led into performing it: to accept his own death and sacrifice." And in a somewhat baffling statement a few pages later, Camus adds: "Faithful to his origins, the rebel demonstrates by sacrifice that his real freedom is not freedom from murder but freedom from his own death."[85] I mention this interconnection only to suggest a background similarity, but as the concluding pages of *The Just Assassins* attest, it also serves as a fitting transition to Camus's haunting play.

The Just Assassins (Les justes). Like Sartre in *Dirty Hands,* Camus in *The Just Assassins* focuses his dramatic engagement with revolutionary means and violence on an insurrectional group who are outraged by the blatant injustices of their society and ruling political regime and are radically committed to ushering in a more just and humane human community. Although some central concerns and actions clearly differ in the two works (e.g., the murder of a fellow revolutionary versus the murder of a nation's political head, the Grand Duke), the issues that the works share are the source of oppositions that later become points of antagonism between their authors.

The Just Assassins, which Camus based on actual historical events, opens in "the terrorists' headquarters" in Moscow. An intense discussion among

81. Ibid., 232–33.
82. Ibid., 242.
83. Camus, *Caligula and 3 Other Plays,* 67; originally published in *Le malentendu suivi de Caligula* (Paris: Gallimard, 1944).
84. Sartre, *Dirty Hands,* 247–48.
85. Camus, *The Rebel,* 282, 286.

the Russian revolutionaries regarding the plot to assassinate the Grand Duke outlines the issues. Disagreements regarding revolutionary motives and means and who should throw the bomb surface immediately. Although all seem to be united in their opposition to despotism and in their wish—in the words of Annenkov—"to set our people free,"[86] they are not agreed about what constitutes a "true revolutionary." This seems to parallel the situation in Sartre's *Dirty Hands*. Stepan, who appears to embody Camus's stereotype of the revolutionary, asserts that "a true revolutionary cannot love himself," and confesses: "I do not love life; I love something higher— and that is justice."[87] Kaliayev, who in his own later words has "chosen to be innocent"[88] and whose commitment is questioned by Stepan, openly states that he loves life, that he joined the revolution because he loves life, and that he wants revolution "for the sake of life."[89] Yet his innocence and celebration of life are challenged, even ruptured, by unjust suffering in an unjust world: he cannot be complicit with it. But to what lengths can he go to correct it? Can murder ever be legitimized—or made morally justifiable—in behalf of justice or human liberation? Can the love of life, or the love of another person or persons, justify killing? What are the moral bounds of revolt against absurd evil in the world? These are some of the issues that drive the ensuing rift between Sartre and Camus. The stands and tensions among members of Camus's fictional revolutionary group reflect Camus's own moral tensions and questions.

Kaliayev's first "attempt" to throw the bomb is a failure. Confronted with the Grand Duke and his carriage, he suddenly catches sight of children, and his arms and legs go limp. "Those two serious little faces, and in my hand that hideous weight. I'd have had to throw it at *them*. Like that! Straight at them. No, I just couldn't bring myself."[90] Stepan is incensed. "Not until the day comes when we stop sentimentalizing about children will the revolution triumph, and we be masters of the world."[91] But neither Annenkov nor Dora—one of the voices of both love and realism, who repeatedly introduces the human dimensions—will tolerate the dismemberment of children, or the view that "everything's permissible," for the sake of rescuing humanity. Says Dora: "Yanek's [Kaliayev's, from his revolutionary name]

---

86. Camus, *The Just Assassins*, 244.
87. Ibid., 243–44.
88. Ibid., 261.
89. Ibid., 243–45.
90. Ibid., 254.
91. Ibid., 256.

ready to kill the Grand Duke because his death may help to bring nearer the time when Russian children will no longer die of hunger. . . . But the death of the Grand Duke's niece and nephew won't prevent any child from dying of hunger. Even in destruction there's a right way and a wrong way—and there are limits." To which Kaliayev, in mounting anger at Stepan, his "limitless" revolutionary brother, adds: "Killing children is a crime against a man's honor. And if one day the revolution thinks fit to break with honor, well, I'm through with the revolution."[92] Obviously in question are the limits of violent revolutionary means for attaining worthy revolutionary goals. Camus is sorting out the ambivalences and "contradictions" that he struggles to resolve philosophically in *The Rebel*—and to some of which Sartre later takes vehement exception.

Once the revolutionary group has decided that killing children would serve no purpose and their comrade Voinov cannot bring himself to throw the bomb, Kaliayev gets his second chance, but not before Dora—who desperately seeks from him, even for an hour, a "simple human" love bracketed from the "ugliness and misery" of "this foully unjust world around us"[93]—sets him straight about his alleged commitment to innocence and love. "Too much blood," she says, "too much brutal violence—there's no escape for us. Those whose hearts are set on justice have no right to love." And she adds: "I love you with the same love as yours: a love that's half frozen, because it's rooted in justice and reared in prison cells." In one of the most poignant and potentially contentious lines of the play, she concludes: "We don't belong to the world of men. We are the just ones."[94] "Love calls for time, and we have hardly time enough for—justice."[95] But committed to the revolutionary fraternity that, in turn, is committed to freeing Russia, Yanek (Kaliayev), in spite of his preoccupation with innocence, assassinates the Grand Duke in a determined effort to resist complicity with the world's evil and bring greater purity to the world and himself.[96] He murders to bring about a "world without murder." To use words Voinov later quotes from him, Kaliayev protests against violence and a "world of tears

92. Ibid., 257, 258, 260.
93. Ibid., 270–71.
94. Ibid., 269, 271–72.
95. Ibid., 273.
96. I am influenced on this point by the insight of David Sprintzen, whose book *Camus: A Critical Examination* (Philadelphia: Temple University, 1988) is, in my judgment, the best philosophical commentary on Camus's works available in the English language. See page 117, e.g.

and blood . . . with all the manhood in [him]," and accepts death as a "consummation" of the "ideal that inspired" his act.[97] The dilemma that revolution poses for an accommodation of justice with interpersonal love and love for humanity is complicated both by love and fidelity to revolutionary brotherhood and by the justification for killing—especially when justification is offered in the name of self-sacrifice for an ideal. Hugo's situation in *Dirty Hands* and Kaliayev's in this play are similar. Each character, to invoke *The Rebel* again, accepts his own "death and sacrifice."[98]

But the revolutionary tensions have still not reached the peak of their intensity. After his imprisonment in the Pugatchev Tower, Kaliayev is challenged by the chief of police, Skuratov, and the widowed Grand Duchess, to mention only the most prominent. Seeming more manipulative than earnestly dialogic (he wants a confession that will lead to the arrest of Kaliayev's comrades), Skuratov yet makes statements that meet Kaliayev on his own terms (his wish for innocence, for example) and thus can hardly be ignored. To Kaliayev's claim, "I threw the bomb at your tyranny, not at a man," Skuratov answers, "I am not interested in ideas, I'm interested in human beings. . . . Murder isn't just an idea. . . . It was a living human being whom [you] blew to bits. . . . If an ideal balks at murdering children, is one justified in murdering a Grand Duke on its behalf?"[99] In short, to repeat a theme raised by both Hoederer and Jessica in Sartre's *Dirty Hands,* can ideals or principles ever take precedence over "flesh-and-blood" human beings? And the Grand Duchess, who insists on seeing Kaliayev, only exacerbates the revolutionary dilemmas. She humanizes the Grand Duke even further and appeals to Kaliayev's shared humanity. "Do you know what he was doing two hours before be died?" "It's your duty to accept being a murderer." "I, too, loved—the man you killed." "I am not your enemy."[100] The Grand Duchess wants Kaliayev to accept repentance and salvation from a transcendent God, but—in line with Camus's stand on "philosophical suicide"—he will have no part of it. "I have given up counting on the agreement I once made with God. But in dying, I shall keep the agreement I made with those I love, my brothers."[101] He rejects the possibility of pardon—from either God or the authorities.

97. Camus, *The Just Assassins,* 294.
98. I refer the reader again to Camus, *The Rebel,* 282.
99. Camus, *The Just Assassins,* 282–85.
100. Ibid., 286–90.
101. Ibid., 289.

But it is Dora's last statements during the revolutionaries' "wait" for Kaliayev's execution that are the most haunting with respect to violence. In reply to the claim that Kaliayev's death will "consummate" the "purity of the ideal," she retorts: "But oh the cruelty of that consummation!"[102] To Annenkov's point that there is no other solution, she responds: "If death is the only solution, then we have chosen the wrong path. . . . With the first murder, youth ends forever."[103] (This statement resembles Caligula's final and revelatory admission to Caesonia at the end of Camus's *Caligula:* "I have chosen a wrong path, a path that leads to nothing. My freedom isn't the right one.")[104] And then, realizing that Kaliayev must be dead, she says to Annenkov what she intends for all her fellow insurrectionists: "Yes, you're my brother; all of you are my brothers, my brothers whom I love. But what a foul taste brotherhood has, sometimes!"[105] This is surely a statement that members of Sartre's hypothetical "pledged group" (in *Critique I*) could also have uttered.

Yet the play does not end here. Dora assures her brothers that there is no need for tears. She asks: "Don't you realize this is the day of our justification?" And she adds: "Yanek is a murderer no longer." He has refused to forsake his "brothers" and has died for his ideals of justice. Having brought together her gnawing sensitivities with a reluctant revolutionary justification of killing, she offers to throw the next bomb, but not without continuing ambivalence. When Annenkov reminds her that it is against their rules to have women on the firing line, she responds shrilly, "Am I a woman . . . now?"[106] Revolutionary murder, though meeting the criteria for a certain kind of "justice," exacts a price from our humanity. This is surely one of the unambiguous conclusions of *The Just Assassins,* one that Sartre rejects in both the *Critique* and his Preface to *The Wretched of the Earth.* But we must not forget even Sartre's acknowledgment, in *What Is Literature?* that violence is always an "inevitable setback."

The sensitive and existentially searching exchanges in *The Just Assassins* help to ground and corroborate our understanding of Camus's contentions in *The Rebel.* But even more important, certain differences between *The Just Assassins* and Sartre's *Dirty Hands*—added, of course, to the blatant

102. Ibid., 294.
103. Ibid., 295–96.
104. Camus, *Caligula,* in *Caligula and 3 Other Plays,* 73.
105. Camus, *The Just Assassins,* 298.
106. Ibid., 301.

differences that a reader would not fail to notice between Camus's *Rebel* and Sartre's emerging *Critique I* and *II*—surely contributed to the intensity of the philosophical divergence between the two thinkers in their 1952 "confrontation." Sartre's disdain for bourgeois purity comes out unmistakably in *Dirty Hands*. "Purity is [only] an idea," Hoederer says.[107] In this regard, it is of interest to note that although, in a later interview, Sartre acknowledges that he "had a great understanding of Hugo's attitude," he is quick to add that "Hoederer is the man I'd like to be if I were a revolutionary."[108] Although Hugo, like Stepan in *The Just Assassins,* is to be admired for his commitment to the party and its revolutionary goals (he refuses to compromise), he is too much of a bourgeois intellectual idealist to gain Sartre's full support. The revolution is not a matter of virtue, Hoederer tells Hugo, "but of effectiveness," and he reminds the would-be but despairing revolutionary that he (Hugo) has a "gift for writing." ("Words! Always words!" Hugo replies, reminding us of Sartre's own self-criticism, as well as his own autobiography, *The Words*.)[109] Although Sartre in 1948 may have viewed himself as a "dialectical synthesis"[110] of Hoederer and Hugo, it seems clear that, in *Dirty Hands,* he chooses "red gloves," "effectiveness," and flesh-and-blood human beings over purity and principles. In contrast, although many of the revolutionary dilemmas in *The Just Assassins* are similar, if not identical, to the tensions in *Dirty Hands,* and although Camus in 1949 may well have viewed himself as a dialectical synthesis of Dora, Kaliayev, and even Voinov, for example, it is evident that he is mobilizing all the arguments he can against revolutionary violence and murder and putting before the reader the human consequences of so-called justified murder. Recognizing that there can be no revolution without violence, but also realizing that Kaliayev's commitment to innocence cannot be sustained completely in an unjust world, he yet—it seems to me—values human beings and simple human love above even the demands of revolutionary "justice." His struggle with the issue of violence is, here, considerably more intense than Sartre's, as is the dialogue condemning it. Some of Kaliayev's and Dora's statements against revolutionary killing would surely serve more to irritate Sartre than to engage him, in spite of similar lines uttered by both

---

107. Sartre, *Dirty Hands,* 223.
108. Contat and Rybalka, *The Writings of Jean-Paul Sartre,* 1:192.
109. Sartre, *Dirty Hands,* 234–35.
110. See Pierre Verstraeten's discussion of the "revolutionary hero" and "dialectical synthesis" in "The Revolutionary Hero Revisited," in *Sartre Alive,* ed. Ronald Aronson and Adrian van den Hoven (Detroit: Wayne State University Press, 1991), 211–24.

Jessica and Hoederer in *Dirty Hands*. But one matter is clear: both plays show Sartre's and Camus's agreement—in the words of Hugo—that "you can't make a revolution with flowers,"[111] that lies and murder are means to revolutionary ends. Yet, though Sartre, through Hoederer, places human beings ahead of destruction, Camus is minimally, through his fictional alter egos, placing moral bounds on violence and insisting on limits to destruction. The "maturing" Sartre of the early 1950s and, as we have noted, of the *Critique* and the Preface to *The Wretched of the Earth* in the early 1960s would not preclude revolutionary killing to stop exploitation, colonialism, and other forms of oppressive de- or subhumanization. While Sartre seems more concerned with effectiveness (*efficacité*) in altering the concrete situations of a corrupt society or world, Camus seems more worried about the morality of using violent and human-destroying means to correct the violences and injustices of the human situation. Although both have serious reservations about what Sartre calls the "maxim of violence" (the end justifies the means), Sartre seems, at this stage, to make accommodations to it in prescribed circumstances.[112]

I fully realize that other writings and differing responses to political issues and events of the later 1940s and early 1950s contributed progressively to a distancing between Sartre and Camus on the issue of violence. As early as 1946, Sartre's support of revolution in his long essay "Materialism and Revolution" can find a contrast in Camus's "Neither Victims Nor Executioners,"[113] in which Camus appears to dissociate himself from ideological Marxism and warns against murder and revolutions that belie the aims and values for which revolutions are, allegedly, intended. (In fact, Camus here says that "takeover of power by violence is a romantic idea that the advance of armaments has rendered illusory.")[114] And although—in contrast

111. Sartre, *Dirty Hands*, 225.

112. In commenting on my manuscript, Thomas Anderson has suggested, in this regard, that Sartre and Camus differ mainly about the *limits* for justifiable violence and the extent to which violence against *innocents* can be justified, not about the necessity and justification of violence to stop oppression. Although there is some substance in Anderson's point, I believe he overstates it and tends to underestimate the intensity of Camus's abhorrence of violence. But I do agree with Anderson's corollary point that Sartre, in particular, too frequently either ignores or fails to make the distinction between violence done to the oppressors and violence done to the innocents (e.g., the innocent victims of counter- or defensive violence). This issue would be an interesting topic for another philosophical investigation.

113. Albert Camus, "Ni victimes ni bourreaux," in *Actuelles I*. See especially the section "La révolution travestie," e.g., 155–60, 178–79.

114. Camus, "Ni victimes ni bourreaux," 156: "La prise de pouvoir par la violence est une idée romantique que le progrès des armements a rendu illusoire."

to Sartre—Camus had been a member of the Communist Party in the 1930s (until he was expelled in 1937), he came not only to reject Communism but to oppose Sartre's and Merleau-Ponty's role (at that time) as fellow travelers and sometime apologists for the PCF (the French Communist Party): more specifically, he opposed the PCF's ideological line favoring the revolutionary overthrow of capitalism. Already in the 1940s Camus had no stomach for any form of totalitarianism—he regarded Stalinism as one—and spoke out against Terror as a means for bringing about international justice and/or social liberation for the working class. Sartre, on the other hand, both in the pages of *Les temps modernes* (of which he was the founding director) and in a work of fiction such as *The Devil and the Good Lord* (*Le diable et le Bon Dieu*),[115] though hardly embracing totalitarianism, openly sided with the Soviet Union in the Cold War. In addition, he supported the program of the Communist Party against capitalism and defended the moral compromise of violence in behalf of the concrete struggle of the workers against their bourgeois oppressors. Much additional evidence testifies to the mounting political tension between Sartre and Camus prior to the publication of *The Rebel* and the subsequent "explosion" regarding it in *Les temps modernes*. For example, Camus had, as early as 1942, rejected an invitation to join the editorial staff of *Les temps modernes*. This suggested that he was increasingly distancing himself from both Sartre's ideological stance and his commitment to "engaged" literature. Moreover, his 1946 "Neither Victims Nor Executioners" indicated clearly that his brand of humanism refused to sacrifice means for an end, no matter how noble the end might be. As Sartre moved further to support the interests of the working class, Camus moved closer to issues of morality.

But this is enough. I believe that the detailed background and preliminary contrasts that I have already provided set the stage for the "confrontation" that is the focus of Part II. And I leave to writers dealing exclusively with this confrontation the task of addressing in greater detail the wider range of divergent issues related to the skirmish—among them, the political, the historical, and the biographical.[116] Accordingly, I now turn directly to

---

115. Jean-Paul Sartre, *The Devil and the Good Lord*, trans. Kitty Black (New York: Random House, 1960); originally published as *Le diable et le Bon Dieu* (Paris: Gallimard, 1951).

116. I have in mind David Sprintzen, in particular, who for years has concerned himself with this dispute and is now in the final stage of a manuscript that he has been preparing on it. In addition, I understand that Ronald Aronson, also, has been working on this issue and will publish a monograph on it in 2003. Judging from a paper he gave at a Sartre Society conference ("Camus/Sartre: The Story of a Relationship," delivered at the 11th North American

the specific articles that constitute this too often philosophically disappointing Sartre-Camus "debate." Because the full exchange in *Les temps modernes* has, by 2001, not yet appeared in English translation, I shall be generous in supplying quotations in English and, by so doing, hope to contribute further to my readers' awareness of the content and intensity of the quarrel.

Sartre Society Conference, Wilfred Laurier University, Waterloo, Ontario, September 16, 2000), I expect that he will develop this confrontation as a casualty of the Cold War. (As I recall, William McBride, in "The Polemic in the Pages of *Les Temps Modernes* [1952]," in *Sartre's French Contemporaries and Enduring Influences* [New York: Garland Publishing, 1997], and Mark Poster, in *Existential Marxism in Postwar France* [Princeton: Princeton University Press, 1975]—among others—have also emphasized this connection.)

the confrontation 8

Jeanson's Attack on *The Rebel*

Francis Jeanson's controversial review-article on *The Rebel,* "Albert Camus ou l'âme révoltée" (Albert Camus, or the soul in revolt), published in the May 1952 issue of *Les temps modernes,* sparked the fireworks between Sartre and Camus. His "exposé" in many ways sets the tone and issues for the tempestuous exchange to follow. A brilliant interpreter of Sartre and, in 1951, a junior colleague at *Les temps modernes,* he does not mince words. He cannot tolerate Camus's suggestion that "a revolution is a perverted rebellion" (*une révolte pervertie*)[1] that, historically, has sought to deify the human being in God's stead. Viewing the Camus of *The Rebel* as construing the origin of all rebellion in metaphysical terms and as seeing history as a "slut . . . more attracted to violence,"[2] he accuses Camus of having "allowed

1. Francis Jeanson, "Albert Camus ou l'âme révolté," *Les temps modernes,* no. 79 (May 1952): 2076. The full article falls between pages 2070 and 2090. In what follows, unless there is a particular need for clarification, I give the page references of the original French and place them in the body of my text. And, unless I indicate otherwise, I use the unpublished Sprintzen/van den Hoven translation (in typescript) that Sprintzen has shared with me.
2. Ibid., 2084: "l'histoire n'était qu'une garce, plus sensible à la violence."

119

himself to be caught up with history [*s'étant laissé prendre par l'histoire*]" and "then detaching himself from it [*se déprendre d'elle*] within history itself," and also of refusing any role to history or economics in "the genesis of revolutions" (2077, 2084). Invoking Camus's "Mediterranean heritage"—which Sartre had also done in his earlier review of *The Stranger* (*L'étranger*) and which today might understandably be viewed as racist—he further belittles Camus's view of history: "Seen from the beaches of Africa, history properly so called is confused with 'the history of European pride,' which is but an endless nocturnal delirium."[3] He goes on to accuse Camus of Manichaeism (a label of analysis for which, as we have seen, Sartre is known) for situating "Evil within history and Good outside of it" and thus beckoning us "to choose *against it* in every way possible" (2085). "How can one deny," Jeanson asks—in what strikes me as a non sequitur—"that rebellion is . . . the *refusal of history,* when the former is characterized by limit [*mesure*] while the other is made the place of excess [*démesure*], of cynicism, of destruction, of unlimited servitude?"[4] He bristles at Camus's contention that Stalinists, and even existentialists, are "prisoners of history," scoffs at what he takes to be Camus's embrace of purity in rebellion, and reminds Camus—in terms characteristic of the developing Sartre—that we are historically situated consciousnesses. "History takes hold of us but we grasp it. We don't cease making it but it also makes us" (2088–89). Finally, challenging Camus to reenter the fray, to have his "rebel" *live* history and the "revolutionary enterprise" rather than become irrelevant to it, he appeals to Camus's concern for the humiliated. And he does so by invoking the capitalism/Communism opposition: "To our incorrigibly bourgeois eyes, it is quite possible that capitalism offers a less 'distorted' face than Stalinism; but what face does it offer to an underground miner [*mineur de fond*], to a civil servant sanctioned for going on strike, to a Madagascan tortured by the police, to a Vietnamese cleansed by napalm . . . ?"[5] With respect to concrete action, Jeanson indicts any suggestion in *The Rebel* of a polite rebellion. (The reader will recall Camus's earlier rebuke of "comfortable violence.") In short, for Jeanson, *The Rebel* shows Camus to be too much of a transcendental moralist and purist, more interested in God than in man, too distant from the concrete problems of human history, and too critical of the need (necessity?) in history for violent revolutionary means to alter the injustices created by human beings. For Jeanson, Camus's

3. Ibid., 2084, translation mine.
4. Ibid., 2086, Sprintzen/van den Hoven translation altered.
5. Ibid., 2089–90, translation mine.

moralistic call for dialogue, rather than revolutionary action, slights human praxis and history and is simply out of touch with the real.

Camus's Counterattack

Camus was shocked and hurt by this harsh and inflammatory critique. In the August 1952 issue of *Les temps modernes,* he responded to it in a pointed seventeen-page letter to the editor,[6] namely, Jean-Paul Sartre, in which he immediately—and revealingly—refers to Jeanson as "your collaborator." (For Sartre, these would become fighting words: they suggested that Camus was invoking a sense of "collaborating" with, not resisting, totalitarianism— hence that this was *not* just *literary* collaboration between Jeanson and Sartre.)[7] He loses no time in saying that Sartre's "collaborator" has made "a travesty of the book which he sets out to criticize," and then vehemently objects to Jeanson's attempt, "against all evidence," to turn his book into an "anti-historical manual and . . . catechism of the abstentionists" (317, 320). He accuses Jeanson of misrepresenting his thesis badly, of criticizing a posi- tion he has never defended, and of bypassing key texts in *The Rebel* that deal specifically with "a limit revealed by the very movement of rebellions" (321)—and, in particular, the relevance of that limit to, for example, revolu- tion, terror, concentration camps, and "authoritarian socialism" (328). Sartre's collaborator "appears to be someone who doesn't want to hear" and whose "tactics are disgraceful [*indignes*]." Jeanson, he says, confuses "his- tory" with "historicism." *The Rebel* amply repeats that in today's world antihistoricism is as dangerous as historicism and that denial of history, as much as belief in history, conduces to terror. It is a total misrepresentation or outright "lie" to say that, for Camus, all evil belongs to history and all good is located outside of it. A "wise critic," Camus adds, would have recognized his "true thesis": "that whoever seeks to serve history for its own sake ends in nihilism" (*aboutisse à un nihilisme*) (322–24).[8] And with a mounting sense

6. Albert Camus, "Lettre au directeur des 'Temps modernes,'" *Les temps modernes,* no. 82 (August 1952): 317–33. Unless clarification or an amended translation is required, I use the Sprintzen/van den Hoven translation and include page references from the original French within the body of my text.

7. Because of Sartre's publications and presentation of some of his plays during the occupation, some had accused him of being complicitous with the German occupiers in France.

8. In this regard, see, for example, Albert Camus, *The Rebel,* trans. Anthony Bower (New York: Alfred Knopf, Vintage, 1956), 246–47: "To choose history, and history alone, is to

of irritation, Camus turns the tables: "Confronted with a work that, in spite of its lack of realism, studies in detail the relations between twentieth-century revolution and terror, your article contains not a word on this problem. . . . It seems to me difficult, if one believes that authoritarian socialism is the principal revolutionary experience of our time, not to come to terms with the terror it assumes and, precisely today, . . . with the reality of the concentration camps. No criticism of my book . . . can leave this problem aside."[9] He adds: "I would find it normal, and almost courageous, if, squarely facing the problem, you would justify the existence of these camps. What is unusual . . . is that you don't speak of them at all in discussing my book."[10]

And Camus's counterattack doesn't stop. "The truth is that your collaborator would like us to rebel against everything except the Party and the Communist state" (331). It is not difficult for Jeanson to take a stand against racism and colonialism, but his internal "contradiction" prevents him from speaking out against Stalinism. (If this comment is aimed at Sartre also, it seems shortsighted. In Sartre's preceding [July 1952] "Les Communistes et la paix," in Les temps modernes, he refers to Stalinism as "the gravedigger of the proletariat.").[11] Sartre's collaborator is in favor of a Marxist revolution whose sufferings and sacrifices, The Rebel has tried to show, can be justified only in "the context of a happy end to history" but whose Hegelian/Marxist dialectic "excludes this end" (330). He is "tempted" by a rebellion "that takes the most despotic historical form" (331). Unable to rebel in the name of a human nature, the rebel of Sartre's collaborator does so in the name of history. But, then, history becomes the only motive and "rule of action" and is deified (divinisé). And if history is deified, revolt is abdicated, freedom and the existential adventure are negated, and nihilism fails to be overcome. In Camus's judgment, "only the principles of prophetic Marxism (with those of a philosophy of eternity) can justify the pure and simple rejection of [his] thesis," but Sartre's collaborator cannot affirm

---

choose nihilism. Those who rush blindly to history in the name of the irrational, proclaiming that it is meaningless, encounter servitude and terror and finally emerge into the universe of concentration camps. Those who launch themselves into it preaching its absolute rationality encounter and emerge into the universe of concentration camps."

9. Camus, "Lettre au directeur," 328, Sprintzen/van den Hoven translation altered. In fact, in an article entitled "Les jours de nôtre vie," in a January 1950 issue of Les temps modernes, Sartre and Merleau-Ponty did speak critically to the issue of the Soviet labor camps.

10. Camus, "Lettre au directeur," 329, Sprintzen/van den Hoven translation altered.

11. Jean-Paul Sartre, "Les Communistes et la paix," Les temps modernes, no. 81 (July 1952): 50; reprinted as The Communists and Peace, trans. Irene Clephane (London: Hamish Hamilton, 1969), 264.

these principles without contradiction. Jeanson's "professed existential-ism"—with its unrelenting freedom—would be threatened to the core if he allowed the idea of a foreseeable end to history (*l'idée d'une fin prévisible de l'histoire*). But again, Camus contends, Jeanson totally avoids any dis-cussion of such an end (330).

Finally—at least with regard to our purposes here—Camus offers another sharp *ad hominem* countercriticism. Sartre's collaborator "seems to say that one can be either Communist or bourgeois, and at the same time—no doubt so as to lose nothing of the *history* of his time—he chooses both of them. He condemns as a Communist, but travesties as a bourgeois." Far from encouraging him to engage reality, this "curious complex" makes him "remain silent about his true thoughts" and indulge in an "abstention."[12] Pleading on behalf of all those who suffer violence, humiliation, and victim-ization through war and power, Camus—surely mindful of the contrast between his own activist role in the Resistance and Sartre's—refuses lessons in effectiveness (*leçons d'efficacité*) from critics who have never done any-thing but "place their armchairs in the direction of history." How dare Sartre's collaborator accuse him or others of being lost in the clouds or denying history (because he rejects revolutionary violence), when Jeanson and his kind have failed to take note of "the police at work at their feet" and have not, themselves, entered the fray (332). (In this general regard, readers familiar with Camus's earlier confrontation with Merleau-Ponty will remember Camus's charge that Merleau-Ponty's 1947 book, *Human-ism and Terror,* which strongly influenced Sartre at the time, had attempted to justify Stalin's purge trials in Moscow, as well as other brutality and police excess.)

The lines were already drawn—and in an acerbic manner—even before Sartre officially entered the "debate." Whether or not Sartre had any part in Jeanson's critical review, Jeanson's article showed marks of Sartre's thinking at the time and reflected the differences and issues that had been both ago-nizing and dividing Sartre and Camus in the preceding four or five years. Violence, revolution, murder, the relation of means to ends, party loyalty, concrete and/or intellectual engagement in the struggles of the time, the role and meaning of history, the Cold War, bourgeois capitalism versus Commu-nism, class warfare, how to deal with Stalinism and totalitarianism, the vio-lence of the Soviet work camps—all of these were parts of a constellation of issues that Sartre and Camus were attempting to address in their philosophical,

12. Camus, "Lettre au directeur," 331–32, Sprintzen/van den Hoven translation altered.

political, and literary works of the period. Camus's *Rebel* simply brought the growing divergence of some of their views to a head. It didn't matter whether Sartre "coached" Jeanson on his review of *The Rebel:* Camus assumed that he had and responded accordingly. And it was precisely to that response, and with that presumption, that Sartre—displaying an untempered acrimony that excelled the anger demonstrated by Camus—responded bluntly and vengefully.[13]

Sartre's Untempered "Response"

Sartre seems livid from the start. He recognizes, I think, that he, as much as Jeanson, has been the object of Camus's biting countercriticism. He, understandably, resents Camus's addressing his response to him—a friend for ten years—as "Monsieur le Directeur." He resents even more Camus's addressing him as though Jeanson's views and attitude were his, or as though Jeanson were his "ghost writer" (*valet de plume*) and "henchman for his dirty work" (*l'exécuteur des basses besognes*).[14] "You bewilder the reader by an artifice of language to the point that he no longer knows which of us you are talking about" (340). Sartre deplores Camus's "guilt by association" but has no difficulty directing barbed and sarcastic *ad hominems* at him: "You have fallen prey to a gloomy immoderation [*la proie d'une morne démesure*], which hides your inner problems and which you call, I think, Mediterranean 'mesure.'"[15] "I don't dare advise you to consult *Being and Nothingness*.

13. Jean-Paul Sartre, "Réponse à Albert Camus," *Les temps modernes,* no. 82 (August 1952). If nothing else, this response provided the world with a clarification of Sartre's emerging views. With regard to its tone and Sartre's developing views on violence, revolution, history, and pacifism, for instance, the response seems to represent a "natural" sequel to the first part of "Les Communistes et la paix," which Sartre had published in the preceding (July) issue of *Les temps modernes*.

As elsewhere, when referring to Sartre's "Réponse," I use the Sprintzen/van den Hoven translation and, unless I clarify or amend the translation, include the page numbers (from the original French) within my text.

14. It is now generally assumed, given de Beauvoir's account, that although the editorial board of *Les temps modernes* felt *The Rebel* deserved a detailed negative critical review, the staff was reluctant to take it on. Finally (perhaps with some encouragement), Jeanson volunteered to do it. See, e.g., William McBride, "The Polemic in the Pages of *Les Temps Modernes* (1952)," in *Sartre's French Contemporaries and Enduring Influences* (New York: Garland Publishing, 1997), 82.

15. Sartre, "Réponse à Albert Camus," 334, Sprintzen/van den Hoven translation altered. The reader may note that the French word *mesure* is not easy to translate. Neither "measure"

Reading it would seem needlessly arduous to you. You detest difficult thoughts" (344). "You have such a mania for not going to the source" (344). "What gives you the right to take on, toward Jeanson, a superiority that no one accords you?"[16] "You are completely insufferable" (351). The personal attacks and derisions go on and on, but they do not preclude Sartre's addressing the philosophical/political views that distance him vigorously from Camus. (In passing, I cannot refrain from mentioning that Sartre's defense of Jeanson [on, e.g., 339] and his repetition of some of Jeanson's central criticisms sometimes serves to confirm, not refute, Camus's hunch that Jeanson and Sartre had collaborated on the stinging review-article on *The Rebel*.)

In one way or another, violence, revolution, and history remain among the central issues. Sartre protests Camus's criticism of Jeanson and, more indirectly, of himself as editor of *Les temps modernes* for (Camus claimed) totally ignoring the violence of the concentration camps. After correcting Camus regarding the coverage of the topic by *Les temps modernes* (he and Merleau-Ponty had criticized them in these pages in 1950) and assuring him that he (Sartre) has never held back from criticizing the Communist "attitude," he agrees that these labor camps are "inadmissible." But "equally inadmissible," he says—as if to deflect the criticism—"is the use that the so-called bourgeois press makes of them every day." They are used as a form of blackmail. "They *summoned* people to denounce the camps under pain of being accomplices to . . . the greatest crime on earth." But, Sartre adds, "the scandal of the camps puts us all on trial—you as well as me. . . . The Iron Curtain is only a mirror in which each half of the world reflects the other. Each turn of the screw *here* corresponds to a twist *there,* and, finally, here and there, we are both the screwers and the screwed."[17] Although he accords Camus the "relative" right to speak of the Russian concentration camps, he bemoans the "sledgehammer argument" (*argument massue*) Camus has offered to justify a "quietism" that seems to make no distinction among masters, or, more precisely, between masters and slaves. (The reader should bear in mind that Camus had, in his "Lettre au directeur," accused Jeanson of quietism with regard to this issue, and that Sartre earlier—specifically in

nor "moderation" is entirely adequate, as Sprintzen has pointed out, although at times I'm willing to use either. Sprintzen usually leaves *mesure* in its French form, and I normally respect his choice. But I frequently translate—as does he—its opposite, *démesure,* as "excessiveness" or "immoderation."
16. Ibid., 338, Sprintzen/van den Hoven translation altered.
17. Ibid., 342, Sprintzen/van den Hoven translation altered.

L'existentialisme est un humanisme (1946)—had to defend himself against the criticism that his version of existentialism lent itself to quietism.) Concluding this part of his defense, he says dismissively and somewhat pompously: "I see only one solution for you: the Galapagos Islands. I, on the contrary, feel that the only way to come to the aid of the enslaved 'out there' [*là-bas*] is by taking the side of those who are here."[18] Although the issue of when and on what conditions one should take sides, politically, is also at stake here (consider Jeanson's criticism of Camus), it must be subsumed under the more basic issue of history, to which Sartre's preceding statement leads and on which much of the quarrel focuses. Of course, it is the Jeanson-Camus disagreement over the role of revolution and Terror in historical rebellion that inevitably forced the discussion of history and continues to pervade the quarrel.

Sartre, without mentioning Jeanson's initial criticism, but, we may assume, having read both Jeanson's review and Camus's reply, continues Jeanson's "antihistory" charge against Camus. He offers it unremittingly and in varying forms. "To deserve the right to influence men who are struggling, one needs first to participate in their struggle, . . . [and] to accept many things, if one wants to change some of them." "History" has presented "few situations more desperate than ours," yet Camus, the exemplary man of the Resistance, "has put himself in a corner all by himself and sulks."[19] With this free act of abandonment, Camus has chosen to stay within the great "classical tradition" that, since Descartes, has been "entirely hostile to history" (347). Acknowledging that Camus's "first contact with history"—his "austere struggle" in the Resistance, "without glory or panache"—involved sacrifice, Sartre, who is still operating, at least in part, at an *ad hominem* level, accuses Camus of having paid "tribute to History" only for the right to return to his "real duties" (*vrais devoirs*)—specifically, his "struggle against heaven" (*lutte contre le ciel*) or "the desperate fight" that human beings wage against their "revolting destiny" (*destin révoltant*) (347–48),[20] that is to say, the revolt against absurdity. Using Camus's "Letters to a German Friend" to confirm his contention, Sartre points to Camus's

18. Ibid., 343, Sprintzen/van den Hoven translation altered.
19. Ibid., 345, translation mine.
20. Sartre takes "revolting destiny" (or "fate") from Camus's Fourth Letter of his "Letters to a German Friend," in *Resistance, Rebellion, and Death* (New York: Modern Library, 1960), 21—the letters originally published as *Lettres à un ami allemand* (Paris: Gallimard, 1948). Sartre relies on these letters for a significant part of his "antihistory" argument against Camus.

admitted reluctance to "enter History": "You didn't think of 'making history,' as Marx said, but of preventing it from making itself. . . . You fought,
as you wrote, 'to save the *idea* of man'. . . : after the war [i.e., "after serving
your five years of History"], you envisaged only the return of the *status
quo*" (348).

Sartre is now charging Camus with taking part in a struggle "outside" of
history, claiming that his revolt is an "ideal revolt" (350), not principally a
revolt against the revolting material conditions and injustices that human
beings have created as part of history. "You were lucky," he tells Camus,
"that the common fight against the Germans symbolized, to your eyes and
ours, the union of all human beings against inhuman destinies,"[21] for—
Sartre claims—the moral demands that Camus articulates are but "idealizations" of the very real needs that well up around him. These "idealizations"
are like the affirmations of the privileged who are blind to the anger of
oppressed and impoverished masses crying out for some material justice. In
line with Jeanson's earlier stinging criticism, Sartre accuses Camus of hating
God more than oppression: "You didn't even want to hate the Germans,[22]
but hatred of God appears in your books."[23] Sartre joins Jeanson in indict-
ing Camus for his preoccupation with metaphysical rebellion, that is, for his
rebellion against God and creation rather than against the historical conditions human beings have created and can change. (The reader will remember that Jeanson maintained that Camus's "rebellion," characterized by
"limit," or *mesure,* with respect to violence, amounted to a "refusal" of
history.) Camus's rebellion can do nothing for the humiliated person whose
body "has been stolen from him all day" (350). What a short time earlier
was Camus's *"exemplary reality"* of solidarity has become a "completely
fruitless affirmation of an *ideal.*"[24] "You decided against history," Sartre tells
Camus, virtually restating Jeanson's point but ignoring, it seems, Camus's
reply.[25] "Instead of interpreting its course, you preferred to see in it but one
more absurdity . . . and condemning humankind, you stood alongside it but
outside its ranks [*à coté de lui mais hors du rang*]" (351). Echoing Jeanson's

---

21. Sartre, "Réponse à Albert Camus," 349, Sprintzen/van den Hoven translation altered.
22. In the Fourth Letter of his "Letters to a German Friend" (e.g., p. 24), Camus dis-
claims any hatred for Germans.
23. Sartre, "Réponse à Albert Camus," 350, translation mine.
24. Ibid., 351, translation mine ("l'affirmation parfaitement vaine d'un idéal").
25. The reader must bear in mind that Sartre's response is to Camus's "Lettre au
directeur" published in the same issue of *Les temps modernes* and is partially a defense of Jeanson against Camus's countercriticisms. Thus, Sartre must have read them.

suggestion that Camus sees history as a "slut . . . attracted to violence"[26]—or, in Sartre's slightly different words, "a pool of filth and blood" (*une piscine pleine de boue et de sang*) (352)—he offers Camus a lesson in history: "History does nothing. . . . It is real, living men who do everything." Anticipating what he'll later say in the *Critique* and the "Rome Lecture," Sartre affirms that history is only "the activity of human beings pursuing their own ends." Apart from the human beings who make it and give it ends, History is only "an abstract and static concept" (352). The point, for Sartre, is not to discern whether History has an end or meaning, but to give it one through our projects and actions. To proclaim that the world is unjust is already to lose the game. For Camus to think that it is unjust not only divorces him from History but distances him from human beings. From Sartre's perspective, Camus distrusts both History and the human being. Viewing History from hell, Camus no longer shares anything in common with the human beings who are creating it (351). Sartre ends his attack with burning words, deliberately invoking against Camus the unwelcome notions of Terror and violence that *The Rebel* so strongly opposed: "You became a terrorist and violent when history—which you rejected—rejected you in turn: you were no longer anything but an abstraction of the rebel [*qu'une abstraction de révolté*]." And Sartre, in effect, terminates his friendship with Camus with the charge that Camus's "distrust" of human beings has led to his "police tactics with Jeanson" (*méthodes policières avec Jeanson*) (353).

Clearly, just as Camus turned the tables on Jeanson, so Sartre has done to Camus. For example, just as Camus countered Jeanson's charge of anti-historicism with his exposure of Jeanson's own form of "abstention" and quietism in history, so Sartre counters Camus's claim with his own relentless attack on Camus's antihistoricism and quietism. Just as Camus counter-indicted Jeanson for his failure to speak out against Stalinist brutality and the work camps, so Sartre, in turn, indicts Camus for his post-1945 failure to "enter" History and for his rebel's greater distress over our ontological condition than over our humanly created atrocities. Moreover, to Camus's charge that Jeanson and his ilk have neglected the police at work at their feet, Sartre returns the barb with the accusation of Camus's "police tactics." Finally, in response to Camus's rejoinder to Jeanson's charge of bourgeois hypocrisy (Camus has said that Jeanson "travesties as a bourgeois"), Sartre not only associates Camus's position with the "bourgeois press" but, in the

26. Jeanson, "Albert Camus ou l'âme révolté," 2084.

manner of a vengeful adolescent, reminds Camus that "you are a bourgeois, like Jeanson and me."[27] In short, in spite of the deep seriousness of the disputed issues, the exchange between Sartre and Camus degenerated into volleys of offended accusations and counteraccusations. And there is no doubt that, whether true or not, Sartre's response gave the appearance of his having a vested interest in Jeanson's initial repudiation of *The Rebel*.

Moreover, given the critical importance of the dividing issue of revolutionary violence and murder, as well as Camus's rebuke of Jeanson for failing to condemn Stalin's violences publicly, Sartre gives relatively little explicit and focal attention to "revolution and Terror." He seems too busy defending Jeanson against secondary counteraccusations, and himself against implied criticisms, to deal sufficiently at a philosophical level with violence and killing as instruments of rebellion. His extended discussion of history keeps revolution and violence—which underlie the issue of history—in the background. From the perspective of what Sartre discusses directly or explicitly in his assault, the criticism that Camus leveled against Jeanson could just as aptly be applied to Sartre: specifically, that he has been reluctant to discuss some of the crucial issues of *The Rebel*—for example, "a limit [regarding violence] revealed by the . . . movement of rebellion itself."[28]

Nonetheless, I believe that, aside from the personal attacks, virtually all the issues of animated disagreement between Sartre (or Jeanson) and Camus in 1952 are relatable to their differences regarding violence—particularly killing—and its roots. Revolution, Marxism, rebellion, Stalinism, justice, gulags, the ends-means relation, history, class struggle, human nature, the limits of revolt, hatred of the bourgeoisie—all of these relate directly to the topic of violence and generate diverging responses from Sartre and Camus.

Even their disagreement about freedom pertains directly to, or has ramifications for, their differing approaches to violence. Throughout this study, I have shown that, whatever his modifications, Sartre sees violence as the exercise of freedom against freedom, freedom acting against freedom, freedom negating freedom.[29] Both in his "Letter to the Director" and in *The Rebel*, Camus has criticized Sartre's concept of "absolute freedom," calling it a "freedom without restraint," a "terrible and incessant freedom," and suggesting that it has led to excess, "necessity," nihilism, terror, and war (330). In *The Rebel*, Camus has told us that absolute freedom is the "freedom

---

27. Sartre, "Réponse à Albert Camus," 335.
28. Camus, "Lettre au directeur," 321.
29. Sartre repeats this general view in his "Réponse à Albert Camus," 344.

to kill," and rebellion, far from demanding it, "puts total freedom up for trial."[30] (Three years later, Merleau-Ponty contends that Sartre's conception of freedom "is unstable and tends towards violence," a charge similar to the one that Benny Lévy later makes in *Hope Now.*)[31] Sartre correctly, I believe, accuses Camus of misunderstanding his concept of freedom and of confusing philosophy and politics, or, I should prefer to say, ontological freedom and practical/political freedom. "Freedom has no brakes," Sartre reaffirms in his "Response": unlike vehicles, "it has no relationship to brakes"; we cannot put brakes on freedom, for, ontologically, we *are* freedoms. (Sartre has made this point repeatedly—in *Being and Nothingness, Existentialism and Humanism,* "Materialism and Revolution," and *Notebooks for an Ethics,* for example. But Sartre is referring to ontological freedom, not practical; and he is quick to add that freedom is always related to a given.) And then, moving to a more political level, he tells Camus: "The limit of a right (i.e., a freedom) is another right (that is to say, still another freedom) and not some 'human nature' [another swipe at Camus]: since nature—whether human or not—can crush man but cannot reduce him while alive to the state of an object." A human being can be an "object" for only another human being (another "freedom")—a point that Sartre has repeated in *Being and Nothingness,* "Materialism and Revolution," and the *Notebooks.* Speaking at a historical and a political (practical) level, he says that today freedom "is nothing but the *free choice to fight in order to become free.*" And "the paradoxical aspect of this formula simply expresses the paradoxical aspect of our *historical* condition" (344–45).Thus, when Annie Cohen-Solal contends that the entire quarrel between Sartre and Camus "hinged on the question of freedom in the USSR,"[32] she overstates and misleads. For although freedom is the core concept in Sartre's ontology and, indeed, whole philosophy, it is the human *violation* of that freedom—that is, violence—as represented in the labor camps and expressed in totalitarian Stalinism, some forms of Marxism, and historical revolutions, that became a central issue in the quarrel over *The Rebel.* Sartre has disagreed vigor-

30. Camus, *The Rebel,* 284.

31. Maurice Merleau-Ponty, *Adventures of the Dialectic* (Evanston, Ill.: Northwestern University Press, 1973), 161. This book includes Merleau-Ponty's protracted discussion of Sartre's view of freedom. See, esp., 159–64, 188–98. In *Hope Now: The 1980 Interviews* (trans. Adrian van den Hoven, with an introduction by Ronald Aronson [Chicago: University of Chicago Press, 1996], 93), Benny Lévy contends that in Sartre's work "there is a profound tendency toward an ethic of violence."

32. Annie Cohen-Solal, *Sartre: A Life* (New York: Random House, 1987), 333.

ously with Camus about the limits to which freedom should go when freedom has turned against itself, when some free human beings have exploited
or oppressed other human beings through social, economic, or political
domination. In impelling his contemporaries to unite in solidarity to "break
the bars," he will not, in 1952, anymore than in 1946 ("Materialism and
Revolution"), condemn violent means out of hand. Sartre, as we have seen
earlier, goes on to defend this position vigorously in both the *Critique* and
his Preface to *The Wretched of the Earth*. And he does the same, but more
sensitively, in his "Rome Lecture" of 1964.

Although Sartre had written his last words to Camus, the quarrel generated by Jeanson's review was not over. And if we assume—as I have—that
Sartre's defense of Jeanson's critique was not incidental, we cannot ignore
either Jeanson's detailed rejoinder in the same August 1952 issue of *Les
temps modernes*[33] or Camus's subsequent undated defense of *The Rebel*
("Défense de *L'homme révolté*"), which was likely written toward the end
of 1952 but only published posthumously by Gallimard in 1965.[34]

Jeanson's "To Tell You Everything"

Jeanson's rejoinder is largely a protracted development of the criticisms and
accusations that he and Sartre had already offered, together with his
response and corrections to some of Camus's interpretations and criticisms.
The rather merciless *ad hominems* do not stop: "Abandon your grandiose
solitude and, to descend among us for a moment, assume . . . a lighter bear-
ing than this marmoreal dignity that prematurely drapes over you."[35] Time
after time, he accuses Camus of being pompous, haughty, aloof, grandiose,
above the battle, too noble, "up in the air," indifferent to human beings,
and moralistic (see, e.g., 365, 370, 371, 374, 375). Of course, all of this is
packaged into his repeated claim that Camus has "refused" history, that he
has rewritten the history of revolution so as to repress it in behalf of "a type
of metaphysical conflict" between "revolt against the human condition"

33. Francis Jeanson, "Pour tout vous dire," *Les temps modernes*, no. 82 (August 1952):
354–83; translated by Sprintzen/van den Hoven as "To Tell You Everything," available only in
typescript form. Unless otherwise noted, I use this translation but include the page references
to the French in the body of my text.
34. Albert Camus, "Défense de *L'homme révolté*," in *Essais*, Bibliographie de Pléiade,
183, with an introduction by R. Quilliot (Paris: Gallimard, 1965), 1702–16.
35. Jeanson, "Pour tout vous dire," 359, translation mine.

and "the 'revolutionary' temptation to deify man" (360). And now, more than in his review-article, he speaks directly—and rather defensively—to the issues that Camus has challenged him to address. "After all, Camus, perhaps revolutions . . . are *especially made* . . . by simple men who try—as best they can and in solidarity—to gain the right to exist as men. . . . Perhaps the ideal conditions of a pure rebellion are not present when real men [*des hommes réels*] rebel effectively against real structures" (362–63). (The echo of Sartre is distinct in these words.) "Bourgeois society maintains itself through violence . . . and nonviolent forms of protest against it are essentially insufficient or already outmoded" (365). "Revolutions are *necessary* for the humanization of bourgeois societies" (366). "My whole [review-] article was intended precisely to recall the simple fact that we cannot restart from zero and that we are born into a world where millions of human beings, rebelling in solidarity against an oppression of very human origins, have already been organizing to make their rebellion effective [*efficace*]."[36] All of this resonates with the evolving views of Sartre in the 1950s, which came to a head in the *Critique of Dialectical Reason* (1960) and are refined in the "Rome Lecture" of 1964. Maintaining that effectiveness must not preclude violence, Jeanson—like Sartre—suggests that "obsession with purity" turns one into an accomplice" (367) of oppression. (The reader will recall that Sartre, in the *Critique*, calls nonviolence the choice of "naïveté" and "complicity.") In this regard, Jeanson sounds like Hoederer of *Dirty Hands* speaking to Kaliayev of *The Just Assassins*. And from this perspective of effectiveness and resistance to complicity, he now, on Sartre's lead, responds to Camus's criticism of his and Sartre's failure to denounce Stalinism. It is not a contradiction, he says, that prevents them from speaking out clearly on Stalinism, but "a difficulty of fact. . . . The Stalinist movement world-wide doesn't appear to us to be authentically revolutionary, but it is the only one that claims to be revolutionary . . . and it brings together, especially in our own country, the great majority of the proletariat" (378). This echoes Sartre's claim in "Materialism and Revolution," six years earlier, that "the Communist Party is the only revolutionary party,"[37] and anticipates what Sartre repeats in his tribute to Merleau-Ponty in 1961: "Whatever its crimes, the Soviet Union has this enormous advantage over bourgeois

36. Ibid., 374, translation mine.
37. Jean-Paul Sartre, "Materialism and Revolution," in *Literary and Philosophical Essays*, trans. Annette Michelson (New York: Collier Books, 1962), 255. Of course, toward the end of his life, Sartre stated that "the party is the death of the left" (Sartre and Lévy, *Hope Now*, 78).

democracies: revolutionary aims."[38] Although critical of its methods, he nonetheless supports this revolutionary movement, for authentic revolution may be "pure chimera," but the "revolutionary enterprise" needs to move on.[39] Violence, for Jeanson, as for Sartre—and as Camus has conceded in his earlier response to d'Astier de la Vigerie—is an inevitable part of history. For Camus to purify rebellion of revolutionary violence, Jeanson again declares, amounts to a withdrawal from history. Camus has made himself the "true Moralist," the "High Priest of Absolute Morality," reigning outside the world of human struggle (382–83).

Thus, except for elucidating grounds for favoring revolution over Camus's metaphysical rebellion, and the violences of Communism (and the USSR) over the violences of oppressive, profit-driven capitalism, Jeanson's rejoinder doesn't add significantly to the "Sartre-Camus confrontation." Yet, with greater length than required, it reemphasizes the pivotal role of violence in the vehement disagreement. From a Sartre/Jeanson perspective, Camus's focus on rebellion against the absurd, rather than on revolt against the rotten conditions and infrastructures that human beings have created and can alter, ignores history and negates human beings. This negation, for Sartre, is, of course, itself violence. His *Critique of Dialectical Reason,* his Preface to *The Wretched of the Earth,* his (as we shall see) "Rome Lecture," and so many of his other writings leave us with that unambiguous point.

But I should think it unfair to conclude an account or discussion of the Sartre-Camus dispute without at least reviewing briefly Camus's undated postconfrontation essay "Défense de *L'homme révolté*" ("In Defense of *The Rebel*").[40] Assumed to have been written a few months after Sartre's and Jeanson's August 1952 contributions to the bitter exchange in *Les temps modernes,* Camus's essay is more moderate and reflective in tone; it clearly rises above the hostility of the earlier exchanges and rearticulates and clarifies some of Camus's points in the light of Sartre's and Jeanson's responses to his earlier "Reply."

---

38. Jean-Paul Sartre, "Merleau-Ponty," in *Situations,* trans. Benita Eisler (New York: George Braziller, 1965), 265. In this connection, it is interesting to note that in the *Adventures of the Dialectic* Merleau-Ponty says, with regard to Sartre's *Communists and Peace,* "The C.P. has, in any case, a negative mission: it is perhaps not the revolution, but surely it is not capitalism" (164).

39. Jeanson, "Pour tout vous dire," 378, Sprintzen/van den Hoven translation altered.

40. Camus, "Défense de *L'homme révolté*," 1702–16. As customary, I use the Sprintzen/van den Hoven translation and, unless I amend or clarify the translation, include the page references in the body of my text.

In Defense of *The Rebel*

By December of 1952—the probable date that Herbert Lottman, in his biography of Camus, assigns to Camus's completion of "Défense de *L'homme révolté*"—Camus appears to have regained his composure after the Jeanson and Sartre spring/summer assaults. He seems here much more interested in clarifying, substantiating, and refining his contentions, and in nurturing his call for human dialogue, than in protracting an intemperate quarrel or counterattacking with a vengeance. One even senses an attempt on his part to offer some grounds for mediation or reconciliation between two exaggerated and mutually misrepresented positions, provoked, at least in part, by the growing political/personal tensions between the two parties in the debate.

While making it clear that he does not want to rewrite *The Rebel*, he makes it equally evident that his work is "the product" (1705) of an existential "contradiction" in which, while revolting against nihilism and murder, thinkers of his generation had also accepted the idea of "murder without limits" (1703). Given his endorsement of rebellion, or "revolt,"[41] his motivating question was, "Can one, without recourse to absolute principles, escape from a logic of destruction?" And now he restates his controversial caution: "One cannot . . . rail against those who rebel in the name of the absolute while justifying revolutionary terror" (1705–6). He adds: "There is but a single nihilism under different guises, for which we are all responsible." *The Rebel* focuses entirely on the frontier "where nihilism turns against itself" and "makes it possible for one to advance."[42]

Mindful of the harsh criticisms that Sartre and Jeanson have leveled against him, Camus tries to put some basic contentions of *The Rebel* "in a clearer light" (*dans une lumière plus précise*). Given my focus and subthesis here in Part II, none of his reformulations is more important than his elucidation of the distinction and relation between rebellion (or revolt) and revolution—a topic on which, I think, *The Rebel* reflects ambiguity. The reader will recall that in *The Rebel* Camus has said that historical rebellion has, by "obeying the dictates of nihilism" and resorting to murder, turned "against its rebel origins" and "travestied" them, and that genuine rebellion and rev-

41. The French word *révolte* can be translated as either "rebellion" or "revolt." In this "postconfrontation" piece, I tend to translate it as "revolt"—perhaps largely because Sprintzen and van den Hoven do so in their translation. I trust that this will not cause the reader any confusion.

42. Camus, "Défense de *L'homme révolté*," 1706, Sprintzen/van den Hoven translation altered.

olutionary murder are contradictory.[43] Now, in his "Défense," he does not repudiate that stance but clarifies it.

"I believed," he says, "that I could then say that these notions only made sense [*ces notions n'avaient de réalité*] in opposition to one another." One can confront historical reality neither with an attitude of absolute but sterile revolt nor with a "revolutionary orthodoxy" that suppresses the spirit of revolt in behalf of historical efficacy. The position he maintained in *The Rebel* was neither a "refutation of revolt" nor "a blanket condemnation of the revolutionary attitude" (1706). Summing up the position he held in *The Rebel*, he continues: "I have simply said that revolt without revolution ends logically in a delirium of destruction; and the rebel, if he does not rebel for everyone ["I rebel, therefore we exist"], ends up by reaching an extremity in solitude where everything seems permitted to him." "Inversely," he adds, "I have tried to show that revolution deprived of the incessant control by the spirit of revolt finishes by falling into a nihilism of efficacy, and bursts out in terror." (Can anyone question that this is intended as a criticism of Sartre?) This nihilism of the solitary individual concludes, one day, by "consecrating terror," either at the level of the individual or at that of the state.[44] Thus, only revolt (or rebellion) has a basis for questioning revolution, for revolution alone has a basis for questioning revolt.

Accordingly, Camus reaffirms what he concluded in *The Rebel*—"the fruitfulness of a tension between revolt and revolution." "In order to reject organized terror and the police, revolution needs to keep intact the principle of revolt that gave it birth, just as revolt itself needs a revolutionary development to find its body and truth. Each one, in the end, is the *limit* of the other";[45] rebellion is the *mesure* of revolution, and vice versa (1710). (Camus is not entirely clear on this latter point; indeed, his attempt at reconciliation seems more than a tad forced.) Far from being a limitless negation, rebellion must be seen precisely as the affirmation of a limit beyond which revolt would negate itself (1709). This *mesure*, Camus insists, is not the casual resolution of opposites (*résolution désinvolte des contraires*). It is, rather, "nothing other than the affirmation of the contradiction." Moreover, to insist that one must hold to a *limit* amounts to saying that one must keep oneself on the most extreme boundary of the struggle, where rifts, fury, and heartwrench do not undermine lucidity or violate rebellion's aim for human

43. Camus, *The Rebel*, 247, 280, 281.
44. Camus, "Défense de *L'homme révolté*," 1707, Sprintzen/van den Hoven translation altered.
45. Ibid., 1709, Sprintzen/van den Hoven translation altered, italics mine.

solidarity (this is also one of Sartre's revolutionary aims), and where lucidity and moderation do not give way to accommodation and indifference (1709–10). Among other matters, this clarification makes more understandable Camus's related—and somewhat surprising—contention that "this critique [in *The Rebel*] does not end up condemning revolution [*ne s'achève pas dans une condamnation de la révolution*], but only historical nihilism, which, by devoting revolution to the denial of the spirit of revolt, contaminates the hope of millions of people."[46]

Camus, still painfully sensitive to Sartre's (and Jeanson's) antihistorical charge, carries this concept of *mesure* to the "more general tension . . . which opposes the individual to history." Only an "initial falsification," he contends, would attribute Manichaeism (man is all good; history, all bad) to his analysis in this regard.[47] On the contrary, revolt appeared to him to be "neither the demand for total liberty nor the exaltation of historical necessity" (another swipe at Sartre!). In it, on the contrary, "both man and history *limited* themselves and made one another productive [*se fécondaient l'un l'autre*]."[48] To be sure, in *The Rebel,* he might have been able to say that murder is justifiable at an extreme limit—say, on condition that one pay for it with one's own life (consider also Kaliayev's position in *The Just Assassins*). But, he is quick to add, "I wanted, for the time being, to do nothing more than to refute legitimate murder and to assign to its demented projects [*à ses démentes entreprises*] a precise boundary."[49]

The "I rebel, therefore we exist" of *The Rebel*[50] continues to permeate Camus's afterthoughts. "The individual only acquires and increases his significance by approaching his own limit, which is self-renunciation for the benefit of others." What human beings make together cannot, except at the price of sterility, negate what is noble in the individual; and, in turn, the individual cannot negate history and the community of human beings except at the cost of barrenness.[51] Though in tension, the individual and history are inseparable.

In short, Camus sees his "Défense" as a refinement, not a retraction, of the position he has taken in *The Rebel*. Rebellion points to a human nature and value that murder would violate. Although *The Rebel* does not propose either a formal or a dogmatic morality, it affirms that "a morality is possi-

46. Ibid., Sprintzen/van den Hoven translation altered.
47. Ibid., 1711, Sprintzen/van den Hoven translation altered.
48. Ibid., 1712–13, Sprintzen/van den Hoven translation altered.
49. Ibid., 1713, translation mine.
50. Camus, *The Rebel*, e.g., 22, 250.

ble" and that "it costs dearly." Even this small step is enough to break us out of nihilism. In fact, says Camus—still taking aim at Sartre's and Jeanson's position—"I have found nothing else which I can justify to oppose nihilism and murder,"[52] nothing else that could have helped him at the moment of that "struggle without hope" of which he speaks in both *The Myth of Sisyphus* and *The Rebel.* "It is only through resolute refusal, and the affirmation of the values it presupposes," that "material liberation" stands any chance of achieving a genuine liberation of the human being.[53] But our efforts will succeed only if we keep ourselves *within limits.* In the public sphere, this means refusing to serve any of the "forces of war" and recognizing the humanity of one's adversary. In a closing statement that would doubtless have both answered and annoyed Sartre further at that time, Camus, mindful of his own emphasis on community and dialogue, says that "each adversary, how-ever repugnant he may be, is one of those inner voices which we might be tempted to silence, and to which we must listen in order to correct, adapt, or reaffirm the few truths we catch sight of in the same way."[54] Yet, in projecting a city of ends, an "integral humanity," Sartre himself, I believe, shared this sentiment in the "Rome Lecture," among other works (e.g., *Hope Now*).

These inspiring words seem to have brought Camus closure to this unmea-sured and acerbic exchange with Sartre, but they can hardly conclude our consideration of it. Nor can they conclude our attempt to study and make sense of Sartre's seemingly unpredictable and conflicting positions in his tra-jectory on violence. The vehement 1952 "debate" between Sartre (and Jean-son) and Camus certainly highlighted issues in the progression of Sartre's thinking regarding violence. These issues included the inevitability and necessity of violence, the place of violence in History, the justifiability of violence and revolutionary killing, the relation of violent means to noble ends, the morality and efficacy of the use of Terror to effect a better com-munity or birth of a "new humanity." But no consideration of this constel-lation of issues would be complete without an examination of the highly important, yet still unpublished 1964 "Rome Lecture." This examination is necessary for a number of reasons: *first,* because the lecture is of such philo-sophical and historical importance and relates so directly to my present

---

51. Camus, "Défense de *L'homme révolté*," 1713.
52. Ibid., 1713–14, translation mine.
53. Ibid., 1711, Sprintzen/van den Hoven translation altered.
54. Ibid., 1715–16, Sprintzen/van den Hoven translation altered.

investigation; *second,* because the lecture, though incomplete and written twelve years *after* Sartre's "Response" to Camus, appears to represent a crucial stage in Sartre's formulation of the "dialectical" (or "second") ethics that he was developing in the *Critique of Dialectical Reason* (1960) and flamboyantly exhibiting in his passionate Preface to (and *defense* of) Fanon's *Wretched of the Earth* (1962) (in fact, as Elizabeth Bowman and Robert Stone allege, this lecture may be regarded as a fitting "ethical sequel" to the *Critique*);[55] *third,* because Sartre, in this lecture, seems to address and philosophically refine his position with regard to key issues in the "philosophy of revolution" that separated him from Camus in their earlier 1952 confrontation; and, *fourth,* because this "Rome Lecture" offers, one might say, *ex post facto* clarification of the 1952 "confrontation" and allows me, in rounding out this study, to provide more of my own philosophical assessment of Sartre's position regarding the "justification" of revolutionary violence and murder. Hence, I intend that my focus on the "Rome Lecture" of 1964 will both enlighten and integrate my subproject in Part II and reveal more of what went "unsaid" concerning Sartre on violence in Part I.

55. Elizabeth Bowman and Robert V. Stone, "'Making the Human' in Sartre's Unpublished Dialectical Ethics," in *Existentialist Ethics,* ed. William McBride (New York: Garland Publishing, 1997), 269.

the 1964 "rome lecture"

9

First, by way of background, I must mention that what is normally called "The 1964 Rome Lecture" may more accurately be viewed as the "Rome Lecture Notes." These "notes," on which the actual Rome lecture was based, take the form of a 165-page untitled manuscript and constitute one part of a trilogy of manuscripts that, together, make up Sartre's "dialectical," or "second," ethics of the mid-1960s. Eyewitness accounts confirm that Sartre consulted bundles of pages in the course of presenting his lecture. Later, his publisher, Gallimard, prepared a 139-page book-length typescript of the "notes," which Sartre, in turn, corrected.[1] According to Robert Stone

---

1. Robert V. Stone and Elizabeth Bowman provided much of this information in "Dialectical Ethics: A First Look at Sartre's Unpublished 1964 Rome Lecture Notes," *Social Text*, nos. 13/14 (winter/spring 1986): 195–96; "'Making the Human' in Sartre's Unpublished Dialectical Ethics," in *Existentialist Ethics*, ed. William McBride (New York: Garland Publishing, 1997), 269–70; "'Socialist Morality' in Sartre's Unpublished *1964 Rome Lecture*," *Bulletin de la Société américaine de philosophie de langue française* 4, nos. 2–3 (1992): 166–67. (This last-mentioned article is reproduced in McBride's *Existentialist Ethics*, 286–320.) I have confirmed these data while consulting the actual documents—or copies thereof—at Yale University's Beinecke Library of Rare Books and Manuscripts. I shall give further details of this collection in subsequent footnotes.

and Elizabeth Bowman, who were among the first to be granted access to the manuscripts and whose pioneering works[2] on Sartre's "second ethics" have prompted me (and a few other) Anglo-American scholars to attend to these writings, the "Rome Lecture Notes" are the most finished, the most conceptually rich, and the most important of these manuscripts. Their judgment, to be sure, is influenced and corroborated by Simone de Beauvoir, who, in a letter to Stone in 1986, opined that the "Rome Lecture" is "the culminating point [*le point culminant*] of Sartre's ethics."[3] The actual lecture, which Sartre presented at a conference on "ethics and society" at the Italian Communist Party's Istituto Gramsci on May 23, 1964—and is, thus, sometimes referred to as the "Gramsci Lecture"—represents only a small fraction of the almost eight hundred pages of his "notes" on ethics but provided his audience with the fruition of his ethical thought since *Critique II*. The full body of his "notes" addressed not only the experience of morality and the grounding of morality in the "need" of the exploited and oppressed classes (as in Algeria), but the moral problems related to need-meeting revolutionary action.

In what follows, I lean considerably on Stone and Bowman's splendid "condensed summary" of the "Rome Lecture Notes"—which appears in the articles I have cited.[4] For my purposes here, their careful synopses, combined with some fragments that have already been published, would be quite adequate. Nonetheless, in deference to my sense of philosophical responsibility, I have also verified and added supportive references by consulting the original materials now available in the marvelous John Gerassi

2. See the articles cited in the preceding footnote. See also Stone and Bowman's "Sartre's Morality and History: A First Look at the Notes for the Unpublished 1965 Cornell Lectures," in *Sartre Alive*, ed. Ronald Aronson and Adrian van den Hoven (Detroit: Wayne State University Press, 1991), 53–82. This article is based on a probable draft of *Recherches pour une morale* (more often referred to as *Morale et histoire*, or *Morality and History*), the title of a series of lectures Sartre was intending to give at Cornell University but eventually declined because of the American bombing and atrocities in the Vietnam War. This 225-page manuscript is also part of Sartre's "trilogy" on "dialectical ethics." It is now available to readers as part of the "John Gerassi Collection of Jean-Paul Sartre," Series II, at Yale University's Beinecke Library of Rare Books and Manuscripts. It is in Box 6 of that series.

3. Stone and Bowman, "Socialist Morality," 189; idem, "Making the Human," 270, 282. See also idem, "Dialectical Ethics," 211.

4. My understanding, when writing this section (2001), is that Stone and Bowman are preparing a book on, and English translations of, the works that constitute Sartre's dialectical ethics. The book—representing more than twenty years of their interrupted work—is to appear, I believe, within the next year and will bring to completion their probing examination of the Rome and Cornell lectures. Sartre scholars are indeed grateful for their dedication and insights.

Collection of Jean-Paul Sartre, which Gerassi recently donated to the Beinecke Collection of Rare Books and Manuscripts at Yale University. In many instances, I shall provide the original French to support my (or Stone and Bowman's) key references or quotations in English.[5]

At the conclusion of my discussion of *Critique I* and the concept of Fraternity-Terror, and at intervals throughout this study, I have raised the likely question, initially suggested by Raymond Aron in his critical commentary on Sartre's *Critique*, of how Terror could ever be an instrument for overcoming alienation and bringing about a new humanity. Certainly, Benny Lévy's climactic interrogation of Sartre in the 1980 interviews and the tensions I articulated in relation to Sartre's *Dirty Hands* and Camus's *Just Assassins,* as well as the intemperate and culminating dispute between Sartre and Camus concerning *The Rebel,* all reverberate this tantalizing concern. And now a consideration of the 1964 "Rome Lecture" requires us directly to confront a variation of this issue: "Does the *end* of revolution, the better state of humanity sought as its goal," Stone and Bowman ask for Sartre, "justify or outweigh the violent, perhaps immoral, acts undertaken as *means* necessary to attain that *end?*"[6] Or, to put it yet another way, is revolutionary killing or Terror morally permissible if it conduces to what Sartre here calls "autonomous integral humanity" or "man as autonomy"?[7] In dealing with this question, we might wish to keep in mind Benny Lévy's challenging (and pragmatic) reminder to Sartre, fifteen years after the "Rome Lecture": "If the idea of revolution becomes identified with the idea of terrorism, it's done for."[8] To be sure, at this late point in his life (1979), Sartre disengaged Terror and the "pledged group" of *Critique I* from both

5. The original manuscripts may now be found in the Bibliothèque Nationale de France in Paris and, usually in photocopy form, in the Beinecke Library for Rare Books and Manuscripts at Yale University. Sartre scholars should be indebted to John ("Tito") Gerassi for making the highly important John Gerassi Collection of Sartre manuscripts and interviews available through his recent donation of same to Yale University. I hereby express my personal gratitude to him and, of course, to the Beinecke Library, which allowed my ready access to, and quotation from, this splendid collection. I shall also make reference here to short fragments of the "Rome Lecture Notes" that appeared in Jeanson's small 1966 book, *Sartre.* Francis Jeanson, *Sartre,* Les écrivains devant Dieu, 9 (Paris: Desclée de Brouwer, 1966).
    6. Stone and Bowman, "Socialist Morality," 193, italics mine.
    7. See, e.g., Stone and Bowman, "Socialist Morality," 170–78, 196; idem, "Dialectical Ethics," 205, 208–11, etc.; idem, "Making the Human," 271.
    8. Jean-Paul Sartre and Benny Lévy, *Hope Now: The 1980 Interviews,* trans. Adrian van den Hoven, with an introduction by Ronald Aronson (Chicago: University of Chicago Press, 1996), 96; originally published as *L'espoir maintenant: Les entretiens de 1980* (Lagrasse: Verdier, 1991), 66: "[S]i l'idée de la révolution s'identifie à l'idée terroriste, elle est foutue."

fraternity and the "origin" of a "new humanity," seeing them as mutually exclusive. Had he done so a quarter of a century earlier, his bitter skirmish with Camus would likely never have occurred.

But we must now systematically view the key aspects of the "Rome Lecture" that combine to bring to a head Sartre's "justificatory" argument for violence in his "second" ethics and become important components of the crucial question that Sartre himself had raised.

(i) *"Making Humanity"* (*Faire l'homme*). I have already remarked the controversial role that Fraternity-Terror assumed in the "birth of humanity" in Sartre's *Critique*. But this frequently criticized "birth"[9] was not the central happening in that major work. In contrast, Sartre gives the "birth" of a new humanity "center stage" in the "Rome Lecture."[10] It provides the key to understanding the other parts of Sartre's analysis and argument in this lecture, as well as his dialectical position concerning the "justifiability" of violence. We should note, in passing, that as early as "Materialism and Revolution," Sartre had viewed "We, too, are human beings" as at the heart of the revolutionary praxis, and human autonomy as the goal of the revolutionary.

Sartre uses "humanity" or "the human"—or even "man" (*homme*)—interchangeably in this lecture. One thing is clear: here, as in some other works, the human, or humanity, *does not yet exist*. Humanity is *incomplete, lacking,* and alienated. Humanity is to be made. Yet humanity functions as an "end" of human conduct ("integral humanity is the end of incomplete man"); and the "oddity of human action is that in it an unknown future, not the past, . . . conditions the present."[11] "The root [*racine*] of morality [and humanity] is *in need* [*le besoin*], that is to say, in the animality of man," and it is need that posits "integral humanity" (*l'homme intégral*), or the human being, as his or her own end.[12] *Need* is the fundamental motive

---

9. For the criticism, see, e.g., Raymond Aron, *History and the Dialectic of Violence,* trans. Barry Cooper (New York: Harper Torchbooks, 1976), 160.

10. Stone and Bowman, "Socialist Morality," 169.

11. Ibid., 170. See Jeanson's "excerpts" from the "Rome Lecture Notes," in *Sartre,* 137: "[L]'homme est à faire. Il est la fin . . . d'un être qui se définit par la praxis, c'est à dire de l'homme incomplet, aliéné, que nous sommes." See also 138: "[L]'homme intégral est la fin de l'homme incomplet." In addition, see the Gallimard typescript of the "Rome Lecture Notes," p. 111 (or p. 134 of manuscript): "L'homme est l'être de l'homme: cela veut dire *qu'il à se faire*. Maintenant. Partout et toujours" (italics mine). As I said in my footnote at the conclusion of Part I, I use "Rome Lecture Notes" and "Rome Lecture" interchangeably to designate "The 1964 Rome Lecture Notes."

12. These Sartrean references to "need" as the root of morality and humanity are from the Gallimard typescript of the "Rome Lecture Notes," p. 79/manuscript p. 100. Stone and

for all human action, for all history making, and every praxis or autonomous action, even the colonizer's, aims at the "unconditional possibility of making ourselves human." As Sartre put it, "History has no reality except as the unconditional possibility for man to realize himself *in his full autonomy . . . as the praxis of all associated human beings.*"[13] This is a distinct refinement of Sartre's contention, in *What Is Literature?* that all our undertakings are reducible to a single one—that of making history. According to Sartre, "man" aims at *the human* even when praxis is alienated, even when praxis is operating within a system's alienated norms or within alienated moralities.[14] The human is presupposed even in the inhuman. But, predictably, aiming at our humanity through repressive and exploitative systems will confine us to the system that oppresses us (and others) rather than free us for our "unconditional future," that is, for the project of making ourselves human, which is *beyond* all systems. Humanity, or being human, is not inevitable but only possible. Yet human autonomy, or humanity, remains the only possible end of praxis—an end "not knowable but graspable as a sense of direction" (*non connaissable, mais saisissable comme orientation*) by the "uncompleted, alienated" humanity that we are (*de l'homme incomplet, aliéné, que nous sommes*).[15]

But humanity as a "capacity for autonomous self-production" has no models: it requires "invention"—a term Sartre uses to mark the possibility of transforming "impossibility into possibility," according to humankind's ends, or "the moment of morality or value-making in historical praxis."[16]

Bowman cite this passage in each of their three articles on the "Rome Lecture": "Socialist Morality," 171; "Dialectical Ethics," 206–7; "Making the Human," 273–74. The quotation in the original reads: "La racine de la morale est *dans le besoin,* c'est à dire dans l'animalité de l'homme. C'est le besoin qui pose l'homme comme sa propre fin." See also, e.g., typescript p. 94/manuscript p. 116 of the "Rome Lecture Notes": "Le besoin est à la base de la praxis." For earlier reference to the importance of "need" (*le besoin*), see *CDR* I:85–88 (*CRD* I:170–72).

13. "L'histoire n'a de réalité que par la possibilité inconditionnée pour l'homme se réaliser dans sa pleine autonomie . . . comme praxis de tous les hommes associés": Jeanson, *Sartre,* 137–38, translation mine. In "Dialectical Ethics," 202, Stone and Bowman present the full quote. Italics in the English translation here are mine.

14. "Rome Lecture Notes," typescript p. 74/manuscript p. 95.

15. This statement originally appeared in the "Rome Lecture Notes," page 48 of the Gallimard typescript, page 65 of Sartre's manuscript. See also Jeanson, *Sartre,* 137. Many of statements made in the body of this paragraph are taken from pages 73–76 of the Gallimard typescript, pages 94–97 of the manuscript of the "Rome Lecture Notes."

16. See, e.g., Stone and Bowman, "Socialist Morality," 171–72; idem, "Making the Human," 275. It may be noted here that "invention" for Sartre makes humanity as the goal of historical praxis "unconditionally possible" ("Socialist Morality," 171). See also Stone and Bowman, "Sartre's Morality and History," 68–69.

(For Sartre, here, morality has its roots in the *struggle* of the exploited classes against the dominant.) Our initial moves toward the end of making ourselves human are devoted to the repetitive reproduction of alienating systems (e.g., of profit) that have made us subhuman. To invoke the language of the *Critique,* we have allowed the *practico-inert* to dominate *praxis* rather than the reverse. This has diverted us from our free project of making ourselves human—that is, of bringing about satisfaction of human needs instead of scarcity, human novelty instead of subhuman repetition, group praxis instead of self-serving serial action.[17] But we must "make the human" *against* the system. We can progress *toward* the end of making ourselves (or humanity) by affirming pure revolutionary praxis, by taking action against the stifling systems and alienating moralities—too readily accepted as *a priori*—that limit our "unconditional future" and foster our subhumanity, even if such actions require us to sacrifice our own lives, as in pure praxis. To use Stone and Bowman's adaptation of Sartre, we "must purify the norm from its practico-inert secretions," which our individual praxes have nurtured. Radical action, unrepeatable life-risking action, as the exercise of pure revolutionary praxis that underlies all praxis, is never precluded, and no *means* can be excluded from the *end* of making ourselves autonomous, of satisfying the incomplete human's need to be completely human.[18] There is no end that is higher. "To the extent," Sartre says, "that the agent's own end implies an overthrowing of the system, it gives to that agent his character as *means* and *end* of history."[19] History becomes for all subhuman agents the process of "making ourselves" through the "building and overthrowing of systems."[20] Moreover, Sartre, linking more closely the issue of means and ends with that of *justification,* maintains that the satisfaction of this *need* requires no additional "justification," because "it is by itself adequate justification for its own satisfaction." All need posits satisfied integral human life, so the satisfaction of this need needs no further normative primacy or external *a priori* principles—which are, in any case, unavailable—to justify revolutionary praxis.[21] And it is this self-justifying revolutionary praxis that gives rise to the human.

17. Stone and Bowman, "Socialist Morality," 173–75; idem, "Making the Human," 273–74.

18. Stone and Bowman, "Dialectical Ethics," 203; see also 212.

19. Quoted in ibid., 212, italics mine.

20. Quoted in ibid., 204. See also Stone and Bowman, "Making the Human," 275.

21. Stone and Bowman, "Making the Human," 273; also idem, "Dialectical Ethics," 209.

This relatively brief account of "making the human" already provides added rationale for what Sartre was vehemently asserting in his 1952 "confrontation" and for what he was arguing in the *Critique* (1960) and contending even more strenuously in his Preface to *The Wretched of the Earth* (1961). In particular, while reaffirming the central role of praxis in history making, this core concern of the "Rome Lecture" has clarified Sartre's meaning, in both his earlier and later works, of the human being as *end* of history and group praxis. The conceptual clarification of this term, though hardly complete, helps us to understand Sartre's identification of the human with both the *means* and *end* of history. It also sheds important light on his acceptance of violence—necessary violence—as part of the praxis-process of bringing about a more satisfied, autonomous, integral humanity of genuine reciprocity. Even his more mature conception of history in terms of "making ourselves human" seems to illumine the passion with which he—I think unfairly—dismissed Camus as antihistorical twelve years earlier.

(ii) *The Means-Ends Relationship.* The relation of violent means to human revolutionary ends certainly appeared to be at the heart of the radical disagreement between Sartre and Camus in 1952. As early as 1948, in *What Is Literature?* Sartre affirmed the need "to meditate upon the modern problem of means and ends, not only in theory but in each concrete case." More generally, he asked: "What are the relationships between ends and means in a society based on violence?"[22] And certainly the justificatory question in the "Rome Lecture," as posed by Stone and Bowman above, is formulated in terms of "means" and "end." Given the preceding subsection, Sartre's own question can be put more narrowly and sharply: "If there's but one way to humanity and it involves *means* incompatible with a human world, isn't action with humanity as its *end* impossible?" Sartre's answer— as had been Merleau-Ponty's emphatic response in *Humanism and Terror*— is in the negative: humanity as end can continually look back at, scrutinize, alter, and moderate the means. Even Terror—in which "subhumans become the means of humanity"—introduces sanctions to accompany its orders.[23]

---

22. Jean-Paul Sartre, *What Is Literature?* trans. Bernard Frechtman (London: Methuen, 1950), 214, 174; originally published as *Qu'est-ce que la littérature* (Paris: Gallimard, 1948), 348, 248. I have taken the liberty of correcting what must be a typographical error in the Frechtman translation. "Mediate" should read "meditate" in the first quotation above: "Nous devons méditer sur le problème moderne de la fin et des moyen" (348).

23. The "Rome Lecture Notes," typescript pp. 133, 135/manuscript pp. 159, 161. The most relevant statement here is taken from page 133 of the Gallimard typescript/page 159 of Sartre's manuscript. The full passage reads: "La Terreur: le sous-homme devient moyen de l'homme. On exige son travail et sa discipline par impératif. On accompagne cet impératif de

But we are not likely to understand Sartre's position regarding Terror or violence here unless we return to Sartre's further elucidation (in the "Rome Lecture") of the means-ends relation.

According to what Stone and Bowman call the "scale metaphor," if a means is immoral, no noble or "good" ends can outweigh that immorality. This presupposes that means are external to, and can be weighed on the other side of the scale from, the "ends"—or conversely. But for Sartre, here, this metaphor is unacceptable, and he offers his developed alternative to the "scale" model. Far from being morally separable or individually weighable, means and ends are "interrelated 'moments' of actual historical undertakings." To use the language that Sartre employs much earlier in *What Is Literature?*—where he first rejects a "quasi-mathematical formula" for assessing means to ends—the end is "the synthetic unity of the means,"[24] that is to say, the "unfolding of all the means" (as Stone and Bowman put it). "Ends" *don't* justify means or specific acts; they are, rather, parts of actions or human "undertakings" that make up history and give them intelligibility. Means also are constitutive parts of human actions, or history-making praxis. The end synthesizes, or "totalizes," the means. The end does not come after the means; it rather pervades their use, keeps them together as means, and even guides them. Conversely, the means are constituent "moments" of the same historical acts. As concretizations of the end that also modify the end,[25] they—to use Sartre's distinguishing word in *Critique I* and *II*—*incarnate* it.

Hence, as inseparable moments of a movement that integrates itself as it proceeds, means and ends are not to be treated as though they can be weighed morally, against one another, with respect to actions or their consequences. On the contrary, they must be weighed together. (In this regard, but with different consequences, Sartre's contention resembles both Gandhi's and Thomas Dewey's approach to the relation between means and ends.) As Sartre puts it in the undelivered and unpublished Cornell lectures, they are an "unfolding totalization" in which the goal of an undertaking is presented "as the totalization of the means used to attain it."[26] On this

sanctions qui s'adressent aux déterminations mêmes qu'il faut cesser." See also Stone and Bowman, "Socialist Morality," 183.

24. Sartre, *What Is Literature?* 213. In the "Rome Lecture," Sartre clearly builds on the foundation that he began in *What Is Literature?* with respect to means and ends. See my subsequent note.

25. Sixteen years earlier, in *What Is Literature?* Sartre said that "the means . . . introduce a *qualitative* alteration into the end and consequently are not measurable" (213).

26. Quoted in Stone and Bowman's "Sartre's Morality and History" (*Morale et histoire*), 68. This article represents their digest of Sartre's "Notes" for the 1965 Cornell lectures. See also *CDR* I:45–47.

ground, the justificatory questions raised above, morally separating end from means, appear to be misdirected and/or to betray a radical misunderstanding of the structure of human action and the means-end "unity" on which Sartre here insists. Accordingly, revolution must now be viewed in a different way. Revolution is a project involving a manifold of acts. Revolutionary means and ends, as a "synthetic unity," are not to be weighed separately or against one another, but together, as one side against another side (e.g., against oppression) on the moral balance.[27] Looked at through these postconfrontation lenses, and in view of Sartre's contention in this "Rome Lecture" that the revolutionary praxis requires no external justification, his emotional defense of revolutionary killing in the 1952 dispute with Camus already takes on greater philosophical force. But we must press on with other elements of what I have called the "justificatory question" in the "Rome Lecture."

(iii) *Limits to Revolutionary Action.* Are there "limits" to revolutionary action? Much of the hostile exchange between Sartre and Camus related to Camus's demand for *mesure* (moderation) and *limits* with respect to rebellion. Given Sartre's emphasis on pure revolutionary praxis against alienating systems, as well as his reconception in the "Rome Lecture" of the means-end relation, we may now appropriately ask whether, in pursuing integral humanity, revolutionary praxis must observe any *limits,* that is to say, whether the *end* of revolutionary praxis would preclude any means as part of its synthetic unity. In short, are all means dialectically synthesizable with the "end" of revolutionary praxis?

Sartre provides a quick answer in the fourth chapter of the "Rome Lecture": "All means are good except those that denature the end."[28] And, indeed, there are some means—for example, Khrushchev's invasion of Hungary in 1956—that are so incompatible with the revolutionary end that they "smash the synthetic unity," or dialectical continuum, that they intend to enter.[29] This becomes, for Sartre, a kind of "revolutionary's criterion." Thus, despite his "synthesizing" refinement of the relation between means and ends, Sartre does define limits. "The revolutionary force" itself must be sacrificed if its continuation would likely "denature" the revolutionary "end" it purports to incarnate—namely, autonomous integral humanity. So, in its

27. Unless otherwise indicated, what I've said in the two preceding paragraphs closely follows Stone and Bowman's account in "Socialist Morality," 193–95.

28. "Tous les moyens sont bons sauf ceux qui dénaturent la fin." From typescript p. 139/manuscript p. 164 of chap. 4 of the "Rome Lecture." See also Stone and Bowman, "Socialist Morality," 195.

29. Sartre, *What Is Literature?* 213.

own way, the revolutionary praxis generates its own limits. The absence of an *a priori* or extrahistorical principle to which to appeal does not imply that all means are morally permissible within the means-end continuum of revolutionary praxis. As early as in *What Is Literature?* (1948), Sartre had expressed serious reservations about systematically lying to a party's militants for the sake of abolishing oppression. (This also calls to mind one of Hoederer's revolutionary dilemmas in *Dirty Hands*.) The lie itself, he contended, is a form of oppression, and lying would, unfortunately, contribute to the creation of a *"lied to* and *lying* mankind."[30] In 1964, though still *not* unambiguous in his stand, he has certainly substantiated his earlier position. In 1952, however, Sartre did not have the worked-out position of 1964 available for support in his distressing debate with Camus, but it is surprising nonetheless that he did not reply to Camus's insistence on limits, even in revolution, with evidence that he was already on record as supporting limits. For even in his 1946 "Materialism and Revolution," where he begins to articulate his "philosophy of revolution," he appears to be calling for limits, or "measure," in the revolutionary project to attain human liberation and autonomy. Of course, in the "Rome Lecture," the limits seem to emerge or be generated from within the synthetic means-end unity. But that does not settle the issue—as Stone and Bowman point out—of the soundness or workability of this "denaturing of the end" criterion. Within Sartre's careful analysis of revolution and the "making of humanity" in the "Rome Lecture," is Terror, we may ask—which figures so prominently in both the *Critique* and Sartre's Preface to Fanon's *Wretched of the Earth*—morally acceptable? If so, in what circumstances and to what degree? And what would be its moral limits?

(iv) *Terror and Its Permissibility.* Sartre refers to Terror as one of the "night time moments" (*moments de nuit*) of "making the human" and differentiates it as action in which "subhumans become the means of humanity."[31] In its original expression, it is a "praxis" of "necessity," that is to say, a necessary act of *counterviolence* in which one, reduced to subhumanity, *uses oneself* qua subhuman as a means to make oneself human (or "make humanity") against and beyond the system that oppresses and dehumanizes.

---

30. Ibid., 213. I am grateful to Stone and Bowman for these references. See their "Socialist Morality," 195–96, esp. n. 46.

31. Typescript p. 133/manuscript p. 159 of the "Rome Lecture Notes." This is quoted by Stone and Bowman, "Socialist Morality," 183. Again, the French, on page 133 of the Gallimard typescript, reads: "La terreur: le sous-homme devient moyen de l'homme."

(One must note here that systems, for Sartre, are "objectifications" of praxis.) Algeria is, again, a case in point, as it was in the *Critique*, the Preface to *The Wretched*, and later, in a modified way, in *Hope Now*. Given the colonization of the natives, given their *need* to break their status as subhuman, they must *destroy* the bourgeois capitalist system that refuses to treat them as human or recognize their need. Counterviolence against this system of violence is *necessary;* Terror is a likelihood. In a world in which being human is made *impossible* by the alienating norms, imperatives, and systems of others, only *counterviolence* can eliminate that impossibility and remake "humanity." In resisting an exploitative system, even at the price of death, this counterviolence of the exploited natives is "irreversible."[32] But let us return more specifically to the permissibility of Terror as the extreme form of this counterviolence.

Sartre, in the "Rome Lecture," appears to answer the kind of challenge regarding Terror that Camus put to him twelve years earlier. He provides four conditions under which Terror—used by subhumans toward the end of creating "the human"—could be deemed "inevitable" and, therefore, on my interpretation, morally permissible. But he makes it clear that such instances must only be "provisional expedients" (*expédients provisoire*). Failing any one of these four conditions, Sartre seems to say, Terror is *not* morally permissible, so another recourse would need to be "invented." These "enabling" or "limiting" conditions for the permissible use of Terror are as follows:[33]

(*a*) Only when Terror can be prevented from becoming an alienating system like that of the oppressing adversary. In short, if Terror is to be used only as a means to produce yet another exploitative system or to keep human beings in a state of subhumanity, it must *not* be permitted.

(*b*) Only—and this seems to be a corollary of the first—if those who employ Terror can preclude and therefore avoid all ideologies of Terror. (Sartre later sees any ideology as a "practico-inert determination.") Stalin's "socialism in one country" is an example of what would *not* be permissible (see *Critique II,* e.g., 164). As a slogan, it was used to nationalize and reinstitutionalize subhumanity among precisely those (e.g., the

---

32. Stone and Bowman, "Dialectical Ethics," 208–10, and idem, "Socialist Morality," 183–84.

33. These conditions are summarized from pages 133–36 of the typescript prepared by Gallimard and corrected by Sartre, or pages 159–61 of Sartre's manuscript. The adjectives "enabling" and "limiting" are mine. I also follow Stone and Bowman's presentation in "Socialist Morality," 184–86.

peasants, or "masses") who were engaged in the struggle against sub-humanization.

(c) Only if no justification of Terror is offered other than its *necessity* (*sans autre justification que sa nécessité*). It should never be chosen for the sake of ease (*facilité*) when a more difficult solution is possible; nor should it be employed to "conceal a mistake" (*dissimuler une faute*). Even while exercising Terror, one must continually work against it; if not, one contributes to the continuation of subhumanity. This means—in keeping with what I've pointed out regarding the self-limiting role that the "end" plays in the means-end synthetic unity—that one must always rigorously *limit* the use of Terror and acknowledge it as *inhuman* to those who undergo it.

(d) Only if Terror has its "origins in the masses" (*naît des masses*) and is taken up by the leaders (*dirigeants*) "in their turn" (*à leur compte*). But—and this strikes me as somewhat surprising—the leaders must denounce it as a deviation, out of necessity, from (integral) humanity as an end, and as "a technique totally unjustifiable outside of its effectiveness" (*une technique parfaitement injustifiable en dehors de son efficacité*).[34] (This appears to be in tension with Sartre's view, which I articulated above, that satisfaction of "need"—in this case the need of the exploited to be humanized—needs no further justification. Yet, admittedly, it is still consistent with Sartre's "denaturing of the end" criterion, which I also outlined in my foregoing account.)[35]

In short, then, only if these four conditions are met would the use of Terror be just or legitimate. But even then its justifiability would appear to be ambiguous, and its *limit* would seem to be mandatory in the light of "integral humanity" (or "city of ends") as the goal of revolutionary praxis. Terror, according to the "Rome Lecture," is always a "revolutionary pause" (*une pause révolutionnaire*) that "marks history negatively" and runs the risk of erecting a *system* (which itself always violates *praxis*) of Terror similar to Stalinism.[36] Nonetheless, with the meeting of these conditions, "Terror

34. "Est-ce possible? oui. Car elle naît des masses, et les dirigeants doivent la reprendre à leur compte" (typescript pp. 134–35/manuscript p. 160 of the "Rome Lecture"). See also Stone and Bowman, "Socialist Morality," 185.

35. "Rome Lecture Notes," Gallimard typescript pp. 134–35/manuscript p. 160.

36. Ibid., typescript p. 135/manuscript p. 161. Robert Stone reaffirms this point in a letter to me dated March 26, 2001. I am grateful to him for the interest he has expressed regarding my project, and look forward to the publication of his and Elizabeth Bowman's forthcoming

becomes *revolutionary justice*," and, as a consequence, "the humanization of terror" becomes "possible *in principle*."[37] Although Sartre, on this account, would allow, for instance, the insurrectional Terror of the Algerian colonized people against the French, or of a popular revolution against Hitler and the Nazis, he would not condone the institutionalized Terror of the USSR, which made Terror the keystone of an "ideologically justified" system of government. This institutionalized Terror, which, in *Critique II*, Sartre himself called a "synonym with *Hell*" (*synonyme d'enfer*),[38] clearly violates the first two enabling conditions above and, arguably, the latter two as well. Although, as Simone de Beauvoir had pointed out in her *Ethics of Ambiguity*, there is "a dialectic which goes from freedom to freedom through dictatorship and oppression," trying to establish themselves in the world, and although Terror may be required and justified in the "assertion of freedom against them," it must not "on the way" destroy the very freedom and end of "humanity" that it is pursuing.[39] That is to say, for Sartre in the "Rome Lecture," as for de Beauvoir earlier, although Terror can in certain circumstances be justified to overcome oppression, it cannot be justified in behalf of an action that—to repeat Sartre's words—"qualitatively alters" the end of making humanity and instead establishes a *system* of Terror. In fact, the "outrageousness" of this new system might be so extreme that—to appeal to a criterion suggested by de Beauvoir—the "outrageousness of the violence" practiced against it could be justified.[40]

---

book on Sartre's "second ethics"—concentrating mainly, I understand, on the Rome and Cornell lectures.

37. These statements, used by Stone and Bowman, are taken from the corrected Gallimard typescript of the "Rome Lecture Notes," p. 135/manuscript p. 161. In the original French they are "La terreur devenant *justice révolutionnaire*" and "L'humanisation de la terreur est possible *en principe*."

38. *CDR* II:116 (*CRD* II:128). I owe this specific reference to Stone and Bowman, "Socialist Morality," 186. I have added the French. Sartre also called Stalinism "the gravedigger of the proletariat" as early as 1952, in "Les Communistes et la paix."

39. Simone de Beauvoir, *The Ethics of Ambiguity* (Secaucus, N.J.: Citadel Press, 1948), 155, also 153. This reminder comes close to what Dora warned in Camus's *Just Assassins*. Note also the closeness of de Beauvoir's implied view of violence to Sartre's view in his *Notebooks* and onward, namely, freedom asserting itself against freedom.

40. De Beauvoir, *The Ethics of Ambiguity*, 97. I have given the full quotation in note 36 to Chapter 5. I recognize, from a recent exchange at the North American Sartre meeting in New Orleans, that Bob Stone disagrees with me regarding the issues of Sartre's "justification" of Terror in the "Rome Lecture." (That symposium, entitled "Sartre on Terror," is tentatively scheduled for publication in *Sartre Studies International* in 2003.) Yet, on the basis of the text—which, again, exhibits some ambivalence—I remain with my position and look forward to Stone and Bowman's challenge in their forthcoming work on the Rome and Cornell lectures.

Thus, Sartre's "Rome Lecture" offers a belated elaboration and refined rationale for what he and Jeanson were militantly contending against Camus in their 1952 confrontation. Even Sartre's restatement of the meaning of "history" in the context of human-forged oppression and systems of violence takes on additional, post-*Critique* emphasis and clarification. But that is not to say that Sartre's proposed resolution here is decisive and completely without ambiguity. Stone and Bowman are right in saying that "Sartre is ambiguous on terror."[41] Though helpful, the "denaturing of the end" criterion does not easily or unambiguously distinguish what is *not* permissible. Nor is "necessity" or "efficacy" or what "originates in the masses" or the "avoidance of all ideologies" of Terror or resistance to the implementation of any system readily or decisively determinable. And acting for an undetermined future doesn't guarantee that future.[42] Sartre's and de Beauvoir's own discussion of ambiguous circumstances in these regards offer testimony to the point. And for this reason among others, I find Stone and Bowman's[43]— and Linda Bell's and Bill McBride's, to name only two others—statements about Sartre's debt to de Beauvoir's insights regarding the justifiability of violence largely exaggerated, if not unwarranted. Sartre, himself, I repeat, had confronted many of these issues both in his formative essay on revolution, "Matérialisme et révolution" ("Materialism and Revolution"), in 1946, and his subsequent 1952 essays in *Les temps modernes* (e.g., "Les Communistes et la paix"). Although he offered his revolutionary views in "Materialism and Revolution" from a somewhat different perspective—for example, he saw revolution as the transformation or replacement of one *system* by another—he still, at least a year before de Beauvoir, pointed to

41. Stone and Bowman, "Socialist Morality," 198.
42. These are not the only shortcomings of Sartre's conditions. In note 112 to Chapter 7, in which I compare Sartre's and Camus's approaches to violence, I mention Thomas Anderson's suggestion of Sartre's failure to distinguish sufficiently between violence done to oppressors and violence inflicted on innocent people (in, for example, an oppressor's homeland). I think he is right in suggesting that this failure occurs also in Sartre's conditions for the justification of Terror and constitutes a significant omission. I am grateful for Anderson's point and suggest that it would be a worthwhile topic for exploration in another work. But, at the same time, I must express my reservation about Anderson's tendency to view and attempt to formulate some of Sartre's "conditions" as though they were parts of the "just war" tradition and doctrine. (See, e.g., Anderson's *Sartre's Two Ethics* [Chicago: Open Court, 1993], 127–28.) Although Anderson does not use "last resort," he says that Terror, for Sartre, must never be the "first resort" but instead is the "sole possible means to make man" (i.e., "last resort"?). He also lists as a condition that it have a "good likelihood of success." This is surely "just war" language, but I do not think that Sartre thought in those terms.
43. Stone and Bowman, "Socialist Morality," 190, e.g.

the ambiguity, or "double character," of the affirmation of freedom in acts of violence. He also depicted violence as the necessary, and therefore only, way to combat the oppressor's praxis of domination and inhumanity, but demanded the recognition of the oppressor's humanity in the pursuit of a "new humanity"—that is, a "solidarity of freedom" or "kingdom of ends." Of course, none of this denies that Sartre and de Beauvoir were in continuing dialogue, were readers and friendly critics of each other's work, and inevitably influenced each other. Yet, I remain adamant in disparaging the game—now too common in de Beauvoir circles—of "who said such and such first?"

In conclusion, I must point out, *first*, that although the position Sartre takes in the "Rome Lecture" is not radically different from that he took in "Materialism and Revolution" or *What Is Literature?* for instance, it is sufficiently different to have made a difference in his confrontation with Camus. For one thing, it is less clear in this lecture that he would always regard violence as a "setback"—though, to be sure, an "inevitable one"—as he did in *What Is Literature* (1948).[44] Although he sees the violence of the established capitalist and colonial system as an agent of subhumanity and even regards revolutionary counterviolence as a possible threat to "[re]making the human," he now, I believe, allows that "necessary violence" practiced through revolutionary praxis could serve as an advance, rather than a "setback," to this human "end." In my judgment, this is the view toward which he was working in the 1952 confrontation and which was coming to fruition in the *Critique* and in his Preface to Fanon's *Wretched of the Earth.* *Second,* in the "Rome Lecture" Sartre seems more comfortable with—and is thus more likely to use—the words "justification" and "justice" with respect to the revolutionary use of violence and Terror. In this regard, the "Rome Lecture" is closer to what he says in his Preface to Fanon. This is in marked contrast to "Materialism and Revolution" and the *Critique,* where, in spite of his pronounced tendency to describe and condone the necessity of violence on the part of oppressed subhuman, he pulls away from the language of justifying it, preferring to speak, for example, of violence "presenting itself" as (justified) counterviolence or freedom "affirming itself" as "justified violence against the practico-inert." To be sure, in the bitter

---

44. Sartre, *What Is Literature?* 214. It may be recalled that in *Notebooks for an Ethics* he even insinuates that terrorist violence is a "dead end," not "a passage towards liberation" (406).

exchange with Camus, Sartre is vehemently contending, *against* Camus, that revolutionary killing can be legitimate. Why, there and elsewhere, and especially in the *Critique,* he shies away from making judgements of moral justification and takes refuge in what I have called "phenomenological description" of defensive counterviolence is difficult to comprehend, unless he was hoping to nurture the *dialectical tension* and *ambiguity* of revolutionary violence that he later brings to a head and tries to resolve in this "Rome Lecture."

In a letter to me of March 26, 2001, Robert Stone says that Sartre "short-circuits much analytical discussion of the 'justifiability' of violence." I am not at all sure that I would describe it in that way. I would prefer to say that until the "Rome Lecture" Sartre tends, for the most part, to evade the *language* of moral justification in his consideration of radical violence or Terror even while offering specific arguments for such justification. His earlier arguments for the necessity and acceptability of counterviolence against the oppressor, whether in the *Critique* or "Materialism and Revolution" or especially the Preface to *The Wretched,* seem to be guised justifications of violence. (In *Critique I,* for example, Sartre speaks of the necessity of *destroying* the "anti-dialectic system of super-exploitation" and states that "the colonialists were for the [African] army the legitimacy of this violence.")[45] And his denunciation of Camus's adamant refusal to legitimize revolutionary killing strikes me as an indirect way of saying that it is *justifiable.* Thus, I suspect that we are viewing, in Sartre's earlier works, an evasion rooted—perhaps mainly—in his concern that employing the word "justification" would imply *moral* justification, when he had not yet worked out the details of his "concrete," or "second," ethics. (In one place in the "Rome Lecture Notes," he even seems to identify "history" with the development of morality.) This tendency seems to be in marked contrast to Simone de Beauvoir's, who, in *The Ethics of Ambiguity,* despite her emphasis on the ambiguity of the revolutionary dilemma, felt freer to use words like "justified" or "legitimized" in a morally judgmental, not simply descriptive, manner.[46]

45. *CDR* I:729–30 (*CRD* I:683–84).
46. De Beauvoir, *The Ethics of Ambiguity,* e.g., 138, 148.

justificational ambivalence: problematic interpretation

10

Throughout this study, I have tried to show the ambivalence that marks Sartre's trajectory on violence—an ambivalence that seems in keeping with the ambiguous freedom that, for Sartre, is at the heart of human existence and both grounds and permeates his entire philosophical system. This ambivalence is not significantly different in his direct engagement with Terror in the "Rome Lecture." In circumstances of oppression, or what Sartre calls "pure violence," revolutionary violence and Terror, because they are "necessary" and inevitable, are permissible and just, but they are bound by limits. In dialectical synthesis with the goal of "integral humanity," violence and Terror must not violate the goal of pure revolutionary praxis (i.e., autonomous humanity) or denigrate the human. Sartre, here, it seems to me, moves beyond "weasel" words and justificatory euphemisms such as "necessity," "unavoidability," and "acceptability"—words that have often frustrated and misdirected readers trying to understand Sartre's overall position on violence and Terror. He does this by linking morality with *need*—in particular, the need of the oppressed subhuman to become human—and then proposing and invoking moral criteria, or "enabling" conditions, that any justification of Terror must satisfy. Although, in line with the *Critique,* the

Sartre of the "Rome Lecture" may still see Terror—to borrow Ron Aronson's words—as a "stage of the dialectic" and an "understandable product of totalizing praxis,"[1] he now formalizes the limiting conditions beyond which Terror *cannot* be *morally* legitimated. After the "Rome Lecture," it is, I think, less easy for Sartre—certain conflicting statements notwithstanding—to say emphatically with Hegel of the Master-Slave relation, or Merleau-Ponty of *Humanism and Terror,* or Fanon of *The Wretched of the Earth,* that human beings have either become human or necessarily "make human-ity" through violence and Terror. To be sure, Sartre has offered the notion of self-justifying revolutionary praxis, but this praxis generates its own limits with regard to its revolutionary end of "integral humanity." Although, admittedly, ambiguity and ambivalence remain in Sartre's analysis, and although he has not, from what I know, presented a specific account of the relation between the self-limiting work of the means-end continuum (or synthesis) and the restraining conditions for Terror (how are the two to be reconciled? we may reasonably ask), he also has not allowed "necessity" and "inevitability" alone to decide what is acceptable—in this case, *morally* acceptable—in conditions of subhuman oppression.

One point is clear and merits repeating—especially given the disposi-tion of some readers to conclude otherwise after reading Sartre's and Jeanson's 1952 denunciation of Camus's position in *The Rebel:* Sartre's endorsement (another morally evasive term?) of violence and Terror is not without bounds. In spite of his dismissal of Camus as "antihistorical" and "but an abstraction of a rebel,"[2] Sartre, from "Materialism and Revolution" onward, at least suggests that revolutionary Terror is not always acceptable ("justifiable") and that it sometimes requires the application of brakes or simply a nonstart. As Camus has said that historical rebellion in the form of revolution with Terror "has turned against its rebel origins," Sartre could say, after the "Rome Lecture," that any Terror that "reinstitutionalizes sub-humanity" turns against its *revolutionary* origins. Had either Sartre or Jeanson, in response to *The Rebel,* made or conceded such a point, some of the vitriolic and philosophically demeaning aspects of the Sartre-Camus dis-pute might never have ensued.[3] Dora's statement in Camus's *Just Assassins,*

---

1. Ronald Aronson, *Sartre's Second Critique* (Chicago: University of Chicago Press, 1987), 181.
2. See the last page of Sartre's "Réponse à Albert Camus," in any available translation.
3. I am, of course, aware that other grueling issues separated Sartre and Camus in their debate, not the least of which was the Cold War. I would expect Ronald Aronson's forthcom-ing book to provide a focused account of their political positions regarding this issue.

"Even in destruction there's a right way and a wrong way—and there are limits,"[4] sometimes resonates in Sartre's works also.[5]

Sartre, Bell, and a Problem of Interpretation

With these comments in mind, I wish, before concluding, to give some attention to another Sartre scholar's attempt to deal with the justifiability of violence and Terror in working toward a new humanity, or what Sartre earlier called a "city of ends." I do this in part to demonstrate how a serious attempt to give a general account of Sartre's views concerning the justifiability of violence may be misled and somewhat marred by Sartre's choice of morally neutral words such as "necessary," "unavoidable," "inevitable," and so forth. I am referring to the account offered by Linda Bell in her sensitive book *Rethinking Ethics in the Midst of Violence*.[6] Although her discussion is limited by her main focus on *Notebooks for an Ethics* and is not informed by the refinements of the "Rome Lecture," it still serves my purpose and allows me to make other related observations.

Bell formulates Sartre's revolutionary dilemma in the following succinct manner:

> The revolutionary confronts a society in which violence is woven through the status quo. Sartre is clear that this violence is *unacceptable* and that it should not be allowed to continue. He is equally clear that *avoiding* all violence is likely to strengthen the status quo and *condone* the violence that permeates it. Yet to *accept* violence as a *legitimate* means to a good end is also unacceptable since that acceptance and use will undermine movement towards the city of ends. If violence is *avoided*, there is no movement toward a better

4. Albert Camus, *The Just Assassins*, in *Caligula and 3 Other Plays*, trans. Stuart Gilbert (New York: Vintage Books, 1958), 258.

5. I shall not repeat here the passages that confirm this point. But let me point out again that, as early as 1946 (in "Matérialisme et révolution"), Sartre seems to preclude the use of Terror that would work *against* his concept of a "new humanism" or reintroduce subhumanity. And a year or so later, in *Cahiers pour une morale* (1947–48), he says that although violence and war are inevitable in history, he would want his time to be one in which some of it could be avoided. See, e.g., NFE 490, but I may be reading too much into his statement here.

6. Linda A. Bell, *Rethinking Ethics in the Midst of Violence: A Feminist Approach to Freedom* (Lanham, Md.: Rowman & Littlefield, 1993).

society; if violence is *condoned,* then the goal of a better society is compromised. [Hence] . . . the goal may *require* revolutionary violence in order not to compromise the goal itself.[7]

Bell concludes that, for Sartre, revolutionary violence is "unavoidable" and "necessary" for the rejection of the violence of the status quo but that this necessity implies neither that violence is "rendered an acceptable means" nor that the "maxim of violence" (i.e., the end justifies the means) is "endorsed."[8]

It will hardly surprise the reader to learn that I concur strongly in Bell's related contention that Sartre's position is "resolved . . . with the affirmation of an ambiguity": namely, that "condoning violence both supports and undermines the actions of the revolutionaries who fight against oppression."[9] In Part I, I have tried to show the "curious ambiguity" and ambivalence in Sartre's overall treatment of violence, and in Part II, I have, in addition, attempted to demonstrate the same with respect to his approach to the "justifiability" of violence. But that is not my main point here. Rather, I want to reaffirm the difficulty posed to interpreters of Sartre by his tendency to evade the specific language of *moral justification* and instead use terminology that circumvents or dodges the moral issues. Look at Bell's use of "acceptable," "unacceptable," "condone," "necessary," "required," "unavoidable," "avoidable," "legitimate," "endorsed." These appear to be words chosen to avoid *direct* confrontation with the issue of *moral* justifiability in Sartre. That is understandable, given Sartre's inclination, as I have pointed out, to do the same, and thus leave the reader frustrated, if not bewildered. Although the "Rome Lecture" provides relief, it, too, by using the language of "permissibility," suggests some moral indecisiveness as well as ambivalence/ambiguity.

Notwithstanding what I have said, I must point out that Bell *does,* at times, use the language of morality when articulating Sartre's position. She says, for instance, that "violence [for Sartre] simply cannot be seen as *moral;* to see it as moral (or justified) [note her apparent identification of the two] is to slip into a complacency vis-à-vis violence that changes the end we seek. . . . Yet in spite of the *immorality* of violence, it is sometimes necessary, [although] it must be *condemned.*"[10]

7. Ibid., 188; the italics, mine, emphasize Bell's choice of words within the context of my contention.
8. Ibid., 152, 189, 192–93.
9. Ibid., 192.
10. Ibid., 188, italics mine.

To be sure, Bell does not have the benefit of the "Rome Lecture Notes" in her account. Nor does she make sufficient use of Sartre's discussion of violence in the *Critique* or the 1961 Preface to *The Wretched*. Yet we observe her saying that, for Sartre, violence is "unacceptable" but "unavoidable," "necessary" but "immoral," and—invoking the *Notebooks*—that violence "appears as unjustified" (note again Sartre's phenomenologically descriptive language). Moreover, at one point she goes further to say that, for Sartre, violence cannot be morally *justified*.

The problem here is at least threefold. *First,* it does not follow that because an action is "unacceptable," it *is* morally unjustifiable or just plain immoral, as Bell, speaking for Sartre, seems to suggest. I submit that an act might be *socially* unacceptable, for instance, without being immoral or morally unjustifiable—for example, telling your hosts that their meticulously prepared multicourse dinner was terrible! Nor does the judgment that an act is unacceptable or cannot be "condoned"—another expression that Bell uses—logically entail that it deserves *moral* condemnation. That would need to be shown. *Second,* I contend that Bell goes too far when she maintains that, for Sartre, violence can never be seen as moral—even if pursued in behalf of the revolutionary end—and must therefore be condemned morally. Bell's best case *is* and can be based on Sartre's analysis in *Notebooks for an Ethics,* but even there Sartre exhibits the ambiguity connected with the revolutionary situation and is often noncommittal about *moral* justifiability in that context. I might add that if Bell's interpretation here is correct, and if Sartre had maintained the position she attributes to him during the four years following the *Notebooks* and preceding the 1952 skirmish with Camus, Sartre's stand would have been too close to Camus's views to warrant the intemperate exchange that followed. (Earlier in this book I have alleged that Camus's position regarding violence in the 1952 debate bears some resemblance to Sartre's position in *Notebooks for an Ethics.*) It must be recalled, again, that in response to Emmanuel d'Astier de la Vigerie, Camus said, "Violence is inevitable and at the same time unjustifiable." Camus didn't hesitate to use the latter word. *Third,* one must ask about the connection, if any, between what is "necessary" or "unavoidable" and what is moral or immoral. The interpretation offered by Bell, and occasionally suggested by Sartre himself, that a given *necessary* and *unavoidable* act—for example, revolutionary violence in behalf of a "city of ends," or autonomous humanity—is immoral and unjustifiable, is, to say the least, questionable. If an act, X, is in fact an act that I must necessarily do or can't avoid doing, given a certain end, on what grounds is it to be condemned as immoral and declared unjustifiable? Wouldn't the category of "amoral" better suit "necessary" action? But what is the sense of the word "necessary" in this context? It is surely not a "necessary" that precludes freedom to do otherwise in this situation. That would violate Sartre's ontology, for even *given* the revolutionary end in this context, we are here *not* dealing with, for example, physical compulsion. The problem is not just Bell's but, as I have said, Sartre's: it is the inexactness of his words as well as the duplicity in his position that moves the reader to seek more *moral* definition or closure with regard to his revolutionary "contradiction" (his word).

But two ancillary points must now be repeated. Despite Sartre's own qualifying words about violence, which I have quoted and discussed earlier in this book, Bell's attribution, in Sartre's name, of immorality to all violence cannot, I submit, be sustained after a study of the "Rome Lecture Notes," or even, necessarily, after a careful consideration of relevant parts of Sartre's *Critique I* (1960), his Preface to Fanon's *Wretched of the Earth* (1961), or his antiviolence *Hope Now*. For, as we have seen, Sartre, in the "Rome Lecture," roots "morality" and "humanity" in human need—specifically in the need of the oppressed subhumans to become human—and offers an account of a "means-end" synthetic balancing that would provide an "internal" justification of violence that is aimed at the revolutionary end of "making humanity." "Inevitable" or "necessary" Terror is, I judge, *morally* allowable (or "permissible"), provided certain limiting conditions are observed within the "praxis-process" of attaining human "satisfaction" and destroying dehumanizing systems. Moreover, despite Sartre's often descriptive but morally evasive language, it would be hard to read either the *Critique* or his Preface to *The Wretched*—or even his and Jeanson's replies to Camus in 1952, for that matter—*without* concluding that Sartre is offering a *moral* justification of the colonized natives' unqualified defensive counterviolence. And Sartre does the same with regard to the student violence at the Sorbonne in 1968. "The demonstrators," he said, "were simply using counterviolence as a response to the [police] violence that had been used against them." More important, as David Drake has also pointed out, Sartre saw the "uncontrolled" violence of their demonstrations as their only remaining way to resist the oppressive "inertized" (my word) societal violence into which they were born and raised.[11] Further, Sartre recognized a *moral* dimension in this violent rejection

11. Jean-Paul Sartre, "Les bastilles de Raymond Aron," *Le nouvel observateur,* June 1968, 179. I am indebted to David Drake for this reference. In this article, Sartre says more fully: "What we have to explain to people is that 'uncontrolled' violence has a sense to it, that it is not the expression of a desire for chaos but the desire for a different order" (184). The translations are mine.

of "the superstructure of the dominant class."[12] Hence, as an overall account of Sartre's position on violence, Bell's seems to me partially flawed and also misleading. This is, in part, because her account is limited by her narrow selection of Sartre's writings. But also, to quite a significant degree, this flaw reflects Sartre's own lack of linguistic, methodological, and heuristic clarity, especially with respect to justification and morality.

To be sure, I understand Bell's own discomfort with the "maxim of violence"—I myself emphatically *reject* it!—and agree that the Sartre of the *Notebooks* shares that discomfort.[13] I should add that in spite of some of his seemingly brash statements to the contrary (e.g., in his Preface to *The Wretched*), he is never at ease, as the "Rome Lecture" attests, with that maxim. But, to my mind, this does not logically entail Bell's conclusion— even if one were to restrict it to her references—that all violence, for Sartre, is immoral. Not even later, in *Hope Now* (1980), where Sartre sees violence as the opposite of fraternity and continues to develop his "third" ethics, does he attribute *immorality* to *all* violence. There (as I have noted), he refers to the violence of the colonized as a "necessary evil"; yet still, in his ambivalent manner, he acknowledges it as "just"—meaning, I believe, *morally* just.

Bill McBride appears to be in agreement with the position I have been arguing when he says, in an early (1969) article that followed the "tumultuous year of revolution and counter-revolution [1968]," that although "social violence is accepted by Sartre as a very central and logical phenomenon of our world, . . . the employment of violence as a means of bringing about a desirable future society simultaneously receives implicit *justification* within Sartre's theory." And in what I believe is an overstatement—but one that bears directly on the Sartre-Camus confrontation—he adds: "Within a Sartrean universe there are no Camusean qualms about the *approval* [note McBride's similar evasion of moral terminology] of violence directed toward genuinely progressive social goals."[14] Although McBride sees the

12. David Drake, "Sartre and May 1968: The Intellectual in Crisis," *Sartre Studies International* 3, no. 1 (1997); see esp. 46–48, 57. Drake's article "Sartre, Camus, and the Algerian War," *Sartre Studies International* 5, no. 1 (1999), is also worthy of note in this regard.

13. Bell, *Rethinking Ethics in the Midst of Violence,* 198 n. 94.

14. William McBride, "Sartre and the Phenomenology of Social Violence," in *New Essays in Phenomenology,* ed. James M. Edie (Chicago: Quadrangle Books, 1969), 290, 310, respectively. Italics are mine. Again, I express appreciation to Bill McBride for making me aware of this article after he had read the core of my first draft of the present work. Note also that I have tried to point out earlier that, in selected writings, Sartre *does* have qualms about the approval of violence.

Critique as phenomenologically descriptive and also, following Sartre, sometimes dodges moral terminology, he clearly suggests *moral* approbation on Sartre's part when he says that Sartre's theory in the *Critique* points to the possibility of a "progressive, humane, and rational approach to violence."[15] But, of course, one could argue, as Ronald Aronson has suggested, that this is exactly where Sartre "goes wrong" against Camus—that, indeed, the acceptance of violence as "the only path to emancipation," as Sartre appears to contend in that debate and elsewhere, overlooks the possibility that it may also be the route to a Stalinist "Hell."[16] This is a point that Sartre clearly understands and acknowledges in the "Rome Lecture." Yet we must bear in mind that this confrontation, as well as the *Critique* itself, precedes the clarifications of the 1964 "Rome Lecture"—even though these clarifications do not imply the *elimination* of moral ambiguity.[17] And I suspect that, whatever our differences, Bell, Aronson, and I, as well as a number of other Sartre scholars (e.g., Aron), would sympathize with Aronson's view that Sartre's acceptance of a connection between violence—particularly Terror—and human emancipation is at least a point of vulnerability in Sartre's political thinking.[18] As much as I should like to have Sartre say, as Bell contends that he says, that all violence is immoral and must be condemned (note: "immoral" means more than a "setback" or "dead end," to use the words that Sartre has ascribed to violence in *What Is Literature?* and in his *Notebooks*), I am not at all persuaded that Sartre's ambivalent texts warrant it. Bell's is a case of overinterpretation rooted in Sartre's own ambivalence and lack of clarity.

---

15. Ibid., 304.

16. Ronald Aronson and Andrew Dobson, "Discussion of 'Sartre and Stalin,'" *Sartre Studies International* 3, no. 1 (1997): 17, 18. I do not suggest that this is Aronson's position, but only that it is for him a defensible one.

17. The reader will remember that in the "Rome Lecture" Sartre views Terror as a "revolutionary pause" that "marks history negatively" and carries the risk of bringing about a system of Terror like Stalinism. I might point out, further, that as early as 1946, in "Matérialisme et révolution," Sartre attacked and attempted to demonstrate the errors in Stalinism. And he certainly assumed and did the same later in *Le fantôme de Staline* (*The Ghost of Stalin*), 1957.

18. E.g., Aronson and Dobson, "Discussion of 'Sartre and Stalin,'" 18. Of course, Aronson's point is more extreme: he refers to this connection as the "Achilles' heel" of Sartre's political thought. But that does not take sufficiently into account the relevant ambivalence in it that I have been arguing.

conclusion

What am I to conclude at the end of this study of Sartre on violence—a study in which I have devoted Part I to Sartre's engagement with violence in his main representative writings and then, in Part II, have attempted both to view the Sartre-Camus conflict of 1952 in relation to their diverging positions on violence and revolution and to clarify Sartre's overall stance regarding the justifiability of violence?

Let me first offer a few comments to round out my expositions and discussion in Part II. The debate between Jeanson/Sartre and Camus in 1952 is hardly one of which any of the participants could be proud. At a personal level, each sounded more like an offended high priest or an indignant adolescent than a reflective, fair-minded thinker. The misrepresentations, insults, *ad hominem* attacks, *petitio principiis,* indirect jibes, by both sides, hardly "became" two literary—and, in the case of Sartre, philosophical—giants. Yet, as I have continually tried to show, the bitter exchange dealt with the perennially important philosophical issues of the limits and justifiability of violence. Moreover, this debate over Camus's analysis in *The Rebel* brought out the differing approaches to violence and revolution—precipitated, to be sure, by diverging political and ontological views—that

163

Sartre and Camus were taking at that time. Both were working under the cloud of the Cold War, struggling to position themselves in relation to Communism, the Soviet Union, widespread oppression, and the threat of atomic destruction. Horrified by the "apocalypse of murder"[1] that he had traced in contemporary revolutions, Camus, though realistic about the inevitability of violence in history, refused any legitimization of revolutionary murder. Sartre, on the other hand, having been "converted" earlier by Merleau-Ponty's view, in *Humanism and Terror,* that violence can be humanizing, yet becoming increasingly critical of Stalinism (e.g., in *The Communists and Peace*), saw Camus's repudiation of violent revolution as bourgeois, privileged, unrealistic, antihistorical, and anti–human being. Sartre adamantly opposed Camus's *a priori* (he thought) imposition of limits, or *mesure,* on rebellion without regard for the oppressive conditions of the proletariat. And by firmly rejecting Camus's refusal to grace revolutionary murders with the word "justice" (Camus unqualifiedly declared them "unjustifiable"), Sartre, though rather reluctant to use the word, was willing to justify revolutionary Terror under certain conditions, given what he regarded as the revolutionary "end" of making a "new humanity." "Materialism and Revolution," the *Critique,* the Preface to *The Wretched,* and especially the "Rome Lecture" (for more considered "moral" reasons) have all progressively clarified and confirmed this. But Camus never pulled away from the *limits* on which he insisted in *The Rebel.* Having been a member of the Algerian Communist Party until he was expelled from it in 1937, he could no longer indulge their revolutionary fancies. If revolution violates its human origins and the spirit of revolt, if it fails to exercise limits and "incessant control," it will end up "consecrating terror." Even in his later "Défense de *L'homme révolté,*" in which he makes some effort, in response to Sartre and Jeanson, to offer points of reconciliation between rebellion and revolution, he, as I pointed out, refuses "legitimate murder" and "assigns a boundary" (*une borne*) to "its demented projects" (*ses démentes entreprises*).[2] If the Sartre-Camus debate had not turned into a battle between offended egos, and if Sartre had entertained even the ambivalent insights of his later "Rome Lecture," he might likely have granted Camus his demand for *mesure.* And given Camus's anti-Communist criticisms, I suspect that the vehemence of

1. I borrow this expression from Mark Poster's citation in *Existential Marxism in Postwar France* (Princeton: Princeton University Press, 1975), 188.
2. See, again, Albert Camus, "Défense de *L'homme révolté,*" in *Essais,* Bibliothèque de la Pléiade, 183 (Paris: Gallimard, 1976), 1713, translation mine ("réfuter le meurtre légitime et assigner à ses démentes entreprises une borne précise").

Sartre's position against Camus had much to do, also, with the militancy of his "anti-anti-Communism" (McBride's expression),[3] to which he had been "converted" (again?) following the spring 1952 arrest of the PCF leader, Jacques Duclos. "An anti-Communist is a dog," he said, just before his exchange with Camus, and he swore his hatred for the bourgeoisie until his dying breath.[4] Soon after, I might add, he began to extend his disenchantment to the views of his good friend Merleau-Ponty, who, at about the same time, was "converting" away from his strong pro-Communist proclivities and, three years later, was sharply criticizing Sartre's "ultra-Bolshevist" views in *Les aventures de la dialectique* (1955) (chapter 5, especially). At the heart of these disagreements, too, was *violence*: To what extent, in the absence of an unqualifiedly good or ideal political party, could one support a revolutionary party that, though purportedly struggling to overcome the pervasive violence of a bourgeois class society, employed measures and means that continued violence, destroyed human freedoms, and generated Terror? Rather than make known his limits, Sartre scoffed at Camus's limits and preferred instead to focus his discussion on the meaning of "history" and (he contended) Camus's failure to understand it or place himself in it. But Sartre scholars can be grateful for his 1964 "Rome Lecture," for it is in it that he more clearly spells out his limits and more directly answers the question of the justifiability of violence and Terror. Yet, even there, Sartre seems curiously enigmatic at points. In spite of the details and attentiveness of that important lecture (in which he grounds morality in human need), Sartre has not convincingly shown how violent revolution and Terror can be the vehicle for overcoming alienation and creating a new humanity. If means and ends are as synthetically intertwined and unified as Sartre maintains in *What Is Literature?* and the "Rome Lecture," it is hard to imagine— as Camus affirms in *The Rebel* and *The Just Assassins* and Sartre suggests in his *Notebooks for an Ethics*—how resort to revolutionary violence and Terror could ever take place without in some way disparaging or defacing humanity.[5]

    3. William L. McBride, "The Polemic in the Pages of *Les Temps Modernes* (1952)," in *Sartre's French Contemporaries and Enduring Influences* (New York: Garland Publishing, 1997), 83.
    4. Sartre gives an account of this conversion in *Situations* IV (Paris: Gallimard, 1964), 248–49; also in translation (as cited), *Situations*, trans. Benita Eisler (New York: George Braziller, 1965), 287–88. McBride offers the relevant passage in *Sartre's Political Theory* (Bloomington: Indiana University Press, 1991), 93.
    5. The reader will remember that in *Notebooks for an Ethics* Sartre shows the non-coexistential and anticommunitarian dimensions of violence. I discuss this thesis in Part I. See

At the risk of tiring the reader, I must say again, in this conclusion, that, even after the Rome Lecture and *Hope Now,* Sartre remains problematic and ambivalent with regard to the justifiability of violence and Terror. His attempt to root morality in human *need* does not seem to do the trick. How, for example, can one move from the "is" of need to *moral* justification, even if means and ends are synthetically balanced? Yet that does not vitiate his point in *Hope Now* that violence can sometimes serve oppressed colonized people by breaking up the "state of enslavement" of those condemned to subhumanity. But nor does his point, *ipso facto,* morally justify the violence. The problem of morally justifying the violation of freedom (i.e., violence) of some people, for the sake of restoring freedom and humanity to others, remains a vexing problem for both Sartre and his critics. Sartre appears to have understood this in his undeservedly maligned dialogue with Benny Lévy in *Hope Now.* In spite of the vehement opposition of de Beauvoir and many others in Sartre's "entourage" to those interviews,[6] I'm prepared to accept Sartre's response to Lévy's interrogation on violence as his "last word" on it. Moreover, I approve of it: he seems here to bring to a head his sense of the antihuman dimensions that violence and Terror constitute for humanity.

In the course of my study, one point has become clear, now perhaps exhaustingly clear to some readers—namely, that Sartre's writings on violence, from beginning to end, are riddled with *ambivalence.* My focus, in Part II, on the Sartre-Camus confrontation and its dividing issue of the justifiability of revolutionary violence and murder has confirmed my finding of a pervasive ambivalence in Part I. Moreover, the meaning of violence, what Sartre himself calls the "curious ambiguity" of violence, as freedom affirming itself destructively against freedom, has not altered as I have moved from one part to another. (Although this is where the core ambiguity lies, one must remember that Sartre, especially in *Notebooks for an Ethics,* also regards the human person's destruction of the world as violence.)[7] Moreover, I believe that my comparative study of Sartre's representative views on violence in Part I informs and enlightens my consideration of Sartre's vehement "break" with Camus. In turn, I believe that my examination of the disastrous "exchange" of 1952, together with my focused discussion of the dominant justifiability issue, has added clarity—and further rationale—to the views of

---

also my sustained discussion of Sartre's point in "On the Existential Meaning of Violence," *Dialogue and Humanism,* no. 4 (1993): 139–50.

6. For my discussion of this opposition and my defense of the interviews, see Ronald E. Santoni, "In Defense of Lévy and *Hope Now:* A Minority View," in *Sartre Studies International* 4, no. 2 (1998), 61–68.

7. E.g., *NFE* 172–74 (*CPM* 181–84).

Sartre examined in Part I. In this regard, I stress again that my direct access to the 1964 "Rome Lecture Notes," made easier by the generosity of John Gerassi and the untiring efforts of Robert Stone and Elizabeth Bowman, have allowed me a retrospective fine-tuning of Sartre's earlier views concerning the limits and moral defensibility of revolutionary violence and Terror—especially when used against exploitative systems and classes that maintain themselves through violence.

Therefore, I say at the conclusion of this book what I said at the end of Part I: in spite of the shifts, modifications, and changes in emphasis in Sartre's thinking regarding violence—often because of changes in the *political* (I use this term broadly) situations he was confronting and considering—Sartre's overall position on violence exhibits an unsteady but tested line of continuity, development, and coherence. Given his profound sympathy for the oppressed, alienated, and disadvantaged, and his intense lifelong commitment—ontologically and politically—to human freedom, it is hardly surprising that he would, in certain circumstances, "endorse" (I use this word deliberately) revolutionary movements that aim to dislodge oppressors and undo oppression, even if their activities suppressed the freedom of capitalist, colonialist, bourgeois oppressors. For him, as for the early Merleau-Ponty—although not for me—the choice is not between purity and violence but between different types of violence. Yet, in spite of his inflammatory statements in the Preface to *The Wretched of the Earth,* my contention should not be taken to mean that Sartre—to use Benny Lévy's word—"exalted" or extolled violence. For both his earliest and latest statements exhibit not only the "curious ambiguity" of violence but also his wish to distance himself from, and even *oppose,* violence. Although in *Hope Now: The 1980 Interviews,* he does not say what he said in *Notebooks for an Ethics* (1947–48)—namely, that violence "is an experience that can benefit no one"[8]—he does make it clear that violence and fraternity (and, surely, human community) are opposites, never "twin brothers,"[9] and that the "fraternal love" of integral humanity can never issue out of Terror or the violence of killing. In his last days and interviews of 1980, though still accepting as restorative the past necessary violence of the subhumanized colonized Algerians, for instance, he appears to recognize—in the words of Camus's Caligula (no invidious comparison intended)—that, in spite of

8. *NFE* 406 (*CPM* 420: "expérience qui ne peut profiter à personne").
9. Sartre, *L'espoir maintenant: Les entretiens de 1980* (Lagrasse: Verdier, 1991), 63–64 (*Hope Now,* 92–93).

guilt, "killing is not the solution." He does not want, any more than Camus, to follow a "ruthless logic that crushes out human lives."[10]

To many, Sartre may appear to "want it both ways," as they say. I confess that, at times, I share that impression. But in a world overwhelmed and scarred by systems and institutions of oppressive violence, in which the vast majority of human beings—that is, the poor, hungry, disadvantaged, and "least favored"—are daily struggling to be recognized and treated as humans, Sartre still stands out as one who, in spite of his ambivalences, errors, temperamental and unfair overstatements, as well as his irritating (but warranted) goading of the privileged and "favored," is always trying to improve the lot and practical freedoms of the "have-nots." This is another line of continuity that runs throughout his *oeuvre*. For this reason alone, one can call a spade a spade, criticize his periodic attempts to approve strongly of the violence of the oppressed, point directly to his apparent duplicity, question, on his own terms, his accommodation of Terror to the project of bringing forward an "integral humanity," yet salute Sartre for his unrelenting devotion to the cause of the marginalized, unrecognized, colonized, and exploited. In this regard, his occasional bow to violence is at least understandable. Although Sartre's philosophy as a whole hardly emphasizes the possibility of a violence-free world, one might contend, as McBride suggests, that a violence-free world haunts the pages of a number of his works.[11]

Finally, although Sartre enjoins all of us, because of our own complicity in maintaining the institutions and systems of oppression, to join in a common praxis to undo the violences of oppression, he has *not* provided a comfortable, unambiguous, resolution of the problem of justifying violence. Given the terms of his trajectory, I do not think one is available in it. Yet with his repeated and admirable goal of a "city of ends," and his dream of a world in which free, autonomous beings live *for* one another in a reciprocity of sharing, Sartre remains—in spite of his ambivalences and deficiencies—an inspiration and prod. Among other contributions, he has exhibited through his living what it means to be an "engaged" (*engagé*) activist intellectual. Our world needs more of them.

10. Camus, *Caligula,* in *Caligula and 3 Other Plays,* trans. Stuart Gilbert (New York: Vintage Books, 1958), 72.

11. McBride, "Sartre and the Phenomenology of Social Violence," in *New Essays in Phenomenology,* ed. James M. Edie (Chicago: Quadrangle Books, 1969), 298.

index

169